Women of Iron and Velvet

Illustration from Gyp's novel, La Fée

Margaret Crosland

Women of Iron and Velvet

French women writers after George Sand

Taplinger Publishing Company
New York

First published in the United States in 1976 by
TAPLINGER PUBLISHING CO., INC.
New York, N.Y. 10003
Copyright ©1976 by Margaret Crosland
All rights reserved
Printed in Great Britain

Library of Congress Catalog Card Number: 75-8202
ISBN 0-8008-8436-1

For my son Patrick
male chauvinist Francophobe

It is very difficult from the standpoint of natural logic, to sympathize with moderate feminism, one could more easily accept feminism in excess. For if there are in nature numerous examples of feminism, there are very few of an equality of the sexes.

Rémy de Gourmont: *The Natural Philosophy of Love*

Eve was certainly not a Frenchwoman. If she had been she would never have become so mixed up with God, Adam and the serpent. How would she have avoided it? That's a national secret. I'd be disloyal to reveal it. I do not know what women in other countries are made of. In France they are made of iron. But around the iron are all kinds of skilful decorations. The result is that when the product is a good one, she gives the impression of velvet.

Françoise Giroud: 'The Second Sex'

Contents

List of Illustrations

List of Illustrations

Preface

I have chosen to write about French women writers because I enjoy reading them and in the course of research over many years have come to know them well, especially those of the last hundred years or so. It struck me that so much has happened in the field of women's writing since George Sand died in 1876, women are writing in France as everywhere else with increased professionalism. Madame de Sévigné, three centuries ago, was thought to be in search of fame, while her friend Madame de La Fayette wrote novels anonymously because she was plain and felt unloved. Now women in France are writing not to find personal compensation but for most other reasons: they are deeply concerned with the improvement of social conditions and especially of their own condition. At the same time they want to entertain, instruct and earn money. They no longer have to sacrifice their personal life in order to write, as Madame de Charrière was afraid they must do at the end of the eighteenth century. Men accused them of over-dedication to their work, while personal feelings took second place.

This is surely no longer true. And my own feelings, which are affectionate, for the French women writers, do not imply that they are 'better' writers than the women of other countries: they are different. France has produced no women writers in any century 'like' Anna Akmahtova, Karen Blixen, Carson McCullers, Gabriela Mistral, Virginia Woolf. Instead they have produced Marguerite Yourcenar (born in Belgium), Simone de Beauvoir, Simone Weil and a whole new generation to follow them. It goes without saying too that these writers are not necessarily 'better' than the men writers. Again, they are different.

Paradoxically, French women, who have always had so little legal and social freedom, have always succeeded in taking and keeping a particular kind of personal, almost secret liberation. At the moment they think they need a good deal more, and the writers are working hard to help achieve it.

I have written principally about writers I enjoy and hope I understand in some way. The book is not a history, although it takes some rapid glances backwards, and follows only an approximate time sequence. Some chapters discuss books and some describe life, while on other occasions the life and work complement each other and the life is the work. The scene in France at the moment is particularly exciting for women writers, since both publishers and readers alike are intrigued by their work, and they reflect the current interest in the 'feminine condition'. How far it will change nobody knows, but the women writers at least are determined that it should; some are militant, some merely go on writing as their predecessors did, convinced that by their works shall we know them, and in our own way, respond.

M.C.

Sussex – Puy de Dôme

1976

Acknowledgements

Many people and organizations have helped me in the writing of this book. I particularly wish to thank the Arts Council of Great Britain for their generous support and my editor Elfreda Powell for her steady and constructive advice.

Historians, critics and biographers to whom I am indebted are listed in the bibliography. Otherwise I am grateful for the help I have received from many sources in England and France: friends, researchers, booksellers, librarians, publishers and secretaries: Neville Armstrong, Armand Avronsart, Marion Boyars, John Calder, François Chapon, R. S. Collins, Irene Cox, Lily Denis, Monique Detry, Hilda Gaskell, Nell Gorecki, Editions Grasset, Margery Hemming, Colette Horn, Marjorie Hunt, Pierre Javet, Dr Marthe Lamy, Osyth Leeston, Jérôme Lindon, Thérèse Mairesse, Jean Mauldon, Peter Owen, Pierre Pain, Jeffrey Simmons, Michael Williams, Tana Wollen, the staffs of the London Library and the Bibliothèque de l'Institut français in London.

M.C.

I

After George . . .

In early June 1876 the French woman writer who called herself George Sand died, probably of cancer, a few weeks before her seventy-first birthday. She had outlived many of her friends, lovers and enemies, but Gustave Flaubert, who had become her friend, came to the funeral and wrote a few much-quoted remarks about it. He told his friend Turgenev, who was in Russia at the time, that he had 'cried like an ass'; it was a wet day and the local country people also cried as they stood about in the mud, listening to, but probably hardly understanding, a long letter from Victor Hugo that was read out by the grave-side. Flaubert may have wept, but true to form he took notes: 'It was like a chapter out of one of her own novels', he wrote to Turgenev.

Since then George Sand and her books have made more friends, lovers and enemies. Any writer who produced a hundred or so books, mainly novels, an autobiography in ten volumes and at least six additional fat volumes of correspondence, some of it published only recently, could hardly fail to make an impact of some sort. Would the impact have been so great, during her lifetime and even now, if she had not been a woman? Biographers and critics are still arguing about her as people argued when she was alive. Her existence and personality are still at the centre of a psychological and social problem. Turgenev had been perceptive enough, a hundred years ago: 'What a good man she was,' he wrote, 'and what a kind woman!' Many women in France had published books before her, many of them had been successful, several influential. But no woman so far had personified the equation: woman + books = writer, meaning professional writer.

She seemed to have been born to symbolize one thing: the chance offered to women by the Romantic movement, the chance for a new kind of freedom. George Sand wanted personal freedom, equality within marriage; without this she did not see how women could take up positions in public life, they must first establish status as individuals in private life. She was full of fine, and not always vague, ideas about what she regarded as socialism; she even mentioned the word communism. But in 1848 she refused to stand as a deputy because women were not yet ready, she believed, for this type of career. The following year a woman did stand and had no success, so perhaps George had been right.

She had not begun writing out of sheer self-indulgence, she had begun to write because she needed money. She was separated from her husband and divorce had been prohibited in 1826. She had tried to earn money by painting and even by doing needlework, but could not earn anything like the amount she wanted. Writing letters had always been easy for her and this gave her an idea; she succeeded after some trouble in finding work as a journalist in Paris and after the success of *Lélia* in 1833 she literally never stopped writing for the rest of her life. In more ways than one she could not afford to: she had to support herself, and intermittently her two children, then writing became her life. Some of her lovers never forgave her for the way she used them in her books, and it is amusing to notice that even some male literary critics of today have the same chauvinistic reaction. In 1975, for example, Anthony West, son of a woman writer who had tolerated an extra-marital relationship with H. G. Wells when society generally condemned such behaviour, seems unable in his turn to tolerate the mere existence of George and other women writers, especially those who wrote in French. He was as destructive as the French writer and critic Barbey d'Aurevilly had been a hundred years earlier. Sand and her kind, believed West, wrote only because of the 'mortal wounds' that life had inflicted on them. But George Sand would surely have shrugged off this attack, admiring the flow of misdirected rhetoric and feeling sorry for someone capable of such self-exposure. Perhaps West could not bear the thought that if men did not support a woman with love and/or money then they had to support her with material for narrative, copy. The critic Sainte-Beuve had had the same terror, he couldn't think of 'anything worse than having an affair with a *femme de lettres*. Because all the time you'd have the feeling that she was giving the whole world what she ought to be keeping for you alone.' Men could give it to the whole world, that was fair, but if women did the same thing that was unfair.

Sand was a feminine, maternally minded woman, she would probably have been much happier as an organizer of normal family life than as a writer. There is no point in condemning her more melodramatic love affairs and her treatment of the men concerned or in allowing these real-life stories to predominate over her own writing. She did not entirely solve her central problem, that of Mary Wollstonecraft and so many other women: only with difficulty, at middle age and after the waste of much psychic energy, did she succeed in establishing a more or less stable relationship with Alexandre Damien Manceau, which in fact lasted fifteen years. Since he died first it is impossible to say whether they would have 'settled down' together emotionally, and whether his image would have obscured all others. Her career had begun because she had to support herself and wanted to support her children. Men are often irritated by a woman who succeeds in doing so, for once she has embarked on even a moderately successful career men, or even a man, can no longer be the centre of her attention. For George Sand it was very quickly too late for 'normal' life. She was forced to compromise in far too many ways as wife, mistress and mother. Everything was compromise except one thing, her own individuality.

Individual achievement by women, and especially among women writers in France, had always helped the ever-present but not very vociferous women's movement that had been in the background ever since the late middle ages. It was not surprising that during the Revolution the voices were raised more than a little, for the eighteenth-century *philosophes* had given some thought to the question. In 1790 the philosopher and mathematician Condorcet published his *Essai sur l'admission des femmes au droit de cité* (Essay on the admission of women to citizens' rights), in which he considered why women should be allowed to have citizens' rights, which included the possibility at least of a local vote. He asked whether men had not violated the 'principle of equal rights by calmly depriving half the human race of the right to participate in the formulation of laws by excluding women from the *droit de cité*'. How could pregnancy and 'temporary indispositions' make them incapable of exercising these rights when nobody had considered similar deprivation for people who 'suffered from gout every winter and caught cold easily'?

He mentioned well-known women of the past: would not Montaigne's adopted daughter (Marie de Gournay) have done more in 1614 for citizens' rights than Antoine de Courtin, a diplomat and writer, who believed in magic? And would the Marquise de Lambert, a highly moral salon-keeper of the early eighteenth century, have made laws as 'absurd and barbarous' as the Garde des Sceaux (Keeper of the Seals) against Protestants, smugglers and negroes? If they looked at those who govern them, 'men have no right to be so proud'.

Condorcet was surely fair and he implied that if women were given the rights they deserved they would not break up family life: 'Women could no more be torn from their ménage than ploughmen would be torn from their ploughs, or workmen from their workshops.'

All this provided inspiration to at least one woman, the violent young widow who called herself Olympe de Gouges, and in 1791 she published the *Déclaration des Droits de la Femme et de la Citoyenne* (Declaration of the Rights of Women and Female Citizens). She had been born Marie-Olympe Gouze, in Montauban, possibly the illegitimate daughter of a poet who had the merit of being hated by Voltaire. At fifteen she had married a former tavern-keeper named Aubry who soon left her a wealthy young widow. She had two ambitions: to have a good time and to write. Of five plays she showed to the Comédie Française, one was performed, but on the outbreak of the Revolution she found mere literature too tame. She took up the cause of women, for after all they had not shrunk from action and had joined in anti-royalist demonstrations.

If women could go to the guillotine, she wrote, logically they could have citizens' rights. Boldly she drew up draft constitutions, nothing was too much of a challenge for her. After her early revolutionary activity she even decided to take up the cause of the unhappy Louis XVI and when he was on trial she wrote to the great Robespierre in indignant protest – would he, she asked, throw himself into the Seine with her? Robespierre's reply was straightforward: he clapped her in gaol and in November 1793 she went to the guillotine, which she had perhaps half-anticipated. (Robespierre followed her but for other reasons.) The newspaper *Le Moniteur* made it quite clear why she should not be forgiven for all she had written: 'She wanted to be a statesman, and the law has apparently punished this conspiratress for having forgotten the virtues suited to her sex.' She and the militant women who surrounded her were said to have been so 'immoral' that they harmed their own cause. It is only too easy to laugh at militants and their excesses, but they have to happen, and in France at least there are still many reasons why they go on happening nearly two hundred years after the Revolution.

If asked in some quiz programme who it was who said 'O liberty, what crimes are committed in thy name!' how many people outside or even inside France would know the answer at once? It was Madame Roland, who edited a newspaper in Lyon, was politically active in the Girondist cause and hated Robespierre. In her turn she also went to the guillotine in 1793 and she spoke the famous words as she approached that blood-stained machine. At the news of her death her husband killed himself. She is not remembered notably as a writer but her memoirs are well worth reading and so is the piece published after her death which she had called *Appel à l'impartiale postérité*, a title which speaks for itself.

The advent of Bonaparte was a setback for the feminists. His own case-history was straightforward: his Corsican background and his relationship with Madame Mère were obviously the joint cause of his reactionary attitudes towards women in general. He was so susceptible to them (although by no means untouched by deep feelings for men) that he was probably terrified, on behalf of the male world, of any possible power they might achieve outside sexuality. That alone was more than enough. Two sentences in the preamble to the Code civil of 1804 are only too well known: 'Woman is given to man in order to have children. She therefore belongs to him as the fruit tree belongs to the gardener.'

The Code civil still horrified Simone de Beauvoir a century and a half after its appearance. She quoted many of its provisions in *The Second Sex* and others have done so since. Article 1124 precluded certain persons from making contracts: minors, married women and those who had been outlawed, namely madmen, imbeciles and criminals. According to the Code, a woman had neither the right to exercise a profession nor to choose where the ménage should live without her husband's agreement. Even if she was supposed to own property in her own right she could not, according to Article 217, 'give, dispose of, mortgage or acquire [it] without the collaboration or consent of her husband'.

Article 222 went further: a married woman had no right to any earnings acquired in the exercise of her profession (if her husband had graciously allowed her to have one) and she could not open a current account at the bank. Incredibly enough, a married woman in France had no legal right to her own earnings until 1907. Where women were forced to provide the family income, or augment it, they accepted, like women in other countries, wretched work for miserable pay.

Until 1874 they could be exploited by employers, again like
women in many other countries, and in La Fortune des Rougon
Zola describes the man who was saddened by the death of a
fourteen-year-old girl, not because she died but because he was
deprived of her wages. During 1874, however, it was decided
by law that women could not work for more than twelve
hours a day. At the same time employers were forbidden to
employ girls under age and no women could work underground in mines or quarries. That was the law but not the
practice. What about equal pay for equal work? Until 1893
women received precisely half the amount that men were paid
for identical work. And in 1900, the year identified with all
that is most picturesque in la belle époque, a description that
could only be applied to its surface glitter, women could not
legally work for more than ten hours a day. But no employers
worried about this would-be protection of their labour force
because most women slaved away at home, surrounded by
their children and/or ageing parents, earning a few centimes an
hour by trimming hats, embroidering or dress-making.

A tolerable, tolerant husband obviously made life more
bearable for women with so few legal rights. But what if he
was or became intolerable? Divorce had been legalized in
France in 1792 and the old system whereby it was achieved
after a three-year séparation de corps was forbidden. In 1804 this
was re-established by the Code civil which allowed divorce
except in the case of temperamental incompatibility: that
would have been too easy, some lawyers thought. When
Napoleon had gone feminists among women and even among
men had hoped that the restored monarchy would remember
woman's cause, but they were disappointed. Early during the
reign of Louis XVIII divorce was in fact abolished, partly
because of the religious revival which followed the collapse of
the Empire. Until 1884 it could only be effectively obtained,
according to Article 217 of the inevitable Code civil, if the
adulterous husband had brought his 'concubine' into the
marital home.

There was continued pressure from the public for a sane divorce system and in 1880 the dramatist Victorien Sardou and one of his collaborators had written a comedy entitled *Divorçons!* (Let's Divorce!) The plot turns on a trick telegram claiming that divorce had become legal, and the wife is ready to go off with her lover, but the husband is too clever: he claims he is now a bachelor again, and therefore interesting. Naturally there is a reconciliation. In other words the play might even have been interpreted as anti-divorce propaganda.

But the 1880s and divorce-law reform were still a long way ahead. Everything would have been easier for women if they had had the possibility of education. However, unless their families had the money and inclination to educate them privately they had little chance of learning anything. At the end of the eighteenth century, during the Revolution, the state schools in France would accept girls only up to the age of eight, after which families had to make their own arrangements. Not until five years after George Sand's death came the special legislation introduced by a Jewish député, Camille Sée: girls were at last allowed to receive secondary education in state schools. It is surprising obviously that women had not started fighting in a more determined way, but everything was against them. The Catholic Church favoured early marriage and many children, the unmarried woman was socially undesirable, unless she was rich: but then she would rarely have remained unmarried.

However, followers of the colourful early-nineteenth-century socialists tried to come to the rescue, for they were particularly enthusiastic about improving the lot of women. Here was a large oppressed 'class' whom they could quickly turn, they hoped, into enthusiastic supporters. The Comte de Saint-Simon himself thought that women could at least belong to political committees. One of his most earnest and idealistic disciples, 'Father' Prosper Enfantin, believed that the human race would be regenerated through the equality of man and woman. In one wild, starry-eyed moment he apparently thought of marrying Madame de Staël in order to achieve 'the ideal marriage of two geniuses'. Fortunately for them both, he seems to have given up the idea and they both escaped such an alarming punishment. However, he even wanted women to enter the priesthood and went to Egypt to look for the female Messiah whom he believed must exist there. He had such high hopes of women that he inevitably let them down, for women were in fact not ready to go forward as fast as he wanted them to. George Sand herself was well aware of this. In the end 'Father' Enfantin decided women were petty, but his attitudes had been over-simplified, over-optimistic; he was defeated, as many men and women have been, by the complexities of the female psyche.

That other would-be reformer, Charles Fourier, wrote stirring words on the subject of women's future: 'Men could only be proud of the intellectual liberation of women, for social progress and change take place through the progress of women towards liberty and social decline takes place through the decrease of women's liberty. The furtherance of women's rights is the principle of all social progress.' In the experimental commune established just after his death near Rambouillet in 1838 women were 'emancipated' in an atmosphere of free love. The experiment was a disaster but Fourier's ideas inevitably influenced several writers among his contemporaries, including George Sand herself.

It is worth while remembering that she also listened to the ideas of the religious thinker Lamennais, who was in no way partial to women. There was in fact no shortage of misogynists, the historian Michelet was among them, and so was the positivist philosopher Auguste Comte, although Clotilde de Vaux, the woman he loved and idealized, finally had some influence over him.

Literary and social change, interacting on each other, were two aspects of Romanticism, no writer or reader could escape it. As the wind of change swept through literature it blew the dust off the alexandrine and all the themes so neatly and coolly expressed by the eighteenth-century thinker. Lyric poetry expressed the yearnings of love in a new way because the poets felt free to yearn with ecstasy that was no longer forced to obey the rules, social and literary. Victor Hugo's Ruy Blas may have told the Queen he adored that he was 'an earthworm in love with a star', but the women who saw this play, identifying themselves with the star, felt that they need no longer remain inaccessible. At last women felt that it was no crime or social sin to *respond*. The Princesse de Clèves had caused a scandal in the seventeenth century merely by admitting that she had feelings for a man who was not her husband. The Romantics did not expect women to be coy, the heroines of their books and plays began to show real-life ordinary women how they could or should behave. Gradually some of them, notably actresses, began to live like the heroines. George Sand, when she was young, seemed the symbol of the Romantic movement and women's participation in it, she not only wrote about Lélia, she *was* Lélia.

This is why she changed the course of women's writing, to which she had already brought the new element of professionalism. Her predecessors had written well enough, or better, but there had been no rallying point, no *chef de fil*, and they had inevitably worked as individualists, usually in isolation. They continued in the same way, and probably always will, but at least they became aware that the isolation was relative and the sum of individualism more worth while than regimentation. Madame de Staël, who had died in 1817, was an unconscious feminist. She was also a failed politician and reformer, failing because she was otherwise occupied, she had only time to keep the liberal idea alive through the massive opposition of Bonaparte's dictatorship; she also failed because her exhausting emotional life almost destroyed her. If she had needed to write for money her imaginative writing at least might have been better organized, and she would probably have become a militant leader in search of more freedom for women.

Two women writers followed her who needed money desperately. Like so many women writing in France, each was unconsciously an innovator. 'She lived, suffered, wept', runs one sad little biography of Marceline Desbordes-Valmore and it is not far from the truth. Everything about her life was melodramatic, nothing worked out well for her and she may have been something of a masochist. Her trouble began when she was thirteen. At that time, 1799, she was in Guadeloupe where her mother, who had lost everything during the Revolution – her father had been a designer of armorial bearings – had hoped for support from a cousin. But the cousin was killed in a negro uprising and her mother died of yellow fever. So at fifteen Marceline came back to France and in order to work her passage entertained the other passengers on the ship by acting and reciting. Having no source of income she went on acting in the north of France – the family had come from Douai – and acted well enough to get herself to Paris. She fell in love, earned herself a son but no more. The child died, and although she married a puffed-up actor named Valmore, ten years younger than herself, she was not happy. She had had hardly any education and could not spell. Yet she published five books of poems during her lifetime and the first appeared in 1818, two years before Lamartine's *Méditations*, usually regarded as the start of the Romantic era. Fortunately she had a natural musical sense and learnt much from the not very good plays in which she acted. She said modestly that she had begun to write because at one point an illness prevented her from singing. She even had to convince her husband that her poems were not written to or about other men. The whole tone of her work is elegiac, she was continually mourning the love she had lost and her range is narrow. Yet she is usually represented in anthologies of poetry, deservedly so; she was the only woman poet of value in France between Louise Labé of the sixteenth century and the Symbolist Marie Krysinska, or the pessimistic Louise Ackermann, who are known only to historians. Verlaine consecrated her reputation, which owed much to Sainte-Beuve, by including her among his *poètes maudits*, or accursed poets. Numerous women wrote poetry during the nineteenth century but who reads it now?

Comte Robert de Montesquiou, Proust's friend, however, would have had everyone reading her, and he was probably her greatest admirer ever. He lectured about her, receiving useful personal publicity at the same time, and set up a monument to her at Douai, her birthplace. Proust's biographer George Painter indicates how important she may have been to the novelist for an important 'clue' is contained in two lines she wrote:

> *Je veux aller mourir aux lieux où je suis née;*
> *Le tombeau d'Albertine est près de mon berceau. . . .*

Could it be that this typically sorrowing reference 'may well have helped in suggesting to Proust the name of his heroine and part of the subject of his novel'? It is evidently not impossible.

Required reading, however, despite the fact that the content counts so much more than the form, are the writings of George Sand's contemporary Flora Tristan, a name inseparable from early socialism and early feminism. Her own life, a desperate tale of poverty and persecution, mostly due to the impossibility of divorce, would surely have led any woman to feminism, if not suicide. Before she could begin any agitation for reform she had to educate herself, for she had to learn how to write, to interpret the law and to organize people. The books she finally wrote are not literature but readable, practical, essential works in social history. Her personal experiences could have left her obsessed by the feminist cause but in fact she looked further, describing social conditions in France and in England, where she had once worked as a domestic servant, and giving an account of her year in Peru when she had searched for her Peruvian father's relatives. But the title of her most important work was significant: *Pérégrinations d'une paria*. From her beginnings as an apprentice to a lithographer (later her cruel husband) she came to know the early socialists and it was she who started the trade-union movement known as the *Union ouvrière*. Sadly she died at the age of forty-one in 1844 but fortunately now her work is studied and appreciated. She was a lonely figure but achieved a great deal after a hard struggle. Another of her unexpected claims to fame is that one of her daughters became the mother of Paul Gauguin. Since she has been described as 'violent 'and 'romantic', the painter might well have inherited some of her attitudes.

George Sand was not the only woman writing during the nineteenth century, although her writing career lasted so long and caused Colette, at the end of her life, to envy her, this 'great bee', as she called her. Sand had enemies, but in comparison to some other women writing at the same period she was both an intellectual and a model of decorum. When Nathaniel Hawthorne complained in 1850 about the 'damned scribbling women' in the United States his phrase might well have applied to those in France. Obviously, while women are struggling for equality and freedom, or what they think is equality and freedom, they can be exceptionally tedious. Some of them would have been tedious even if they had not wanted to be writers, but few could have been potentially more destructive to their own cause than Louise Colet. Born in 1808 in Aix-en-Provence, she had come to Paris as the wife of a minor composer and music teacher and was soon hungry for love affairs with well-known people, especially writers. She succeeded, through sheer persistence, in creating involvements with Alfred de Musset and Flaubert, but she soon received hate, ironic coolness or, worst of all, ridicule instead of love in return.

Flaubert's letters to her are some of the most interesting he wrote to anyone; they reveal much of his own nature, especially his terror of having a child, his immature feelings about his mother and the fact that women on the whole did not mean much to him sexually. Art meant everything, men a good deal. It seems strange that he was involved with Louise

Colet for a total of eight years, with some interludes: was she really only a good-looking vain young woman from Provence whose urge to acquire literary lovers was only equalled by her urge to write poetry? Disappointingly her poetry was plainly bad, it had no music, no depth. Flaubert was too polite to tell her and the Académie Française, which refused to admit women, was somehow so wrong-headed that it 'crowned' three of her books. Chateaubriand refused to write a preface for her, but she brazenly published his letter of refusal. Sainte-Beuve, so interested in women writers of merit, refused to have anything to do with her. But she must have been persuasive. She even talked Victor Cousin, the philosopher, and Minister of Public Instruction at the time, to accept an affair with her and when she was pregnant in the 1840s the news got about that she was suffering from *une piqûre de cousin*, literally a gnat bite. The journalist Alphonse Karr congratulated her in his gossip column on the imminent birth of 'something other than an alexandrine'. She was so angry that she seized a rusty kitchen knife, followed him to his house and tried to stab him in the back as he opened the door. But she failed to cause him any harm and he hung the knife up on his study wall as a souvenir.

Yet Flaubert would surely not have written to this tiresome creature so much and so deeply if she had not had something more than a seductive face and body. She complained that he wrote too much about art, but the strange thing is that he wrote so much about it to her. Perhaps she had some curiosity and a talent for response, even on paper; some scholars are convinced that Emma Bovary became more like her as Flaubert worked on. If Louise herself had been less greedy sexually and socially she might have become a better poet by working harder and learning some humility. We shall probably never know much more about her or the relationship, owing to much burning of correspondence, but unfortunately nothing can make Louise Colet's own work anything more than mediocre. Some of her poetry was included in the third volume of *Le Parnasse contemporain* which was published in the year of her death, the same year as Sand's, 1876. Only one other woman writer, Louise Seifert, was included, and she is now unknown. The same volume included work by Anatole France, Mallarmé and Verlaine. And that same year Mallarmé published *L'Après-midi d'un faune*.

That same year again, a woman died who might have been her friend. Like Louise Colet, she had watched George Sand and learnt something from her, but greatness is not contagious. This was the Comtesse d'Agoult, originally Marie Flavigny, daughter of a French officer and a German mother, born in Frankfurt in 1805 and known as a writer under the name of Daniel Stern. She published the novel *Nelida* in 1845, a few years after her long liaison with the glamorous pianist and composer Liszt had ended in bitterness. She portrayed her ex-lover as a painter called Guermann and was no kinder to him than George Sand had been to Musset in *Elle et lui*. At the end of the book he died – and serve him right, the author seems to indicate. The novel was published in Brussels two years before the revolution in France of 1848 and the interest of the book now is less personal than social, for 'Daniel Stern' was not entirely occupied with her unsatisfactory emotional life. She moved on to essays about political liberty and no sooner had the 1848 revolution taken place than she began to write a history of it. She even wrote a play about Joan of Arc which was successfully performed in Italy. Philosophy fascinated her and she believed that women should learn from the thinkers of the past and transmit their lessons to their children: while mothers fed their babies, she wrote, they could 'dream with Plato and meditate with Descartes'. She was devastatingly serious. The writer Barbey d'Aurevilly even talked unkindly about a 'triumféminat' of George Sand in the Academy, Daniel Stern at the Academy of Moral and Political Sciences and Rosa Bonheur (the painter) at the Beaux-Arts. Daniel Stern's *Souvenirs* published in 1877 are well worth reading but it is only fair to admit that she is remembered more for her association with Liszt and her jealousy of George Sand than for her books. Her daughter Cosima – Liszt's daughter – eventually married Wagner. Stern is not infuriating all the time, like the persistent Louise Colet, but the two are fine examples of how easy it had become for women to turn emotional 'copy' into what they hoped to be literature. They had seen the Romantic poets, Lamartine, Hugo, Musset, use their experience in this way but the men usually followed a more highly educated and increasingly more professional tradition. Women writers in the past had nearly all come, like Madame de La Fayette, from those well-endowed classes where parents gave some education to their daughters, although they saw it mostly as a useful social accomplishment. Very few women had the type of solid education which would have allowed them to think of 'professional' writing, even if they had been encouraged to do so, which they were not. Men 'processed' their experience before it reached the public in poetry, novels and plays. Women hardly ever did so because they had not had the chance to learn this specialized editorial art. They wrote intuitively, out of their own experience, and the term *littérature féminine*, women's writing, crept in and is still with us. There is a tendency to regard the term as essentially pejorative, and indeed the male chauvinists find it extremely useful.

Several generations of higher education for women have proved that they are perfectly capable of adding the element of cerebral control to their writing if they so choose. But why should one not accept that organic difference which Anthony Burgess has described through the complementary alternatives of yin and yang, the yielding and the forceful, 'the feminine and masculine poles in a pre-sexual, or, if we like, metaphorical sense'? Women writers in the Anglo-Saxon tradition, like Anglo-Saxon women generally, have too often tried to imitate men and sometimes succeeded. In France, the women writers gradually began to use some of the same techniques as men, and often took masculine or sexless names, but they did not try to be men. They knew they would have lost more than they gained – they would have lost the instinctive approach, an approach that is not exclusively self-centred and exists alongside the analytical approach. It is not limited to women, although in the past men, with years of solid education behind them, rather assumed that it was the one privilege available to what used to be called the weaker sex.

But even during the nineteenth century women did not all spend their time writing emotional entanglements out of their system. By one of those extraordinary accidents which have so often brought women into the limelight in France – this time a more gentle, long-lasting light – a whole series of books was written at this period by the daughter of a previous governor of Moscow (the one who outwitted Bonaparte). They were destined to educate at least two generations of children and are still read, studied and collected: in other words Sophie Rostopchine, Comtesse de Ségur, wrote the famous *Bibliothèque rose*; *Les petites filles modèles*, *Les Malheurs de Sophie*, *Un bon petit diable*, and so many others. They still entertain children, and adults too, particularly because they reveal a whole society: a study of these extraordinary little books, with their red and gold covers, tells the whole story – where your house was and how many rooms it had, at what age people married (husbands were noticeably older than wives), what they ate, what they believed in, why and how they punished their children.

Was she heartless and cruel? Was she a snob? These questions are still hotly discussed in France. For the social historian the Comtesse is a mine of information but the picture of life during the Second Empire is hardly edifying. A whole range of facts become lamentably clear: a great number of people outside the middle and upper classes had no education and indeed most adults living away from the towns could not even read. The poor were, of course, a race apart, but their betters, who had a sense of duty towards them, believed that they had the chance to improve themselves, despite their long working hours. It is sad to reflect that married life was so beset with problems that a wife – of the middle or upper classes, of course – preferred to discuss ideas, social or political, with her brother rather than with her husband. The Comtesse was obviously something of a feminist without being aware of it, and in her last books she seemed to have an inkling that a new generation of emancipated girls was slowly appearing, even in the aristocratic drawing-rooms. And although many of those naughty children are punished, the Comtesse did seem to realize that a relationship of love should replace one of fear. For social problems generally she had a ready-made solution: believe in God, He will restore order to this harsh world. When her complete works were published in France in the 1930s they filled twenty volumes. Few writers for children have 'lived' so long, although her own dates were 1799–1874.

She was not the only Russian woman writing in French at the time. In about 1873 Marie Bashkirtseff, aged nearly thirteen, was at work writing her journal, as many other girls were doing in many countries. But her journal, in eighty-four volumes or so, was different from all others, so frank and uninhibited that Anaïs Nin is pale and dull in comparison. This is because Marie did not subject her unconscious mind to any censorship. Her conscious mind and memory were not always accurate, but that was less important. Her death at twenty-four from tuberculosis was tragic, especially since her paintings are well worth attention and would probably have improved. On the other hand, if she had lived, there is the possibility that she might one day have lost her yearning for fame and decided to liquidate her early private writing. Less tragic but ironic and only recently explained (by Doris Langley Moore in *Marie and the Duke of H*) is the way her journals suffered at the hands of her contemporaries. The late nineteenth century was, after all, a great age of the novel, and when Marie's mother entrusted the manuscripts to a minor but unsuccessful novelist, André Theuriet, as editor, what could she have expected? He could hardly give the story a happy ending, as Tolstoy's first English translators tended to do, but he made Marie into a touching, amusing little angel, which she wasn't.

Theuriet could not resist temptation, he fictionalized the story and 'purified' the heroine. Fortunately enough of her sincerity in self-exposure came through for the elderly Gladstone in England to be impressed and write a long article in The Nineteenth Century in 1889.

One day perhaps the record will be put straight, the Bibliothèque Nationale in France will supervise the publication of the diaries as Marie wrote them and she and her writing will survive as herself alone. She and her work, in writing and painting, move in and out of fashion even eighty years after her death and a whole literature has grown up round her reputation. Her mother gave many of her paintings to art galleries in Russia. Women writers especially, as well as readers, have been intrigued by the story and by the intensity of her longing for immortality. Her family built her an ugly, would-be imposing tomb in the cemetery at Passy, which is worth a visit, although it is neglected. Even in the 1920s its pseudo-Gothic splendour was not so well kept as her admirers would have liked. Colette, in an article entitled *Mausoleums*, referred to the scrubbing and cleaning that was going on at the time and decided there would be no harm in restoring the tomb (although she preferred attention to be given to the living, not the dead), for she knew just how much Marie had yearned for fame, she 'would have given ten years of her delicate and burning youth for one sprig of official laurel'.

Many women went on writing without always knowing why, and when it came to pen-names men's names were still popular. In the 1880s the successful magazine *La Vie Parisienne* received an anonymous manuscript which the editors liked so much that they published it at once and asked the author to give his name. In fact it was her name and it was full of memories. Sibylle Gabrielle Marie Antoinette Riqueti de Mirabeau was a great-niece of the famous Revolutionary figure and the last of the line. Her own story had been strange enough so far. Her parents were separated while she was very young and she was brought up by her grandfather, a former colonel, in

Nancy. She was bright and as she grew up she met many writers. She helped copy out letters for her uncle and god-father Adolphe de Bacourt when he was editing the memoirs of Talleyrand and never missed anything from the conversations of adults. As a result she went to buy a copy of Pascal's *Lettres Provinciales* when she was still a little girl – for she had overheard that he shared her anti-Jesuit views. She met Sainte-Beuve, Lamartine, George Sand's editor friend Buloz, and Marceline Desbordes-Valmore. Only Lamartine spoke to the poor lady, she remembered. Later acquaintances included Paul de Musset, Octave Feuillet, Cora Pearl and an assortment of the aristocracy. She married the Comte de Martel de Janville when she was very young and spent the rest of her long life – which lasted until 1932 – pouring out novels with intriguing titles: *Autour du divorce, Ohe! Les psychologues, Sportmanomanie, Trop de chic* and endless others. It might be true to say that they are more entertaining for the modern reader than the books themselves but this is unfair because 'Gyp', as she cheerfully called herself, had value for three reasons. After the languid descriptions and moody apostrophes of Romantic writing her dialogue was and still can be good entertainment, for it hurtles along at a fantastic pace, much of it in fact set out as though intended for the stage. A drawback now is her love of slang; she had a good ear, a good memory and a love for new expressive words that society, and especially young people, found amusing to invent. Who was to know which ones would last? Pity the translator but enjoy the chat for what it is worth. Her books were popular in England, but London Library readers must have enjoyed them in French, for they can still choose from four full shelves. Those with drawings and photographs are particularly fascinating.

Many of her novels contain young girl heroines who no doubt represent memories of her own adolescence, and French critics have seen them as earlier versions of Claudine at her silliest, busily trying to shock everyone, although Gyp was not touched by the decadence of the 1890s. The heroine of *Le*

Mariage de Chiffon is a genuinely attractive, independently minded tomboy. At least one of her heroes was a great success, 'Petit Bob', aged eight, who is taken everywhere by his grandfather or his father and makes naïve comments which are of course far from innocent although never shocking. He goes to art exhibitions, the circus, the zoo and the Chambre des Députés. At the Chambre he tries to make his father explain the difference between the right and the left, and to say why the Abbé, his tutor, believes his mother to have advanced ideas.

Of Gyp's writing nothing remains but her influence and her memoirs, giving significant details about how children of the upper classes were educated at home and at school – a convent in her case, which she hated. Yet among all the earnest outpourings of her contemporaries her books are cheerfully refreshing. Nietzsche, in *Ecce Homo*, even rated her as a psychologist along with Maupassant and Jules Lemaître the critic. Cocteau, when puzzled by this statement, asked Lemaître to explain 'this heterogeneous list of names'. The older man told him at once: 'Nietzsche is talking about what you can see on the station bookstall at Sils-Maria.' However, the English critic Geoffrey Saintsbury justifiably admired her gift for lively storytelling. What nobody can admire is her late involvement in politics, when she became a supporter of the ridiculous and wrong-headed General Boulanger. While taking part in a demonstration she was even kidnapped. Understandably she did not write up this story. Deplorably she expressed strong anti-Semitic attitudes, but at this period in the history of France she was by no means alone, and in that she was typical of her time. She knew very well that her work would not last, and she wrote to entertain herself and her readers.

Among late-nineteenth-century women writers whose names are known today it was rare to find any with such reactionary views, and it was no excuse for Gyp that she was a Mirabeau and a Martel, or that she had once met an old man who had been a page to Louis XV at Versailles. Two very different women took a basically liberal view: Juliette Adam was a founder-editor of the republican *Nouvelle Revue* in 1879 and wrote well about foreign affairs. Her (second) husband was both politician and journalist, while she herself had written poems and *récits* ever since 1858. Her salon, where Gambetta was a frequent guest, became more firmly left wing and she herself wrote novels, with evocative titles: *Païenne* (Pagan) in 1883, *Chrétienne* (Christian) twenty years later. She was the obvious person to attack the paradoxical Pierre-Joseph Proudhon who considered himself a social reformer: if women had imagination, judgement and memory, he said, he still believed they had no ideas and had not even invented their own distaff.

Another valuable journalist was Caroline Rémy, known as Séverine, who entered the profession through Jules Vallès, left-wing journalist and novelist himself. For a time she edited her own paper called *Le Cri du peuple*, but later moved to free-lance work. Like Gyp she had been temporarily led astray by General Boulanger and even succumbed for a time to the reasoning of the anti-Dreyfusards. Fortunately she soon recovered and at the end of a long career was pro-Dreyfus and unswervingly left-wing.

In that last quarter of a century between the death of George Sand and 1900 women writers had come a long way. Some, like Marcelle Tinayre, were uncommitted at first but soon began to link feminism, even of a non-militant kind, with the need for social improvement. In 1899 her well-educated heroine Hellé, who gave her name to a novel, declined to marry a successful and fashionable writer because she was drawn to a man who cared for underprivileged people, men and women trying to educate themselves. Under his influence she befriended and employed an unmarried mother and soon, naturally, she became the happy wife of the young man who had seen that philanthropy was not enough. Literature was not enough either if women hoped to gain recognition as citizens on equal footing with men. If the word 'suffragette' officially came into the English language in 1880 (according to the *Oxford English Dictionary*) it did not become French and is still only defined in the *Encyclopédie Larousse* in relation to Britain. Women seemed to think the chance of winning the vote was so unreal that their campaigning was less militant, less direct, than in other countries.

However, the last years of the century saw hectic journalistic activity in the field of feminist magazines. They did not always last very long, but their titles were significant: *La Revue féministe, La Femme de l'avenir, Les Droits de la femme*, and several others. Not surprisingly the women overdid their special pleading and naturally the men laughed at them. But who now has heard more than faint echoes of their attackers, such as Albert Cim, who singled out would-be women writers as his target in *Bas-Bleus*, written as early as 1894. André Billy, literary historian of *la belle époque*, has quoted that only too memorable little rhyme '*Si tu veux être heureux, n'épousez pas un bas-bleu*' (If you want to be happy, don't marry a bluestocking). As for the vote, that was far enough away. The French writer Françoise Parturier has pointed out that at the turn of the century 'Madame Curie did not vote, but the boy who swept out her laboratory voted, like Pierre Curie'. Not until 1944 did General de Gaulle realize the usefulness of votes for women and two years later the right was at last written into the constitution. In the meantime women writers worked for women's independence, often, as it happened, by not making obvious demands. Their names are not forgotten, hard work seemed only to improve their health and many who were well known in the 1880s, Judith Gautier, Rachilde and Séverine among them, lived and worked well into the twentieth century.

By the end of the nineteenth century women had written out the most urgent of their personal problems, as George Sand had done, and even if they did not all write so well as her they were learning to handle their material more selectively and they were moving out beyond the purely personal, the intuitive, although they never abandoned this element, fortunately. Gradually women were becoming better educated: in 1891 a woman of thirty-seven had won her way through the Baccalauréat examination, usually taken now at eighteen or so, via the University of Lyon. Ten years later it was possible for a woman to register with a faculty of letters and take the equivalent of an ordinary degree. Over half a century was to pass before women would be allowed to take the entrance examination to the *hautes écoles* in France, schools such as the École polytechnique which give a more practical training than the universities and demand an extremely high standard. When these examinations were opened to them young women embarrassed the examiners by taking some of the first places.

But this was in the future. In the meantime women generally, supported unconsciously by the women writers and by women such as Yvonne Sarcey, who opened the Université des Annales, a kind of adult education establishment, looked ahead and went ahead, but in unexpected, unorthodox ways.

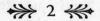

2

Before Lélia

The women of the late nineteenth century in France, many of whom had probably been brought up on the satisfying moral tales of the *Bibliothèque rose*, may not have realized how many women had already contributed to their culture and their literature, long before Lélia or her inventor were born. The French language had struggled into existence during the ninth century and two hundred years later produced a masterpiece, *La Chanson de Roland*. At this stage few people were educated, but when they had the chance to learn, usually through the Church, they learnt thoroughly, and it can be assumed that many of them began to write. This was true of women as well as of men. Women may well have written works of value in several European countries just after the dark ages but few such compositions are known to us. The earliest woman writer in France did not write in French but in Latin, as did her teacher, lover and husband, the scholastic philosopher known as Abélard, correctly Pierre Béranger. The few surviving letters that Héloïse wrote to him have been translated into French and deserve to be better known, they are one of the first expressions of an intelligent woman's total love for a man. The brilliant Abélard could not have loved his pupil as he did had she not been intelligent and perceptive (she even argued rationally against the usefulness of marriage) and her letters are still quoted today by analysts of 'le couple', such as Suzanne Lilar. These are the letters of a realist who had experienced all the pleasures of love, physical and emotional, and in her convent exile she forgot none of them. Even during Mass, she wrote, she was obsessed by her memories. These letters perpetuated her existence and gave her name to that

41

remarkable novel by Jean-Jacques Rousseau which in one way inaugurated the whole modern era of literature: *Julie*, much better known by its sub-title *La Nouvelle Héloïse*, published in 1761. Héloïse is nearly always curtly dismissed by Anglo-Saxon editors of reference books: 'See Abélard', they usually say. Older editions of the *Encyclopédie Larousse* allow her a life of her own, and even mention the *opérette-bouffe Héloïse et Abélard* composed by Henri Litolff in 1872. The excellent music is said to compensate for the choice of subject (*singulier*) and the libretto (*d'un goût douteux*). George Moore's treatment of the story is regarded as one of his greatest achievements but the fine version by Helen Waddell the British scholar is, as its title *Peter Abelard* suggests, more concerned with the hero than the heroine, his poems are quoted more than her letters. A French academic (a woman) has put forward a theory that these letters were 'improved' by Abélard but brilliant as he was, he is not thought capable of 'inventing' them.

The dates of Héloïse's birth and death are known (1101–1164) and her body is said to have been brought to Abélard's tomb in the Père Lachaise cemetery. In contrast hardly anything is known of her presumed contemporary Marie de France who wrote, in the later part of the century, narrative poems called *lais*, fables translated from English and an adaptation of a Latin tale about the trial of a sinful knight. 'Marie is my name, I come from France,' she stated and that is the limit of our direct information. It is known indirectly that she was born in Normandy and seems to have lived and worked in England at the court of Henry II and his queen, Eleanor of Aquitaine, who were, of course, both French. Marie dedicated her lays to the King and there is a theory that she may have been one of his half-sisters, for Geoffrey Plantagenet may have been her natural father. Other theories are that she may have been a well-educated nun – for many anonymous nuns were known to write in prose and verse – or a kind of female *jongleur*. There is an irresistible charm about her writing which is naïve only in expression, as in the *Lai du Chèvrefeuille*, which compares the

love of Tristan and Iseult to the honeysuckle twined round the
hazel-tree:

> Mais si l'on veut les séparer,
> Le coudrier meurt promptement,
> Le chèvrefeuille également.
> Belle amie, ainsi est de nous,
> Ni vous sans moi, ni moi sans vous.

A translation can only convey something of the telling
simplicity:

> But if the two be put apart
> The hazel dies at once,
> The honeysuckle too.
> Fair friend, it is the same with us,
> No you without me, no me without you.

There is nothing naïve, however, about the story of Eliduc,
the man who had to deal with two women, and the psychology
of the solution is fascinating: one of the women, the legal wife,
took matters into her own hands, told him it was wrong for
him not to live with someone he loved so much and decided
that it was time to get herself to a nunnery. So she established
one herself and presumably lived happily ever after, substi-
tuting the love of her flock for that of her husband; either she
loved him enough to let him go or else she preferred power –
probably the latter.

Goethe thought of Marie in a truly romantic way that 'the
mists of time, which grow thicker between us and her, make
her poems more exquisite and more dear to us'. The historical
interest of the lays is that they show a new attitude to love,
equally far from the primitive violence of the *chansons de geste*
and the subtleties of courtly love as expressed in poems such
as *Le Roman de la Rose*. Marie is thought to have heard the old
Celtic tales in Brittany and was obviously intrigued by the way
they presented love as an overwhelming, unexplained feeling,

mysterious and often melancholy, sometimes only consummated in death. The atmosphere of several stories seemed almost to anticipate Romanticism, it was so different from the poems of courtly love, with their complicated symbolism and code of behaviour which tended to make the love relationship into a kind of superior social game. By writing these stories in French, in England, she brought the two countries more closely together at a time when England owned parts of France and earned ill-fame for one of the greatest crimes of the middle ages, the murder of Becket, and the possible *crime passionel* when Queen Eleanor was said to have plotted to kill one of her husband's mistresses, Fair Rosamond. The lays diverted the nobility of both countries, partly because some of them may have told true stories about recognizable people; they were never forgotten in France, understandably so, for they are the first sign of French preoccupation with the psychological novel, and of women's involvement in this kind of story-telling. During the nineteenth century various writers (men) tried to improve them by assimilating them to the taste of the time, but they failed. More may be discovered one day about Marie de France, or even about women writers who were her contemporaries, and a long time passed before any other women in France wrote for publication.

Christine de Pisan did so because like so many women writers who followed her she needed money. She was Italian by birth, born in Venice in about 1365, the daughter of an astrologer. After he had been called to the court of Charles V in France she married there, but was left a widow at twenty-five with three children to support. She wrote many poems, much prose, some of which has yet to be published in France, and combined the business of earning money with the defence of women against male chauvinism. Understandably perhaps not all men were prepared to swallow the inevitable absurdities of courtly love and it was a pity that the intelligent Jean de Meung, who completed Guillaume de Lorris's great poem *Le Roman de la Rose*, belonged to this group. He did not believe in

44

love – no doubt he accepted sex – and he had no patience with women. His attitudes were clearly expressed in the poem and the widowed Christine was determined to speak up for her sex against him. He was a highly educated *clerc*, not of noble birth, and as far as women were concerned he advocated orthodox politeness but mistrust of them:

> *Dames honore et demoiselles,*
> *Mais point ne se fie trop à elles,*
> *Car il pourrait s'en repentir:*
> *Combien a-t-on vu en souffrir!*

> Honour ladies young and old,
> But do not be too trusting,
> This is something men may regret:
> How often has one seen them suffering!

Courtly love seemed a little old-fashioned now to the growing intellectual class and Christine de Pisan realized that many women needed other activities than that of being adored. Like many women writers in succeeding centuries she had been well educated by her father but when her husband died nobody helped her in her legal struggle to inherit his money. When she began to write poems she attracted attention and sympathy and even an invitation from King Henry IV of England to visit his court, because her son had gone there. However she procrastinated until he was back in France, for she was afraid to move away from her protectors. Then, again like many women writers who followed her, she protested too much and was found to be tedious. However, she was determined to press on with the cause and *La Cité des Dames* (The City of Women) of 1405 was in fact the first work by a woman about what is now called the women's movement. The figures of Reason, Fairness and Justice appear to the author and urge her to tell the world about the virtues and capabilities of women. She believed that education was the first step and insisted in her *Livre des trois vertus* (Book of the Three Virtues) that women from different types of social background needed different types of education. There was to be one sort for 'princesses and great ladies', another for ladies in court circles and a third for '*femmes d'état*, bourgeoises and women of the common people'. Many centuries were to pass before much was done to help this third group of women.

At least one male historian has called Christine 'cantankerous', a usual attitude when a woman attempts to defend her own sex, but it is worth remembering today that she was not over-ambitious on their behalf. The educational programme which she set out in so much detail was not intended to bring them into open competition with men and she does not seem to have seen any future for them in politics and the professions. She was so reasonable that she did not even wish to see men ground into the dust and like some other feminist writers in later centuries she even enlisted one of them to help her. This was Jean Charlier de Gerson, a learned churchman and chancellor of the University of Paris who respected her intelligence and sided with her in her attacks on the narrow-minded Jean de Meung. Like most precursors and pioneers she did not have a particularly happy life, which ended with retirement to a convent, a poem about the glorious life of Joan of Arc and her own life-story. It was no compensation to become a chapter in the history of feminism but the important thing is that her poems have their own value and are regularly included in anthologies of French verse compiled by editors unconcerned with the rights of women.

As a writer she was followed by a woman who was even more of a great lady then the mysterious Marie, for the princess who became famous as Marguerite de Navarre was the grand-daughter of the poet Charles d'Orléans and elder sister of François Ier, Princesse d'Angoulême, and born in 1492. Her second marriage made her queen of the kingdom of Navarre and she was destined to become the grandmother of Henri IV. She had a gift for languages and in addition to the Latin,

Italian, Spanish and English current among the well educated at the time she learnt Hebrew and began Greek when she was forty. She felt inferior because she could not study the ancients in their own language. She wrote poems, plays and prose. Her best-known work is the famous *Heptameron*, written perhaps with the help of collaborators, not published until after her death but now usually available in translation. It consists of a set of stories modelled on those of Boccaccio in the *Decameron*. Although the author enjoyed a good story and was no prude, she was aware of changes in the moral climate and through the characters (including herself) who tell and discuss these tales she made a firm attempt to instruct, refine and civilize her readers. In fact she took the concepts of the medieval courts of love forward into the Renaissance and at the same time protected religious thinkers and writers with avant-garde views at the time, including Calvin. At Nérac in the Lot et Garonne her court, full of writers and rarely attended by her rather younger husband, anticipated the salons of the future. Marguerite de Navarre has been described as humanist rather than writer, moralist rather than poet. She was certainly courageous and although not autocratic she was better placed than many people, even eminent theologians, to write what she wanted.

Some of her religious works were circulated during her lifetime but her *Dernières poésies* were hardly known, and certainly not published, in France until 1896. By chance one of these poems, *Le Miroir de l'âme pécheresse*, had been available in principle to English readers for several centuries in a manuscript bound as a small book, formerly in the Royal Library at Whitehall Palace and now preserved in the Bodleian Library at Oxford. Its translator was none other than Princess Elizabeth of England who wrote out a careful prose version of it in 1544 when she was eleven. The original copy in French may have been brought to England by Elizabeth's mother Anne Boleyn, who had been in Marguerite's service in France. The Princess was a skilled linguist and wrote poetry herself, but she probably translated this poem as a thank-offering to Queen

Katherine Parr and for this reason embroidered her initials on the cover she worked herself in gold and silver for the manuscript. She had to thank her stepmother because she herself had for some reason earned her father's displeasure and relied on Katherine to mention her when she wrote to her husband. No doubt the young Elizabeth chose this poem as her gift because the title at least implied remorse. She called it 'The glasse of the synnefull soule', but unfortunately did not mention the author. The poem is not of high literary interest but Marguerite's Calvinist sympathies may themselves have been mirrored in the absence of any references to saints and martyrs. Princess Elizabeth did not attempt to render the author's rhyming decasyllables but she made a smoothly flowing version, writing on faintly drawn lines in a fair rounded hand:

Where is the hell full of travayle, payne, mischieve and turment, where is the pytte of cursydnes, out of the wich doth springe all despaire. Is there any hell so profunde that is sufficiente to punishe the tenth parte of my synnes, wich be of so great a number that the infinite doth make the shadow so darke that i can not accompte them, or els scanth se them. ffor i am to farre entred amongest them and that worse is, i have not the power to obtayne the true knowledge of one.

Fortunately Henry VIII forgave his daughter, although nobody knows what 'wrong' she had done.

During the reign of Marguerite of Navarre there was much discussion about the education of women in the middle and upper classes and the same women all hoped they could be like Laura and inspire a poet as great as Petrarch. Few of them did, but the sixteenth century produced at least two women who profited from a splendid education.

The first was a dazzling poet. Louise Labé came from Lyon, which was then a city more of culture than of commerce, where the women considered themselves superior to those of

Paris. *Galanterie* preoccupied everyone and a whole group of women poets flourished there. Outside the world of the specialist only Labé's name is known, for twenty-three sonnets, three elegies and a 'debate' between folly and love. One longs to know more about her: she was married to a rope-maker and described as *'la belle cordelière'*. She would be the ideal heroine for a dashing film, for she is said to have dressed as a boy, joined the army at sixteen and fought at the siege of Perpignan as 'Capitaine Loys'. She is said also to have been a lesbian and addressed her intense poems to women, not men. Her concentrated, polished manner, her skilled and flexible prosody, have been compared to that of Shakespeare but her sonnets were more intense, if equally ambiguous. They were the poems of someone who relished every moment of love-making and could never have enough of it:

> *Baise m'encor, rebaise moy et baise:*
> *Donne m'en un de tes plus savoureys,*
> *Donne m'en un de tes plus amoureux:*
> *Je t'en rendray quatre plus chaus que braise.* . . .

> Kiss me, kiss me once and again:
> Give me the kiss that is sweetest,
> Give me the kiss that is deepest,
> I'll give you four kisses hotter than flame. . . .

She knew Latin, Spanish and Italian (her first sonnet is in this language) and had as many talents as lovers. She believed all women could and should equal or surpass men 'not only in beauty but in learning and *vertu*'. Jean Larnac, chronicler of French women writers, has pointed out that in her epistle to Clémence de Bourges, another woman poet of Lyon, she distinguishes, as Proust was to do, between genuine memories and those which are 'arranged', consciously or unconsciously, to produce a particular effect.

There could be no greater contrast than the eccentric, argumentative spinster Marie Le Jars de Gournay, who lived with her two cats and worshipped Montaigne. In fact he regarded her as his 'daughter by alliance' and she produced no fewer than eleven editions of his Essays after his death. When not engaged in this work she wrote poetry, moral dissertations and literary debate. Montaigne and all his admirers owe her a great deal.

Towards the end of her life (1645) she saw the seventeenth-century battle of the sexes, when the poet Agrippa d'Aubigné regretfully turned down his daughters' plea for education, maintaining that it was really only necessary for princesses and great ladies. Many men sincerely believed that women were not unintelligent and at this stage men were not afraid of rivalry in the professional field, not even in the literary world. They seemed to be afraid of excess, namely pedantry, as though any sudden chance to learn, so far available only to a favoured few, would distract them from what should have been their proper study, i.e. the men themselves, and generally go to their heads. And of course it did, leading to Molière's attacks in his two plays *Les Précieuses ridicules* and *Les Femmes savantes*. Surely Molière has not let women down; that a man of such perception, such humour and such humanity should have gained a reputation as an anti-feminist is a disaster and is probably inaccurate. One of his characters conceded that women should be well informed; but they should not be too informed and sometimes – most women soon learn this – they should even conceal what they know. Molière had no doubt suffered from too many dealings with actresses.

The *précieuses*, even when not *ridicules*, were fair game, but before their excesses became boring and obvious they had established a few types of influence of wider and more realistic scope than the courts of love or the literary circles that formed Louise Labé. They had invented the salon, which men found helpful. These social occasions allowed the men to develop friendships and love affairs and to advertise themselves by reading and discussing their writing. The Marquise de Rambouillet, who was half-Italian, was one of the first to organize a salon in the famous room with its blue velvet walls decorated in gold and silver. The Hôtel de Rambouillet, built to her own revolutionary design and unfortunately demolished when the Louvre was built, became a cultural centre for a whole generation until preciosity in fact destroyed itself. The Marquise had little literary ambition herself but enjoyed fostering it in others. The famous *Guirlande de Julie* is a set of poems each written by a different writer and addressed to her daughter. As for the Marquis de Rambouillet, he is never mentioned but presumably paid the heavy expenses needed to keep these literary party games going.

The *roman à clef* was one of these, but the formidable Mademoiselle de Scudéry would have been shocked at so frivolous an association. She was a spinster of great stamina who had obviously read Honoré d'Urfé's *L'Astrée* carefully. Her two best-known novels, *Le Grand Cyrus* and *Clélie*, ran to ten volumes each and she lived until well over ninety. Her brother Georges, who wrote mainly plays, helped her a little but he was decidedly inferior as a writer. All the salon society of the time appeared in the books under grand classical names (Madame de Rambouillet was 'Arthénice' and the author herself was 'Sapho'). 'Le Grand Cyrus' was probably Le Grand Condé, whom the Scudérys supported in the civil wars of La Fronde. These interminable works were translated (even into Arabic) and enjoyed by endless readers including Mrs Pepys, reprimanded by her husband for telling the stories to others as she devoured them.

The Scudéry family had gone to le Havre from Provence and then to Paris. Madeleine was ugly, lived with a dog, a monkey, three chameleons and a parrot to whom the physicist Leibniz wrote poems in Latin. If her unreadable novels belong to literary history they belong to the history of feminism too. Their author thought that marriage was a form of slavery and pointed out in *Le Grand Cyrus* that women spent years learning how to dance (and they could not dance for very long) but hardly any time learning how to think, talk and act. She too was against pedantry and insisted that there was a degree of education somewhere between *la science* and *l'ignorance totale*. It is all very well now to laugh at the *Carte de Tendre*, the 'map' of 'tender' feelings set out in *Clélie* (1654–60). It was an immense success at the time and the attempt at the analysis of emotions and behaviour places it above the level of romantic novels. 'The main features of the map', according to *The Oxford Companion to French Literature*, 'are three cities of Tendre, on three rivers, Tendre sur Estime, Tendre sur Reconnaissance, and Tendre sur Inclination. Three roads, all starting from Nouvelle Amitié, lead to the several cities, passing through stages appropriate to the respective goals, such as Sincérité, Probité, or Petits soins, Empressement. But wrong turnings take the traveller to the Lac d'Indifférence or the Mer d'Inimitié.' Theses are written about the *Carte de Tendre* even if no one reads *Clélie* or defends its author. But something of the Scudéry spirit has remained in French literature all the same.

The Scudéry novels were admired by one of the author's friends who did not live so long but exists for ever – Madame de Sévigné, who herself appears in *Clélie* as 'Clarinte'. The famous letters were once required reading for English schoolgirls who usually found them a bore because the mother–daughter relationship seemed too intense even if some sense of contemporary life and history came through. Their value was in their natural style, all the more remarkable when one thinks of the artificialities which surrounded their writer. She did not have an easy life, she was orphaned before she was eight, and widowed at twenty-five, when her spendthrift husband was killed in a duel. She adored her uninteresting daughter and in writing to her at length continually all her life she wrote the history of her times without making any conscious effort to do so. Her letters were read aloud in salons and she earned the friendship and respect of everyone she met, including the Sun King himself. She was a splendid example of what a woman could achieve by simply being herself, and if her daughter failed to respond to her mother's outpourings of affection it was no doubt because this mother was too overwhelming. If her daughter had responded or spent more time with her mother then there would have been fewer letters and fewer descriptions of court occasions and town gossip. Madame de Sévigné would probably never have sat down to write a novel and as a result she wrote spontaneously, a good thing for posterity. And although women had no vote in France until after the Second World War it is worth noting that after her husband's death she was allowed to take his place in the Breton 'parliament', the États de Bretagne.

Indirectly, therefore, the seventeenth century in France, age of the Sun King, the start of Versailles and the great classical dramatists, owed a great deal to the women who did not all write in an organized way or in a style likely to last. The social scene was hardly one of ease and refinement, the civil wars of the Fronde dragged on from 1648 to 1653, the air was full of violence. The early salons, even the activity of the *précieuses*, contributed a calmer atmosphere to conversation and behaviour. The way was being prepared for the age of reason and the modern world. Many women wrote, some of their work still intrigues us, even if the novels especially are more consulted than read, less well known than, say, the fairy tales of Madame d'Aulnoy. Many wrote far too much for our taste, two of them wrote hardly enough and one of these hardly at all.

This was Ninon, correctly Anne de Lenclos, who lived in Paris from 1620 to 1705. Her father was famous for his duelling, she was orphaned at eight and little is known of her education. She led a hectic nymphomaniac existence and fascinated every man she met, including Cardinal Richelieu, who is said to have made her an allowance for life. She was no great beauty but had indefinable charm and endless wit. The *précieuses*, she said, were the Jansenists of love. Her talent for transforming lovers into friends led to a lifelong relationship with the *libertin* critic Saint-Evremond who spent many years in

England as a political exile. Their surviving letters, written when they were approaching old age, make good reading, and she is credited with some dramatic sketches. When she was young, jealous wives and mothers (including Madame de Sévigné) would try to keep their menfolk away from her. But it was impossible to ignore her. Saint-Simon wrote about her in his *Mémoires* and she was 'Clarice' in *Clélie*. As she grew older women began to seek her friendship because she was accepted as a symbol of taste and wit, young men were even advised to pay their respects to her, and her salon had one new virtue: she was far from being a snob and her policy was to bring together friends from both the aristocracy and the ever-rising middle class. Molière is said to have asked her advice when writing *Tartuffe* and at the very end of her life she made a symbolic bequest. She had met a very young man whose intelligence impressed her, and she left him some money to buy books: his name, the name he took, was Voltaire.

One of her friends, also a close friend of Madame de Sévigné, was a very different woman and one of the finest novelists France has produced: Madame de La Fayette. So far there had always been narrative in all forms, and ever since the time of Marie de France the strongest interest of the story had been psychological, even if Scarron's *Roman comique* had to be written to put all the romantic novelists in their place. Madame de La Fayette invented the psychological novel that still persists today in spite of all the attempts that have been made to demolish it. Sheer reaction to the effusions of Honoré d'Urfé, Madeleine de Scudéry and others, as well as her taste for concentrated, reticent narrative, led her to invent as it were the short novel. Her type of treatment was consciously revived by Raymond Radiguet's imitation of her in *Le Bal du comte d'Orgel*, published in 1924. Madame de La Fayette's closeness to the royal circle, and again her own character, led to an insistence on anonymity which many women writers in France and other countries still felt bound to keep.

Madame de La Fayette had been married very young, had

two sons, lived in Paris while her husband was usually in the Auvergne. She enjoyed the company of literary men in the city and it has always been known that the famous writer of maxims, La Rochefoucauld, and others took some part in her writing. They certainly discussed it and advised her. Her earlier work had been influenced by the Scudéry romances but by the time she published her masterpiece *La Princesse de Clèves* in 1678 (after eight years of work and interruptions) the only influences were her own good taste and possibly her own experience. She was concerned not with the 'happily ever after' but with the not-too-happy now, within marriage and within love. She was the first emotional realist among women writers or even among novelists, women or men. At the same time she went to great lengths to remove her story from the reality of contemporary society, using a plot based on an episode from Brantôme's *Lives of Gallant Ladies* and set in the mid-sixteenth century. She took her writing seriously and there were even two writing desks in her house, one of them in her bedroom. Desks were surprisingly rare in aristocratic houses of this period — writing was done by secretaries in their own more modest dwellings. Like La Rochefoucauld she watched and listened, assessing and analysing human behaviour. Through her friends at the court she heard many stories which were potential plots for novels and she heard much that led her to present, like the classical dramatists, the conflict between love and duty. Unlike most of them however she admitted, through her writing, that the satisfaction of being dutiful was overrated.

The publication of *La Princesse de Clèves* was a literary and social event. Some people had heard readings from it and when it actually appeared there was such a rush to buy it that those unfortunate enough to live in the provinces had to wait three months for their copy. The scene where the Princess confesses to her husband that her conduct might have fallen short of perfect caused a scandal and to the author's (or authors') chagrin *Le Mercure galant* published a long, anonymous, well-reasoned and merciless attack on it. Madame de La Fayette denied authorship of the novel to many people but admitted it in a purposely obscure way to an old admirer whom she met again in 1691 after La Rochefoucauld had died. The novel seems inexhaustible. Perhaps one day scholars will discover more details about how the book was written and they are already at work on the analysis of its unconscious sexual symbolism. It pleased Cocteau, in *Le Secret professionnel*, to dwell on its aristocratic quality. 'Nothing is more disconcerting', he wrote (this was in 1922) 'than aristocracy in any form. This fairy-tale, at once so divine, so human and so inhuman, makes novels dealing with what Tolstoy calls the high spheres look terribly vulgar. Compared with Madame de La Fayette's book the *monde* portrayed in the best novels becomes the *demi-monde*.'

But none of her other work reaches the level of *La Princesse de Clèves*. In 1959 a short novel was discovered in a private library in Baltimore, Maryland: *Isabelle, ou Le Journal amoureux d'Espagne*, and there seems evidence that Madame de La Fayette might have written it. The Library of Congress in Washington has stated that it was wrongly attributed to one of her imitators and the Bibliothèque Nationale in Paris has not been certain that she did not write it.

So the seventeenth century ended and at this point it is worth glancing at an unusual woman who lived half-way into the eighteenth, not precisely a writer but a translator who suddenly found herself involved in a major literary quarrel. The story of Madame Dacier proves that a woman could earn some reputation as a scholar even at this time without lapsing into the tedious excesses of *les femmes savantes*. She was born in 1651, daughter of a Protestant from Caen who had settled as a teacher in Saumur. He taught her Greek and Latin which she learnt more quickly than his other students, all young men. Her father and other scholars entrusted her with work on the classical poets and she quickly married André Dacier, her father's most brilliant pupil. The two young people had been courting each other by exchanging compliments about each other's comments on classical texts. Although she was more intelligent than her husband she skilfully concealed the fact (taking Molière's advice) and quietly proceeded with translation from the classics. She published her translation of The Iliad in 1711 and of The Odyssey in 1716, earning praise and popularity.

Unexpectedly she found herself involved, and violently so, in one of the most important literary arguments that have ever raged in the argumentative country of France, the quarrel of the ancients and the moderns, which everyone had thought to be over. It was impossible to decide where the greater literary quality lay: with the old world or the new, for how precisely were they to be compared? Houdar de La Motte produced a versified translation of The Iliad based on that of Madame Dacier, and she denounced it as hardly Homeric. La Motte had aimed to adapt the Greek poet to the social requirements of the early eighteenth century, as Pope did in England. There was a tremendous row and the two translators were not reconciled for a long time.

It is to Sainte-Beuve that we owe a fair account of Madame Dacier's work. Her translation is obviously not acceptable today and her style was even old-fashioned for her own day, but she was the first of the many women translators who have worked for two centuries trying to make major works accessible to everyone. She was so highly esteemed that the King made an exceptional arrangement: she was to inherit her husband's post as keeper of the royal library, a rare honour for a woman in those days. Sadly she died first. Hers had been a life of hard work and reasonable recognition, but when she was asked by a German admirer to write something in his album she might have seemed reactionary: 'Silence is the adornment of women', she wrote, as though agreeing with Molière. But, as Sainte-Beuve added, she wrote it in Greek and in fact she was adapting a line by Sophocles.

As the eighteenth century came and progressed women

began to do practically everything they wanted or thought they wanted, or dared to want. None of the better seventeenth-century women writers had been obvious feminists and if Mademoiselle de Scudéry said her say on the subject her remarks were well hidden in the ten-volume novels. But the achievements were there, the best proof that women could write well and were read by intelligent people. The gradual spread of education for women, even if it did not yet reach the masses, increased the audience for writers of all kinds. The eighteenth century brought not only the famous salons, those of Madame du Deffand, Madame de Tencin and Madame de Geoffrin, but a whole series of women novelists writing with competence and charm but destined mostly to oblivion now were it not for Sainte-Beuve's enjoyment of them.

More absorbing today are the writings more closely connected with life, Madame du Deffand's correspondence with Horace Walpole, the passionate love letters written to the Comte de Guibert by Julie de Lespinasse, or the memoirs of the sensational actress Clairon, although they may not have had much connection with fact. Both men and women applied themselves seriously to the question of women's education, the priest Fénelon wrote a practical and even democratic treatise on the subject, Diderot invited a few women to contribute to the *Encyclopédie* and women who could not aspire to literary heights learnt the pleasures of amateur writing, prose and verse, and could see themselves in print in magazines especially produced for them. Finally it was a woman, Madame de Graffigny, who scored a great success with the partly satiric, partly romantic *Lettres d'une Péruvienne*. It has been described as a 'skilful pastiche of [Montesquieu's] *Lettres persanes*, with a touch of *Pamela* and a pinch of precious metaphysics'. She also achieved some success as a dramatist, never very easy for a woman at this time.

In fact women seemed to be doing well. Madame du Châtelet wrote commentaries on Leibniz and Newton while Madame de Pompadour it was said ran the country. Madame de Genlis educated the royal children and theorized about education generally, although she seemed too good to be true. In 1766 was born the woman who lived and wrote through the Revolution and the great divide that changed the whole constitution of France. This was Mademoiselle Germaine Necker, Madame de Staël, whose *curriculum vitae* contained at least two significant coincidental dates: in 1789, when the Revolution broke out, she divorced her husband while her complete works were published in the year that her old enemy Napoleon died, 1821.

If Mademoiselle de Scudéry had had stamina, so had Germaine de Staël, of a different kind. She had enough energy for politics, writing, salon-keeping, care for her parents, love and sex. One can only pity her lovers, especially Benjamin Constant – but at least he wrote brilliantly about the experience – and remember that Madame de Staël has been described as the only man whom the much-loved Madame de Récamier ever loved in return. If Germaine had been able to love and hold a man more intelligent than herself she might have been almost happy; but Constant was not prepared to accept such a terrifying responsibility. So she is remembered as ugly and unhappy and not read as often as she deserved. Her strength as a writer was not in her novels. *Delphine* and *Corinne*, for instance, are enjoyable for what we can see of her, her friends, heroes and ideas in it. Yet *Dix Années d'Exil* (Ten Years of Exile), first published in London in 1821, is excellent reading, especially her description of Russia, which she saw just as Bonaparte's army reached Moscow and were foiled when the Governor Rostopchine set fire to it. All her analytical essays, such as *De l'Influence des passions*, are written with readable, reasoned clarity. She bridges the gap between the restraint of the eighteenth century and the excesses of the nineteenth. Her own excesses were despairingly personal rather than literary and not even the amateur acting at Coppet and her arguments with Bonaparte could absorb all her surplus energy. The male chauvinist will always applaud the Emperor's words to her when she asked him which woman he admired most: the one who has the most children, he replied. Others, men as well as women, will surely not forget her intellectual courage and the solitude to which it condemned her, despite the crowd of admirers and hangers-on who surrounded her. Until education for women became formalized in France long after her death she knew no rival as an analyst of ideas. She was the first writer to point out what is now taken for granted: the inevitable links between literature and the social background against which it is written.

3

Romantics and Realists

Just as Madame de Staël had drawn the eighteenth century into the nineteenth and the early signs of Romanticism, so a few individual women drew the strands of late Romanticism together, tied them in knots of new colours, carried on old traditions and began new ones.

They were more creative than the salon-keepers and memoir-writers who were more active and varied after the Revolution than they had been before; the salons were no longer limited to the aristocracy and there was yet a new 'class' now, the *noblesse d'Empire*, who of course survived the restoration of the monarchy. Some of them had amassed riches, some of them received pensions from the new regime. Bonaparte had created General Junot Duc d'Abrantès and when the latter killed himself in 1813 his widow, who had been used to a brilliant existence, found herself very poor. She decided to earn money by writing, produced many novels which are totally forgotten, but her eighteen volumes of memoirs are highly readable, if only partly accurate. Balzac is thought to have helped her to compose them. She also wrote absorbing records of what she had seen and heard in the salons. Later in the century the salon held by Louis-Napoléon's cousin, Princesse Mathilde, who enjoyed painting, was a centre of artistic, literary and social life frequented by such writers as Flaubert and Théophile Gautier. The creative writers tended to belong to the minor landed gentry or the middle professional class, for writers now relied more on professionalism and less on patronage. Salons, however, were still useful to them for in the early days of Romanticism many writers had come to realize the value of publicity.

Théophile Gautier enjoyed publicity, but not domesticity or the conventions of marriage. He had adored Carlotta Grisi the dancer from the middle distance and made a suitable 'arrangement' with her sister Ernesta, a singer, which lasted twenty years. Théo already had a son by a previous mistress, now he had two daughters – Judith, born in 1845, and Estelle. Neither he nor Ernesta could cope with small girls and he even threatened to glue Judith to the ceiling to keep her out of the way. She adored her nurse and stole from her parents to help her, for she had noticed the poverty of the woman's home. Her grandfather helped to bring her up and a convent school helped in other ways: she did very well in geology, astronomy and physics and showed great talent when it came to confession. She invented sins so horrible that her confessor would laugh and the *sacristine* muttered that she was perverse enough to corrupt a priest. She had no religious feeling but she was convinced (and a spiritualist dancing-teacher supported her) that in a previous incarnation she had lived in the East, a feeling that was to colour her whole life.

Théo soon saw he had an intelligent daughter and asked her to help with his research on *Le Roman de la momie*. Judith became so fascinated by the subject that she decided to mummify her dolls – and Théo was fascinated by the accuracy of her method. Orientalism was becoming extremely fashionable in Europe generally and especially in France. As a girl in 1862 she came with her father to the International Exhibition in London, full of oriental displays, and she was barely grown up when an unexpected incident seemed to confirm her early premonitions about the East. A friend had met a Chinese wandering helplessly along the street and discovered that he had been sent to France to complete a French–Chinese dictionary, but his patron in China had died, he was now penniless. Théo allowed him to stay in his house and instructed Judith to learn Chinese, which she did, and by her early twenties in 1867 she had published a translation of Chinese poems, called *Le Livre de jade*, which received extravagant praise from Victor Hugo. She was apparently not courageous enough to use her own name at first, unless Théo dissuaded her, and the book was signed Judith Walter, the name she had used when she published an analysis of Edgar Allan Poe's complex essay *Eureka*, which took her a mere week. The critic Rémy de Gourmont at first refused to believe it had been written by a girl of twenty.

Théo is on record as saying that his elder daughter's brain was detached from the rest of her personality, but he doted on her, came to rely on her help and forbade her to marry her first suitor, a Persian prince. All the writers and painters who met her were impressed by her beauty, which had been noticed by Baudelaire when she was still a child: he described her as 'Grecian'. As she continued to write adaptations of works from oriental languages, followed by novels of her own on oriental themes, she naturally met literary personalities, possibly had a brief love affair with Victor Hugo, and decided to accept, in secret, the admiration of the writer and critic Catulle Mendès. The Chinese Ting acted as postman and go-between for them. Judith's father cared not at all for the clever young Mendès, who was said to employ ghost-writers and had the misfortune to be Jewish. Théo opposed the marriage for so long that Mendès thought of abducting Judith. In the end the marriage took place in 1866, Gustave Flaubert was one of the witnesses ('a sad story', he wrote), but Théo refused to attend. He remained distant until his younger daughter Estelle was married six years later. Judith continued to write and the titles of her books are self-explanatory: *Le Dragon impérial* in 1868, her first and probably best novel, later came *Isoline et la fleur de serpent*, *Poèmes de la libellule*, this latter being translations from the Japanese. The Orient for her was a distant dream and she preferred to keep it that way. She did not go to the Far East, although she wrote about nearly every country located there; instead she and her husband, accompanied by the writer Villiers de l'Isle-Adam, went on a shorter pilgrimage to Lucerne to visit someone they deeply admired: Richard Wagner.

Judith might have inherited a love of Italian music from her mother but she preferred her music to be German. She had published articles about Wagner when this was a courageous, unpopular avant-garde activity. At fifty-six he was flattered and fell in love with Judith, who was only twenty-four, and he wrote her heartfelt, revealing, if sometimes mystifying, letters over ten years. Some of them were exchanged through a barber in Bayreuth. Was their relationship truly sexual or not? It is impossible to tell from these strange letters in which Wagner (and Cosima) arranged for Judith to do a good deal of shopping in Paris; they needed gloves, for instance, and Wagner in particular needed glamorous scents, satins and a Japanese robe. Although buying many gifts for Cosima, Wagner was deeply preoccupied with Judith. He asked her to find a perfume she liked and then send him 'half a dozen paper sachets of powder, so that I can put them among my fresh linen, which will help me to be *en bon rapport avec vous* when I sit down at the piano to compose *Parsifal*'. He asked her to think carefully about their *parfum de correspondance*. 'Perhaps Rimmel's "Exquisité", if you like it. I would also like pure Rose, but strong. . . .' His own sense of smell, he said, was not strong. And the silk brocade coverlet for his chaise-longue would be called 'Judith'. Writing of striped silk he said, *'Je ne veux pas du stylé, je préfère le caressant.'* He wanted a particular pink which could no longer be found. Chamois or flesh colour was offered instead: '(Ah! if it was the colour of your flesh, I would have the Pink I want at the same time!) . . .'

A photograph of Judith by the famous Nadar shows her to be richly feminine in the way Wagner liked, and her literary aura attracted him too. She translated the libretto of *Parsifal* and she wrote sonnets to him, but he did not set them to music as he had done with Matilde Wesendonck's poems. There was a possibility at one point that Wagner might have used her Persian story *Iskender* for a music-drama, but the project obviously did not go far. He owed her a great deal, for it was she who pleaded with Liszt to accept his daughter Cosima's

Madeleine de Scudéry, 1607–1701

Marie Madeleine Pioche de la Vergne,
Comtesse de La Fayette, 1633–1693

Marie de Rabutin-Chantal,
Marquise de Sevigné, 1626–1696

Anne Louise Germaine, Baronne de Staël Holstein,
'Mme de Staël', 1766–1817, by Gérard

Marceline Desbordes-Valmore, 1786–1859
by Hilaire Ledru

Marie d'Agoult, Comtesse de Flavigny,
'Daniel Stern', 1805–1876

liaison with Wagner. In old age Judith remembered how the
composer had talked in his vague wild way about his love for
her and about what might have been. But Cosima was there,
Cosima was indispensable, and Judith had to be content with
being godmother to Siegfried, Cosima's son by Wagner.
Wagner stopped writing to Judith, but after his death she
exchanged copious letters with Cosima until 1898, when the
two women seem to have fallen out over a 'performance' of
Parsifal in Judith's miniature theatre in Paris.

Music and drama occupied the romantic Judith, but as she
approached middle age they did not bring her personal happiness. Catulle Mendès was unfaithful to her, as her father had
said he would be, with the beautiful rich and musical Augusta
Holmès (who also wrote); the marriage disintegrated, while in
any case Judith had a limited sense of reality and preferred her
oriental visions. After years of separation she and Mendès
were divorced in 1896. The Wagners in their letters – written
by Cosima – began to send their regards to the admirer of
Judith who had long ago replaced her husband, a minor composer called Ludwig Benedictus and especially interested in
oriental music. When Judith wrote a novel with a contemporary setting, *Lucienne*, about an unhappy kept woman, Cosima
Wagner wrote apologetically saying that she found it depressing. She remembered Judith's romantic oriental heroes and
heroines, 'and I thought how far these noble and pure figures
were more worthy of your fine talent than these examples of
present-day corruption'.

The unreal, theatrical world was her place, whether she
liked it or not, and since her mother had been a Grisi this was
hardly surprising. This remarkable Italian family had produced not only the Carlotta who created the role of Giselle in
Théo's ballet, but also Giulia and Giuditta, both singers. They
were cousins to Ernesta Grisi, which is why her daughter was
named after Giuditta. Towards the end of her life Judith wrote
down something of the family story in *Le Roman d'un grand
chanteur*. In the meantime she had a moderate success herself as

a playwright, and adapted her story *La Barynia*, which had a Russian setting, for performance at the Odéon in 1894. She created her own miniature marionette theatre, Le Petit Théâtre, where she supervised productions of her own works, making all the exquisite miniature figures and décor herself. It was here that she expressed her long-lasting admiration for Wagner by the production of *Parsifal* which earned Cosima's displeasure. Some earlier Wagnerian soirées in Nadar's studio had been more successful. Judith also wrote a play in collaboration with Pierre Loti, best known as a novelist now, and for some time Sarah Bernhardt was interested in it. When finally she decided not to act in it the authors were naturally disappointed.

However, life was not all disappointment, although the success of Judith's writing was not matched by her earnings. Théo had died, not rich, a long way back in 1872. Judith was lucky through someone's else's carelessness, for a publisher who lost one of her manuscripts compensated her indirectly with the gift of some land by the sea, at Saint-Enogat, near Dinard. She built an ugly house there, having found that she had unthinkingly signed a contract to do so. She had to borrow money, but the house was a success, she called it 'Le Pré aux Oiseaux' and went there whenever she could, accompanied by the faithful Benedictus. It was a good place for writers and Pierre Louÿs is said to have written his most famous novel, the erotic *Aphrodite*, in a summer-house there.

Judith Gautier wrote over thirty books, but no one reads them now. Her articles on Wagner were praised, and the composer Dukas thought highly of her notes on oriental music, probably written with the collaboration of Benedictus. But she has a place of her own in literary history. In 1875 the Academy had 'crowned' her novel *La Sœur du soleil* (Sister of the Sun) and it was agreed that had she not been a woman she would have been one of their members. In fact the statutes of the Academy do not expressly exclude women, but certainly at this period male opposition was as conservative as it was strong. Her

writing alone did not bring her success, as with so many women
writers in France at this time; she earned publicity through her
personality and especially when she was young through her
beauty. Rémy de Gourmont praised her 'sculptural' qualities,
another contemporary described her as possessing 'the soul of
an artist in the body of a goddess' and she was also called 'her
father's masterpiece'. She had admittedly inherited some of
Théo's defects, she went on writing but became so plump and
placid that she seemed to drift rather than to live. She made a
short journey to Morocco but did not stay long, for she had
always preferred the romance and the ideal to the reality. In
1910 came the success through which she is best remembered
now. The Académie Goncourt had been in existence for seven
years and its annual prize had been automatically awarded to
a man, for the views of the brothers Goncourt about women
were only too well known. In 1910 Jules Renard died and
there was no firm favourite to take his place. Lucien Descaves
proposed Judith and she was elected by seven votes out of nine.
Her election set a precedent and after many more years had
passed Colette became the first woman president of this much-
criticized but still useful group in 1949.

Judith Gautier spent most of her remaining seven years at
the hideous house near Dinard. She was poor, old-fashioned
and forgetful now. She died in 1917 and her tomb in the local
cemetery carries an inscription in Chinese. Hers was literally
a picturesque story, an unconscious prolongation of Romanticism which only a woman could have achieved at that period,
while the better educated men, who were more interested in
experiment, went on to the new schools of Parnassus, controlled Symbolism, and all that followed.

The Parnassian poet José-Maria de Hérédia had a gifted
daughter who married that other distinguished poet Henri de
Régnier and wrote poetry and novels herself. She felt she could
use neither of the family names and invented a man's personality for herself: Gérard d'Houville. She was born in 1875
and at the turn of the century was publishing novels. At

middle age, in 1925, she published poems in prose; her output has always been characterized as classical and of high technical standard.

Who could have been more different from this highly educated, reticent writer than the extraordinary woman who was born Marguerite Eymery in the Périgueux in 1860, and died at a great age in 1953 after decades of literary life under the name of Rachilde? She received little formal education but her family background was odd enough, with Brantôme himself (author of the famous *Lives of Gallant Ladies*) several centuries earlier, while her great-grandfather had left the priesthood to be married. Legend used to say that for five generations the descendants of such men are accursed and turn into werewolves on Candlemas night. Her mother's family was traced back to a member of the Spanish Inquisition. However, her father was an army officer, brought her up in a damp château and allowed her no candles for reading in bed. She could read, and write, only when the moon was full. Her grandfather gave her the key to the library when she was fifteen and censored nothing, so she read all the eighteenth-century classics plus the works of the Marquis de Sade before she was sixteen. Her parents decided when she reached this age that she should become engaged to an army officer. She therefore tried to drown herself. Having failed, she at least earned some freedom and began openly to write articles which she published in the local newspaper, although under a pseudonym.

She came to Paris when she was in her early twenties, and soon became one of the half-dozen women totally engaged in the business of writing. Fortunately a cousin of hers ran a magazine for women called *L'Ecole des femmes*, and here she made a start as a journalist. Like George Sand she wore men's clothes because they were convenient and saved her a good deal of money. Travelling and reporting was easier and apparently she made one evening suit last ten years merely by changing the facings whenever fashion decreed a change of style, width and colour. Like Colette twenty years later, she cut her hair short, but more dramatically so: she sold it to the former grand chamberlain of Alexander III of Russia, who kept it in a specially designed coffer. She now called herself Rachilde and chose to write in the mood of the moment, which happened to be 'decadent'. This preoccupation with what can briefly be described as 'unnatural' had grown out of certain Romantic works such as Théophile Gautier's *Mademoiselle de Maupin*. The writers who represent it best are Joris-Karl Huysmans, famous for his novel *A Rebours* (Against the Grain), Barbey d'Aurevilly, Villiers de l'Isle-Adam and the more extreme, more ridiculous and lesser-known Joseph Péladan. The 'unnatural' subjects included sexual abnormalities (and the writers made no plea for 'normality') of all sorts: the hermaphrodite, the androgyne, the sadist, the lesbian. Pleasure, crime, vice and horror were inseparable, the whole atmosphere dangerously dark.

Women of a particularly nasty kind appear in these books, which fascinate the twentieth-century literary historian and disappoint the reader; sometimes they are inventive, sometimes tedious and nearly always unintentionally funny. The heroines are reminiscent of Sade's Juliette and the women painted by Gustave Moreau. That a woman should try to write such books was a new departure, but Rachilde was particularly good at choosing titles, she had studied her models and she tried hard enough. *Monsieur Vénus* was about a virile woman, Raoule de Vénérande, and a feminized man, a gardener called Jacques. In 1884 women tried to stop their husbands reading it and it was not surprisingly banned in Belgium. But Jean Lorrain, a novelist who specialized in perversities of all kinds, composed a portrait of the author, whom he called 'Mademoiselle Salamandre', and five years later Maurice Barrès wrote a preface to a new edition, from which the name of an earlier collaborator disappeared. In spite of its shock title and theme the book has no horrors to offer us today. The poet Verlaine told the author that if she had invented a new vice she would have been a benefactor of humanity. There was nothing vicious about Rachilde – she kept her eyes open, remained shock-proof herself and saw that society was full of monsters, some of them only thinly disguised. She was also kind-hearted, hospitable and kept white mice; she looked after Verlaine when he was ill and made him drink chocolate. But as soon as she had gone he would send out for absinthe. The titles of her books, *La Marquise de Sade, Madame Adonis, L'Animale, Les Hors-nature* (The Unnatural), and a little later *L'Heure sexuelle* (The Sexual Hour), make her sound like a monster; but she was no such thing, even if she went to the famous Bullier dance-hall dressed as a man. The poet Albert Samain introduced her to the journalist Alfred Vallette there and in 1899 she married him; one of her admirers reports that on their wedding night the couple, along with Samain, talked about books until four in the morning.

Nobody reads Rachilde now, for her titles are so much better than her books and her inventiveness, a kind of social science fiction, *anticipation*, as the French call it, was not matched by the quality of her writing. She had long eyes with heavy lashes and the men who knew her when she was young maintained that she was totally innocent. She herself maintained that *Monsieur Vénus* was 'the most remarkable product of hysteria which had reached a climax of chastity in a vicious milieu'. Decadence can hardly be learnt, after all. She was usually a firm, fair critic and her regular reviews in *Le Mercure de France* are still worth reading. She said of herself that she was not a critic but a 'passionate reader'. She was a courageous publisher too and it was *Le Mercure de France*, the imprint she ran with her husband, Alfred Vallette, which published in 1903 Colette's description of Claudine in love with a woman: *Claudine en ménage*. It was signed Willy, but it was the only Claudine book not published by Ollendorff, one of Willy's regular publishers.

Rémy de Gourmont, a perceptive critic of the symbolist school, if an unhappy man, had a word to say about the women writers of this era and maybe of other eras too.

Women's writing, he said, was their polite way of making love in public. Was he thinking of Rachilde and her like? Unfortunately, unfairly perhaps, he probably was.

But nobody could say that Rachilde evaded reality. In 1925 she attended a banquet at the Closerie des Lilas, the famous Montparnasse restaurant, in honour of the elderly symbolist writer Saint-Pol Roux. Many surrealist writers attended too, along with their leader, André Breton, but they were not pleased by the presence of Rachilde and the actor–producer Lugné-Poë, who during the First World War had been in the counter-espionage service, the Deuxième Bureau. Rachilde herself had recently made some anti-German remarks to a newspaper, saying among other things that no Frenchwoman could think of marrying a German, and of course the surrealists could not tolerate such old-fashioned sectarianism. They began to shout insults and just when some 'rather dismal' fish in white sauce was being served they climbed on to the tables and shouted even more loudly. Some guests went off to find the police. 'But the comic thing,' said André Breton later, 'was that in the general confusion it was Rachilde, by now in a great state of agitation, who was arrested.' She was a mere sixty-five at the time, and if as Breton said this episode marked the final break between surrealism and all the conformist elements of the period, it is a strange irony that the person symbolizing most closely this very conformity should have been the woman whose Monsieur Vénus had caused such a sensation in 1884.

Who could have been more different again than Lucie Delarue-Mardrus, still remembered by the older generation of France. Living from 1874 to 1945 she was both a romantic and a realist, a link through time and subject-matter between the two centuries. She was born in Honfleur and remained devotedly faithful to Normandy all her life. Her poetry, which she began to publish when she was about twenty, is best characterized by the collection entitled Ferveur. Fervent indeed she was, even the old photographs show it, and so intense that

Colette, who knew her well, could not resist teasing her and often called her 'Ferveur'. The eldest of six daughters, she spent a happy childhood in the north before her lawyer father brought the family to live in Paris. She was still very young when she went to see the popular poet François Coppée and his reply would have made anyone into a feminist: he advised her to find something to do, such as sewing or housekeeping. Her immediate reaction was indirect, she decided to study the history of French poetry along with Théodore de Banville's treatise on the writing of it. Women writers are steadily criticized for their failure to study technique, but this could not have been said of Lucie Delarue, as she still was. She worked hard, met many writers and published her poems. The intense, shy dark girl attracted attention and she earned her first money through working for an all-female magazine called *La Fronde*, run by a courageous woman called Marguerite Durand. But when Lucie found that an enemy of Dreyfus was well regarded by the journal she broke off all contact with it. She was later much more at home with that famous literary magazine *La Revue blanche*, where Léon Blum wrote theatre criticism. In the meantime an unknown army captain called Philippe Pétain asked for her hand in marriage, but with the backing of her parents she refused him. She cut short her dark hair and took to riding a bicycle. Sarah Bernhardt noticed her, grew fond of her and gave her a ring; she had tended from early adolescence to fall in love with women, but in 1900 she met a well-known man and married him ten days later.

He was the handsome Dr Mardrus, of Egyptian origin, known for his much-praised translation into French of the *Tales of a Thousand and One Nights*. He enjoyed publicity – authors had to arrange it for themselves in those days – and enlivened a quiet wedding by insisting that his bride should be dressed in a cycling outfit complete with bloomers, a checked tunic lined with blue and a straw boater. The ménage was known as 'Princesse Amande' and 'Calife Œil', and for a time lived and wrote happily together. The story was told in Paris at the time that the doctor took such good care of his talented wife that when she was working he would feel her feet every hour to make sure she was not getting cold. Flattering critics of the Mardrus translation said that his wife must surely have made occasional suggestions about style and the book became very fashionable. It was also considered shocking and in *A la Recherche du temps perdu* the narrator's mother, having given it to her son at Balbec, suddenly realizes that she should not have done so.

Lucie did not want children and became aware later that heterosexual love was not for her. Her marriage disintegrated and she spent much of her life alone. Consciously she wrote about subjects that were still considered difficult and one of her earliest novels, *Marie fille-mère*, is one of the first modern stories by a woman of an unmarried mother, a propaganda story, although it was not presented as such. Her poetry never lost its early 'fervour' and she brought fervour to an understanding of the differences between women and men. 'The *esprit géométrique* of men will never admit the secret, unexplainable, formidable eddies of women's ocean-like nature. They want reasons. Does anyone ever ask the waves of the sea for reasons?' She seems to have been one of the first poets to write about the subject that Simone de Beauvoir still found taboo in 1949 – menstruation. Lucie saw no point in taboos of any sort. She did not write great poetry but campaigners for the women's movement might be surprised to find a woman writing in the early part of the century who decided to say her say about any subject that interested her, including abortion. A far cry indeed from Anna de Noailles, with whom she had almost had a confrontation; unknown to herself she had been asked to recite poems at a literary soirée because the hosts wanted to find a rival to the over-effusive countess. The organizer of this undignified event was Proust's friend Comte Robert de Montesquiou.

Eventually Lucie Delarue-Mardrus knew something like personal happiness and settled down for a time with a singer called Germaine de Castro. Her ex-husband continued to write to her in Arabic, so that she would not forget the language. She wrote about fifty books and her non-fiction titles included *Les Amours d'Oscar Wilde*. She knew success, refused the Legion of Honour, but lived long enough to see her 'fervent' style go out of fashion. Her *Mémoires* of 1936–8 and her 'moral testament' written when she was forty-seven are well worth reading, they give at least part of her neglected story, while the rest is in her novels. *Le Roman de six petites filles* is an intriguing example of how autobiographical material, notably family life, is transposed into fiction. This is something that women novelists used to do more often than men, not because they were necessarily less inventive but because it was harder for them to escape from it and they tended to be more sensitive to all its details and emotional undercurrents.

Lucie herself said she met her husband through Romanian friends, but others have maintained that they met at the salon of Natalie Clifford Barney. This could have been possible, for just before and long after the turn of the century a great number of people met there. Most chapters in the long life of Natalie Clifford Barney were more like fiction than reality. More foreign writers have written in French than in any other language and she was one of the most intriguing Americans ever to do so. She wrote equally well in her own language. She was once called 'the wild girl from Cincinnati' because she was born near there in 1876, the year George Sand died; Colonel Joshua Barney, one of her ancestors, was famous for his part in the American War of Independence. Her father had made an apparently inexhaustible fortune from the Barney Railroad Car Foundry and was able to pass it on to his two daughters, Natalie, and Laura, who married a Dreyfus and became concerned with oriental religions. Their mother, formerly Alice Pike, was so keen a painter that she took lessons in Paris from Whistler. Mrs Barney's best-known ancestor was none other than Judge Miller who had signed the documents for the purchase of Louisiana from France in 1803. Judge

Miller had married a Frenchwoman who had fled to the United States from the turmoil of the Revolution. Natalie had one more link with France – another Barney had brought documents to Benjamin Franklin and met Marie-Antoinette who, as Jean Chalon recounts in his *Portrait d'une séductrice*, 'embraced in his person the New World'.

Natalie visited Paris as a girl and with her sister was sent to the school of Fontainebleau called 'Les Ruches', the establishment described in that intriguing documentary novel *Olivia*, by 'Olivia'. Natalie gloried in her femininity and had once been in love with a girl cousin. But she could not bear to accept the whole of femininity, for puberty and menstruation horrified her; when the latter form of suffering first occurred the head-mistress had to comfort her and chose to recite to her a famous poem by the eighteenth-century poet André Chénier: *La Jeune Captive* (The Young Captive). It could never be said that the French education system failed to find resource in literature.

After boarding-school Natalie returned to the United States, but was soon back in Paris where she felt at home. It was 'Paris-Lesbos' that she wanted, for at this point in the 1890s lesbianism, 'saphisme' as it was charmingly called, was immensely fashionable. Since so many girls of the middle and upper classes were politely 'sold' as wives, a high percentage of marriages could hardly have been happy. In Paris at least the men had a good deal of scope and if they could afford it they could buy high-class prostitutes, the *grandes cocottes* and the actresses. The women, including the *grandes cocottes*, consoled themselves with each other.

It so happened that the young Natalie saw the most splendid of these ladies, Liane de Pougy, riding in the Bois de Boulogne. Casting aside all male admirers and even a tolerant fiancé she succeeded in a difficult enterprise – she tracked down Liane and they became lovers. 'Liane', a little older, was Anne-Marie Chassaigne, daughter, as far as it can be known, of a petty squire in Brittany, educated at a convent and married to a naval officer who tried to shoot her in a fit of jealousy. From then on men could only be considered useful as rich buyers of sex, and Liane found reading and writing more enjoyable. She not only read authors such as Baudelaire, Nietzsche and Swinburne (her English was excellent), she wrote to Natalie superb emotional letters and in one of them she wrote: 'The prison of ourselves. Who could have said that? Only in myself do I find space, infinity. Prison is other people, the world, society, life.' It is not far to the famous phrase by Sartre in *Huis clos*, 'hell is other people'.

Liane called Natalie 'Moonbeam', because of her fair hair. The love affair and the letters they wrote to each other were highly charged, and they have not turned yellow, like old lace. Two such women could hardly be expected to settle down together, Liane could not afford to refuse her male clients and Natalie liked to seduce every woman she met. They went through the usual emotional phases of any love affair and they both wrote about it. Natalie published her first poems in 1900, *Quelques portraits-sonnets de femmes*, with a frontispiece by the fashionable painter Carolus Duran and further illustrations by her mother. Liane had already published several novels, notably *L'Insaisissable*, but apparently Moonbeam herself contributed some scenes to the new one, *L'Idylle saphique*, which appeared in 1901. The idyll was, of course, their own story and Natalie appeared in it as Florence, a pseudonym she had used socially in order to conceal, when necessary, her love affair with the woman whom she later described as 'the perfect androgyne'. Over the next thirty years Natalie was to appear in novels, as though she were a character too large for normal life, born ready-made for a place in fiction. Colette introduced her as 'Miss Flossie' in some of the Claudine books, but that was only the beginning.

Natalie-Moonbeam-Flossie believed that life was for loving. Endless romantic associations hover round her memory and many strange stories will come to light when all her correspondence is published. The year after publishing her first poems she was deeply in love again with one of the most mysterious and exotic of all her lovers, 'Renée Vivien', another foreigner who wrote in French, and within limitations wrote very well. She had been born Pauline Tarn in London, and was a few years younger than Natalie. Her father was a Scot, her mother an American subject born in Hawaii. The young Pauline was sent to a convent in Britain which she did not enjoy. She was in love with Lesbian love and taught herself Greek in order to read and adapt Sappho. When she fell in love with Natalie she was totally innocent. Natalie sent her a meaningful present, an antique flute, and taught her at least something about love, the result in 1901 was Renée Vivien's first book of poems, Etudes et préludes. Poetry was perhaps the greatest love of her life, but she needed Natalie, whom she called 'Lorelei', before she and her poetry were to reach the literary world. Eventually she published several volumes of poetry as well as scraps of narrative which are best described as poetic prose. When her books were first sent to critics she signed herself René Vivien, as though, like so many women, she thought a man's name would carry her more easily into the approval of literary critics. René soon became Renée and she needed no help, only love, which she received.

She was slender, beautiful in a mysterious, mid-brown un-smiling Pre-Raphaelite way, and floated about her 'dark, sumptuous, changing apartment' in the avenue du Bois clad in purple draperies. It was not easy to see her among the exotic furniture and the Buddha figures for she preferred to live in semi-darkness. There were antique instruments in the music room and, according to Colette, Renée liked change. 'A collection of Persian gold coins gave way to jade, were replaced by a collection of butterflies and rare insects.' When Colette was invited to dinner she would bring a small paraffin lamp with her for she liked to see what she was eating. Lucie Delarue-Mardrus once ate 'little roasted birds' in the same apartment; the hostess could not tolerate red meat and preferred to nibble grilled almonds and grapes. Lucie remembered Renée as brown-eyed, with drooping shoulders, carelessly dressed but

77

speaking perfect French. The novelist thought she looked very English, 'une jeune fille à marier'. Her most remarkable feature was not her eyes but her eyelids, which were both heavy and delicate, fringed with long black lashes. The windows in the apartment were nailed up. By this time the 'Lorelei' was not the only woman in her life, for the Sapphic poet had met and attracted many others. Sometimes she would disappear during a social function, summoned by an autocratic, unattractive but usefully rich admirer who was said to be a baronne, known un-flatteringly as 'La Brioche' and like everyone else in this charmed circle able to write and publish poetry. Lucie Delarue-Mardrus saw and described another of Renée's admirers. She emerged from the draperies a 'slender, astonishing creature, a true Dante Gabriel Rossetti heroine'. She wore a medieval-type dress of dark purple velvet which emphasized her angular figure, and two plaits of red hair were wound round her head like a laurel wreath. She had blue eyes, her face was that of an Italian primitive and she spoke with an English accent. She sounds remarkably like Eveline Palmer, heiress of the biscuit empire and in love with Miss Barney from an early age, for a time intimate with Renée, finally the wife of Raymond Duncan's brother-in-law.

'Paris-Lesbos' may sound like a crowded country, but Lorelei was never far away from Renée. There were two problems, closely related: Lorelei enjoyed life, and that in-cluded sexual life, but Renée, 'la muse aux violettes' as she was called, preferred dreams and unreality. However, they made journeys together, visiting the former Empress Eugénie of France at Farnborough in Britain, and leaving, with splendid idealism, for the island of Lesbos. Here they hoped to find a culture inherited from Sappho where women would live happily and creatively together. They had intended to take with them an English poet called Olive Eleanor Custance, whom they had christened Opal, after one of her book-titles, but in the end she did not come and to everyone's surprise made a runaway match with Lord Alfred Douglas, whom

Natalie herself had refused. As Renée and Lorelei stepped ashore on Lesbos they were greeted by a noisy gramophone record of a song that Maurice Chevalier was to sing many years later: *Viens poupoule* . . . but there was sunshine and sea and violets and at last some physical response from Renée to Natalie's ardour. The women rented two little villas linked by an orchard and thought about their Lesbian colony, but not only did the behaviour of the inhabitants discourage them but La Brioche threatened to arrive. So Renée went back regretfully to join her in Holland and Lorelei returned to Paris.

Renée Vivien was a prolific poet. Between 1901 and 1909 her bibliography contains twenty-seven items: books of poems, prose poems, stories, a novel, translations from Sappho and at least eight other Greek women poets (one had forgotten there were so many). Seven more volumes after her early death (in 1909), her collected poems in two volumes 1923–41, subsequently reprinted.

The scent of violets can soon pall, and few people can spend the whole of life in mist and moonlight listening to the sweet moan of female lovers. The prose is too vaporous to make an impression and even Renée Vivien's admiring editor Yves-Gérard Le Dantec, editor of Baudelaire, cannot accept it. The translations from the Greek have been filtered through Swinburne first. Yet many of her own poems have a languid beauty, they show an extraordinary command of the sonnet form and the rules of French prosody. Renée Vivien was not exclusively obsessed with Sappho and the Greeks, she was far from forgetting other aspects of her cultural heritage and often wrote about the Norwegian fjords (she saw them briefly, along with the rest of Europe and the Middle East), while there is a feminized Wagnerian atmosphere here and there in this strange writing.

Earlier this century literary critics were forced to spend far too much effort explaining why her subject-matter must not lead to moral condemnation, or how her Lesbos had been influenced by Baudelaire. Charles Maurras assumed she had made God feminine, as Laura Riding and others are said to have done since. Some men have appreciated the way she worked discreetly outside social conventionality and never argued or thumped any tubs. 'At Nice', wrote Colette, 'I often surprised her sitting on the edge of a cane divan, writing verses on her knees. She would get up with a guilty air and excuse herself: "I've just finished. . . ." ' *Her voice was ever low, an excellent thing in woman* – she never laughed (at least not in her writing) and it was only too easy to laugh at her. But she wrote as a civilized woman, exclusively about women, at a time when cheap would-be shocking books about 'abnormality' were only too easy to write and fashionable to read. Her appeal to the mass was nil and will never be wider, for her best poems would not be easy to translate, but her writing at its best is outside fashion and time.

Her early admirers were quick to praise her well-disciplined verse, adding that her prose gives away the vague untidiness of her mind. She did not think, she felt: while her friend Natalie Clifford Barney did exactly the opposite. If poets, as Cocteau wrote, walk slightly above the ground, Renée Vivien was hardly conscious of the ground at all; she floated, in her purple draperies, a mile or so too high, but it is worth watching her for a moment, the sound of her minor-key Baudelairian music ringing in your ears.

Neither verse nor prose nor red-haired girls brought her any real happiness and her attempts to keep a nymph-like figure led her to give up eating and try to live on glasses of wine. She was barely thirty when she joined Marie Bashkirtseff in the cemetery at Passy where her tomb is unfortunately not Greek but Gothic. Colette, writing twenty years after her death, thought it best to let the ivy grow over it, for the occupant did not mind at all if she were forgotten, in a sense it would be fitting.

Yet she and her form of liberation were not forgotten. It was one answer to the social situation of 1900 and significant that she chose to write in French. She probably did not realize that her work would appear on the shelves of university libraries, which is the case in Britain, but in a selfless bid for immortality she founded the Prix Renée Vivien, which was to be awarded to a woman poet. Lucie Delarue-Mardrus accepted it once, having refused others.

Renée died and Natalie, who was now approaching her mid-thirties, settled permanently in Paris. That same year, 1910, Liane de Pougy decided to marry. If one had to dwindle into a wife there was no harm in becoming Princess Ghika; ironic journalists regretted her 'retirement' while she, who felt particularly guilty about her love affair with Natalie, decided to sell her Louis XV bed. Natalie married a house, number 20 in rue Jacob, just behind the church of Saint-Germain des Prés on the left bank. The house had romantic, semi-literary associations: the dramatist Racine is said to have walked in the garden with the actress La Champmeslé, and later another actress, Adrienne Lecouvreur, interpreter of Racine and mistress of the Maréchal de Saxe, lived there. Rumour had it that she was poisoned by a jealous rival. She may have built the little stucco Temple de l'Amitié which was apparently used for civil marriage ceremonies during the Revolution. Natalie found the temple irresistible and there was space in the ivy-grown garden for the hammock in which she liked to idle away the time. Her attitude was the reverse of that shown by so many of the women who surrounded her: she was unconcerned with social climbing, politics, success in the arts or the discovery of the first wrinkles, the first grey hairs.

This house was to become famous for decades as an international rendezvous for the known and the unknown, from diplomats to dancers and for all those who belonged to what Jean Chalon has called 'Paris-Lesbos'. Some male visitors from the United States felt sorry for the ladies, imagining them lonely, until it was pointed out that they were blissfully free and happy. Writers of every kind, from Anatole France to André Gide, came to the house and Natalie, whose own writing was gradually becoming known, was a curiosity for some and

an irresistible charmer for many. The American-born painter
Romaine Brooks was one of the many people in love with her
and probably the one whom Natalie almost loved in return,
for fifty years or so, in a long love-story with a sad ending. It
was she who painted the well-known striking portrait of the
Amazon, the fair-haired, grey-eyed Amazon who never seemed
to grow any older.

Everyone who met her remembered those grey eyes, steely
grey, hard perhaps, and they still look out with a penetrating
gaze, hard even then, from the old photographs taken at the
turn of the century. These pictures, which usually show her in
a riding-habit, are a reminder of that extraordinary book by the
Symbolist critic Rémy de Gourmont, the *Lettres à l'Amazone*, for
she was the 'Amazon' to whom this perceptive, solitary, intel-
lectually courageous man, obsessed by his ugly skin disease,
and further embarrassed by a stammer, wrote these letters of
analytical passion. Back in 1890 he had already written a novel
called *Sixtine*, a 'novel of cerebral life', and followed it in 1904
with an 'essay on sexual life'. He was now stimulated by
Natalie's sudden interest in him – his house in rue des
Saints-Pères was very near hers – and by what appears to have
been her teasing sexual approach.

The *Letters to the Amazon* were published serially in *Le Mercure
de France* from 1912 to 1913 and in book form in 1921, four
years after the author's death. When Richard Aldington translated and introduced them to English readers in 1931 he did
not reveal himself exactly as an admirer of the Amazon, he said
nothing about her and pointed out the criticism of her often
implied in the letters. 'The irony is velvet,' he wrote, 'but it is
there.' The Amazon seems to have remained untouched in the
end and was temporarily engrossed in 'owning' de Gourmont
and showing him off to her other friends. She even persuaded
him to come to a fancy-dress ball because his diseased face
could be hidden by a mask. She appreciated no doubt the
psychological finesse of the letters and their themes. The
recurring phrase 'She has a body', followed by sonnets in prose

towards the end of the collection surely indicate that de Gourmont idealized the woman who would not or could not become his mistress, but there were rumours that the Amazon had in fact accepted the role. Gradually she deserted him and he died unhappy in 1917. She was heard to say that in any case they no longer found anything to say to each other. But without her the *Letters to the Amazon* would not have existed.

Normally she was never short of anything to say, and spoke so well in a succession of quotable aphorisms that her friends decreed she must meet Marcel Proust; surely, they thought, the talk would be brilliant and unorthodox. Since Natalie went to bed early and Proust got up late, it was arranged that they should meet at midnight. But the meeting was a non-event, and Amazonian seduction failed. Proust's conversation remained at the level of small talk and he was indiscreet enough to mention other women, including the Comtesse de Greffuhle. Jean Chalon put it best: 'Sodom and Gomorrah were face to face and found nothing to say to each other.'

Yet her salon, her Friday-afternoon tea-parties, were not a waste of time for everyone. She had always known when people needed or deserved help, from the time early in the century when Colette had had her first experience as an actress (not very successful) at one of her garden-parties. Indirectly she helped the poet Paul Valéry and also her compatriots T. S. Eliot, Djuna Barnes and many others. In the recollections of writers she seems ubiquitous and eternal because she was the centre of an organized social life until her death at ninety-five in 1972. She would have been remembered if she had not written anything, and among her many appearances in fiction was Valerie Seymour in *The Well of Loneliness*. Early in the century she had written slim volumes, even harder to find now than those written in her company by Renée Vivien. Later the books were still slim, but infinitely more durable: *Aventures de l'esprit, Souvenirs indiscrets, Pensées d'une amazone, Portraits de femmes*: all clear-sighted, unsentimental writing, some of it about people she had known, some about people in general. If she had needed to earn money or wanted to become a professional writer she could have achieved a serious, straightforward reputation. But all this interested her not at all, she at least affected to believe that the writing of books was a substitute for living, and she preferred living.

But she wrote all the same, including one book in English, extracts from which appeared in the American periodical *The Dial*. Later it was published in London in a very limited edition in 1930 by Eric Partridge, whose interest in slang and unconventional English may have obscured his penchant for Anglo-French literature. It was called *The One who is Legion*, or *A.D.'s After-Life*, and included two illustrations by Romaine Brooks. One of her surviving French friends has described it as 'not at all like her', but perhaps it *was* her, for after its faintly Gothic start it is a genuinely serious attempt to describe the androgyne, the complete woman-man figure. Did she anticipate Eliot's *Tiresias*, in which the two sexes meet? It could be possible, but the book seems old-fashioned now, while her other writing has not dated. Her intentions were clear enough, for she prefaced her book with lines from *Paradise Lost*:

> . . . For spirits, when they please,
> Can either sex assume, or both;

She explained what she hoped to show: 'For years I have been haunted by the idea that I should orchestrate those inner voices which sometimes speak to us in unison, and so compose a novel, not so much with the people about us, as with those within ourselves, for have we not several selves and cannot a story arise from their conflicts and harmonies?

'Let us seize the significance of life where it is unique, not where it is repetitive. Our thoughts more than our actions represent us.'

She was in fact more responsible than she knew. The First World War led her to write not stories, like Lucie Delarue-Mardrus, not newspaper reportage, like Colette, but more of the maxims that she always preferred and composed brilliantly in the classic French tradition. Not since the forgotten eighteenth-century Madame de Sablé (a possible collaborator with La Rochefoucauld) had any woman written them so well, and in fact few women have ever written maxims at all, although Ninon de Lenclos seems to have uttered them. In her *Notes sur le courage*, *Bas Côtés* and *Petites Répercussions* she was able to say in a few pages all she felt about war and those mainly responsible for it: men. 'Men, who tend to accept ready-made feelings and even prefer them summed up as clichés, find in the word "honour" an incitement to courage. This word, without any other excuse, almost always conceals vested interest which is sometimes collective or simply one of the voluptuous pleasures of hatred. Women, who are more truthful about what is essential, often despise it.' She was not the first to note that exposing oneself to danger was a sign of carelessness rather than of courage: 'not to be afraid of a shell striking you on the head proves atrophy of the imagination'.

But she was far too clear-sighted to think of all women as heroines. She saw nurses as Cocteau saw them in *Thomas l'Imposteur*, which was not published until two years later: 'Women in search of romance, or sadistic vampires.' She saw the compensatory aspect of war: 'The Hotel, transformed into a military hospital, is ready, with its four hundred beds, for the vast birth.' Her translations of current journalistic phrases look forward to those which followed in the Second World War and in all wars, including those of ideology: 'Evacuation: no perceptible change.' 'The wounded are arriving: we are making progress in Lorraine.' 'The new Pope also disapproves of the tango: we have recaptured La Bassée.' 'The Crown Prince is said to have been wounded: We are withdrawing slightly near Vailly.'

So much for the war, during which the Amazon refused to do any active war work, as all her friends did. That was her protest, and in fact her creed was better expressed a generation later by young people from her own country: 'Make love, not war.' She never knew the meaning of guilt but she seems to have gone to great trouble to underplay the value of her writing, both in themes and style. There is an unfashionable splendour about her selfishness and she was so confidently selfish in love that she was able to seduce a new lover at the age of eighty, keeping the secret for several years and causing terrible unhappiness to Romaine Brooks, who was perhaps the only one of her many lovers capable of telling her in austere fashion to go to hell. 'Our thoughts more than our actions represent us', the Amazon had written, and that is why some of her attitudes might seem strange and contradictory. There is a rumour that early in the century Dr Joseph Mardrus suggested that he and she should have a child, which would be equally 'shared' by his wife Lucie, who did not want any children of her own. Natalie was not flattered, she did not want anyone's child, she was exclusively concerned with herself, a luxury attitude today. When in the 1960s unmarried motherhood became socially 'normal' Natalie's reaction was to say that she hated conformism.

Yet her self-preoccupation was creative in the end, despite herself. Richard Aldington, after his earlier silence about her, at least in print, described her as 'more gifted for literature than she thought'. If Renée Vivien belongs to the past, her imposing, strong-minded, highly readable friend Natalie Clifford Barney will be better known and appreciated in the future.

When Natalie and Renée had first come separately to Paris as young foreigners they may not have realized how fast life was changing for French women and especially for the women writers. Women had won some personal freedom through the reintroduction of divorce, they now had a choice of feminist magazines to read; at the same time writers generally had to break a way out of the sterile, depressing darkness that came with the end of symbolism, and here the women took the lead. The poet Maria Krysinska, although associated with the symbolists, was one of the first, the first, she claimed, to throw away conventional rhyming schemes and write *vers libres*. Women wanted light and air, and in her early poems Anna de Noailles began to write about nature with an emotional intensity that outdistanced the early Romantic writers. Colette's husband Maurice Goudeket once told me à propos *Claudine à l'école*, which appeared in 1900, that half its impact was due to a reaction against the cerebral, analytical approach of the symbolists: '*C'était frais,*' he said, '*c'était gai.*'

And we can only be charmed by what Joris-Karl Huysmans wrote in 1905: 'The strange thing is that women – and it will be a clever man who can explain it – have more talent today than men.' Presumably he said 'today' because he thought the phenomenon was sudden and/or temporary. On that score he was wrong.

4

Sunshine on a Summer's Day

Every country has its self-taught writers and artists but it is significant that painters such as Douanier Rousseau or Grandma Moses come to mind more easily than novelists or poets. The achievement of literary work by the unsophisticated is not easy, for words have to fulfil two functions: they are the usual form of communication between people and they must also express ideas. To some extent Jean-Jacques Rousseau himself was self-taught, for there were many gaps in his academic education but he was even able to teach himself while teaching others.

The best known of the French *autodidactes* was a woman, and in comparison Rousseau had a fairly easy life, apart from the miseries which he inflicted on himself. Marguerite Audoux was born at Sancoins in the Cher in 1863, her mother died when she was three and her sister younger. The father took to drink and abandoned his children who were rescued by an orphanage in Bourges, where Marguerite was befriended for a time by a nun who was a loving mother-figure. At twelve she was sent to a farm in the Sologne where she looked after sheep and was often frightened when out in the fields alone for hours at a stretch. She yearned to read and to write, for she had been well taught by the nuns at the orphanage, but there was not a single book in the house, nobody there could read or write and nobody even received any letters. One day while cleaning the attic – it was the traditional autumn cleaning associated with All Saints' Day – she found a tattered old book among the rafters. She remembered enough to be able to identify it and of all things it was the eighteenth-century classic *Télémaque* by Fénelon. Life was changed for the girl, her farmer-friends found

old almanacs and books of songs for her and life was crystal-
lized in the book she herself published eventually in 1910,
Marie-Claire. It was not a forgotten masterpiece occasionally dug
up by didactic critics but a work which was translated into
several languages and in 1975 it is still usually available in the
best known of the French paperback editions. In it Marguerite
Audoux described her early life with straightforward fidelity
and no sentimentality whatsoever. Critics and literary historians have written the same things about this book ever
since it was published but for once the new reader cannot argue
with them. Marguerite Audoux, apart from her few years at the
orphanage, had to teach herself everything. She could not
marry the farmer's son with whom she fell in love: as a mere
orphan she could not be a worthwhile wife. After five years
at the farm she returned to the orphanage to collect her
accumulated wages – she had not received any while working.
Her favourite nun was leaving to become a missionary and
advised her not to enter the Church herself.

Marguerite Audoux knew how to sew, came to Paris and
somehow supported herself by working as a dressmaker. Her
sister, whom she had not seen since the convent days, succeeded in tracing her but not out of affectionate family feeling
– she wanted someone to look after her baby. Having found
Marguerite, she disappeared again and the underpaid dress-
maker worked to support the child as well as herself. Through
an accident with lime she almost lost her sight, was temporarily forced to give up sewing and worked in the laundry of
the Hôpital Laënnec. She must have had a gift for friendship
because she became the close friend of an actress married to
a singer and looked after their daughter. Her niece in the
meantime, whom she had adopted, disappeared as her mother
had done. Marguerite met a young man called Jules Iehl, who
was working for his *licence de droit* while doing clerical work for
the Railway. He had some literary ambitions and had met
Gide, who liked him. Through Iehl (he later wrote novels as
'Michel Yell') Marguerite Audoux met Gide and also Charles-

Louis Philippe, best known for his realistic novel *Bubu de Montparnasse*. He died of typhoid in 1909 at the age of thirty-five. But in the meantime he had introduced Marguerite Audoux to the successful journalist and writer Octave Mirbeau and told him that she was slowly writing a book about her early life. Nobody reads Octave Mirbeau now, although he was an efficient, entertaining writer, but he was surely sincere about Marguerite Audoux's sincerity: 'I am convinced that good books have an indestructible power . . .' he wrote in his preface to *Marie-Claire*. 'From however far they come, or however deeply buried they are in the unknown wretchedness of a workman's house, they always reveal themselves. . . . True, they're hated, rejected and insulted. What does that matter? They're stronger than everything and everyone.' He spoke of the author's taste, simplicity, truth, elegance of mind, depth and novelty, he stressed the power of the interior action, the gentle, pleasing light which shone over the book, like sunshine on a summer's day.

In 1910 *Marie-Claire* won the Prix Fémina. The author, who had grown up with a capacity for happiness and little hope of ever finding it, was happy. She never regarded herself as 'literary', she liked writing and her experience was too limited for her to produce much. Her few later books are forgotten now but they have the same gentleness, and use the same technique which seems to anticipate film editing, the clean cuts so much more eloquent than explanations. It could be argued that *Marie-Claire* is not really a novel, since nothing is invented, but it reads like one. Before 1910 women had produced comparatively few 'realistic' novels of any value, although Lucie Delarue-Mardrus had written *Marie Fille-Mère* (Marie, Child-Mother) and other similar books. *Marie-Claire* was no imitation, feminized Zola or Maupassant, it won sympathy because it asked for none and like so many books that French women of all kinds have produced this century it was a document of more than literary value. It was rare in one thing, its power of understatement, which does not exist in a much more famous book about childhood experience, *L'Enfant* by the socialist Jules Vallès, published in 1879. *Marie-Claire* led to a whole series of imitative books with varied regional backgrounds but they had no more than commercial value. The story of Marguerite Audoux is complete in itself, and her friends remembered that she never complained, although she worked and wrote in near-isolation in a small room where she did all her sewing work and was forced to move the dress-maker's dummy in order to sit down at her sewing-machine.

The loneliness of her early years found a kind of compensation in the friendships with writers which seemed to come so easily to her later. Alain-Fournier, author of *Le grand Meaulnes*, that great novel which deals with adolescence in the country, as Marguerite Audoux's book did, met her when she was writing it. The writer Charles Péguy had introduced them. Alain-Fournier admired both her and her work so much that he gave copies of *Marie-Claire* to several of his close friends. He also wrote to Marguerite Audoux and took her into his confidence about his love affairs. When she died in 1937 his name was the last she was heard to utter.

❧ 5 ❧

Mitsou to Madame de . . .

The First World War brought the nineteenth century to a close and produced some fine writing in France as in other countries: Le Feu by Henri Barbusse in 1916 and later Le Grand Troupeau by Jean Giono, who was to become a militant pacifist. The masters such as Gide and Valéry went on writing even if publication was restricted, and the war did not colour their books as much as it might have done. The activities of Dada intrigued young men, such as Breton, Aragon, Radiguet, although they soon moved away from it, but it failed to attract young women. Lucie Delarue-Mardrus was one of the few women to write stories about the war and some of them were later translated into English.

At the end of the war one woman had been writing regularly since 1900 and was to go on doing so for the next thirty years: Colette. Those who do not respond to her work believe her to have been so omnipresent that other women writers failed to attract sufficient attention from publishers or public, while at the same time she soon acquired second-rate imitators. If the latter is true, they are unheard of now, and if the former is correct surely these writers would somehow have come to light. Colette never sought out a place in literary life and never indulged in literary polemics. She admitted that hers was a spirit given to partiality and later in life the people to whom she was particularly partial were in fact women writers. In the meantime, however, she was deeply preoccupied with her own personal life and her work; it would be wrong to say 'career' because she never thought of her writing that way. Few writers, however, and especially few women writers, had had such a hard training in the Grub Street of Paris, the ghost-

writers' factory run by the neurotically over-industrious, pub-
licity-minded, misunderstood 'Willy', correctly Henri Gauthier-
Villars. Colette admitted, when writing prefatorial notes for the
publication of her complete works, that she had never been
able to escape from Claudine, who occupied her from 1900
to 1907, while the moving novels *La Vagabonde* and *L'Entrave*
(Shackle) hardly diverged from her own story, her attempted
breakaway from marriage or some other sexual partnership
and her indecisive acceptance of it. As she wrote out the story
she wrote on behalf of thousands of women who were, and
indeed still are, trying to solve this unsolvable problem. Like
Mary Wollstonecraft and George Sand before her she knew
that men were treating her badly and she also knew that she
could not live without them. This emotional tug-of-war gave
a new edge to her writing and humanized that arch mannerism
which makes the much-praised *Dialogues de bêtes* so artificial,
despite their perceptive humour. Her writing before 1914 had
already grown rich and varied in theme and style, but it still
relied almost wholly on her personal experience, it was not
inventive.

In 1912 she had made a second marriage, happy for a time,
to Henri de Jouvenel, editor of the influential newspaper *Le
Matin*. Their daughter Colette, born in 1913, soon provided an
ideal subject for light prose sketches, but again this was
reportage, not invention. Journalism was easy for someone so
observant and now, at middle age, able to add more interpretation of her own to anything she wrote. Her husband's
career in the newspaper world was interrupted by mobiliza-
tion, but Colette, after a short spell as a nurse, began to con-
centrate on journalistic work of a more adventurous kind.
She joined her husband for a time when he was stationed close
to the front lines near Verdun, and wrote some vivid articles
and letters which made good war reporting. She directed her
readers to think of peace by writing *La Paix chez les bêtes*,
describing how soldiers at the front became fascinated by small
wild animals such as squirrels and rabbits, which the town-

dwellers among them had scarcely noticed before. Colette hoped that the discovery of this new world might lead them to see human life differently.

As for her own life, her marriage had meant the end of her theatrical appearances for the time being but she escaped from the war atmosphere by writing the amusing fairy-tale libretto for Ravel's opera *L'Enfant et les sortilèges* (Boy and the Magic), which contained animals, birds, insects, animated furniture and crockery. The composer was at the front in 1917 and did not receive the text until several months after she sent it. Eight years went by before the first performance of the opera and before then Colette herself had become involved in theatrical work again: in one way or another she was close to the theatre all her life, and she was by no means the only woman writer in France this century to be involved in this way. Writing was not enough, books and their authors had to be identified together as an entity just a little larger than life.

It was during the First World War also that Colette made her first attempt at writing a novel in which the heroine was not herself in thin disguise. This was *Mitsou*, where many pages are set out in dialogue form, as though in a script prepared for the stage, a device also used in the novels of Gyp and no doubt helpful in the past to those who enjoyed reading aloud. The book earned high praise, especially from Proust, who wrote a much-quoted letter to the author. It is the most sentimental piece Colette ever wrote – perhaps the only one – but the war may have affected her more than she knew. The love affair of Mitsou, the actress, and the 'Blue Lieutenant' against a background of leave from the front – always too short and often cancelled – could hardly be presented in the same way as the liaisons in the earlier books, complete with boredom or self-indulgent passions for effete, time-wasting men. The war in fact enabled Colette to see the sufferings of other people, not merely her own, and she grew in stature as a result. *Mitsou* is one of her least satisfactory books but it took her forward to the major novels, notably *Chéri*, serialized in *La Vie parisienne* and also published in book form during 1920. Of all her novels it is probably the one most closely identified with her name, the one that has been most adapted for the theatre, the screen large and small, and still, a quarter of a century after Colette's death, often serialized on radio and in magazines of varying kinds. The story of a middle-aged woman who finds she is in love with a very young man is perpetually fascinating and elusive, especially because Léa, the heroine, knows she is not obeying the social rules. The psychological depth of the theme is masked to some extent by the setting in time and place, Paris at the end of *la belle époque*, which seems so foreign to readers outside France, in spite of the documentation recently produced on the subject. Although obviously modelled on what Colette had seen and heard it was, strangely enough, after twenty years of writing, her first truly inventive fiction. The characters in fact were so 'real' to her, going far beyond the various originals who have been identified, that she wrote a sequel six years later which is if anything more impressive than *Chéri* itself, because it chronicles the sudden post-war change in society, but of course the two novels are complementary.

And what better publicity for *Chéri* than Colette's decision to play the part of Léa at the hundredth performance of the stage adaption in 1922? For the next three years she acted the part in Paris, the provinces and in Belgium. She could not resist the stage.

It is not after all surprising if her work dominated so much other writing, especially writing by women, at this time, although she herself did not grow rich as a result; the 'twenties, which coincided with her own fifties, produced several of her most long-lasting books: *Le Blé en herbe* (Ripening Seed) in 1923, the novel about teenage lovers of fifteen and sixteen which had so shocked the readers of *Le Matin* the previous year that serialization was stopped. *La Seconde* (The Other One) of 1929 may seem at first reading a small-scale novel of adultery, but it is much more: a subtle and fascinating study of a relationship between two women, wife and mistress respectively of a not very interesting if successful man. It is also the study of a *ménage à trois*, a blue-print for what is now called the 'extended family'. To the 'twenties also belongs the carefully fashioned and selected memories of childhood, *La Maison de Claudine* (1922) which has become a classic for both schoolchildren in France and for adults anywhere with a taste for nostalgia. Its sequel *Sido* in 1929 is an intensely sad book, no doubt cathartic but not yet the last of Sido. Willy and Claudine were finally exorcized, but Sido never, thus giving support to those who decry Colette as a merely 'instinctive' writer, dependent entirely on her own experiences and personal relationships. But her writing could only take shape, as Keats said poems should come, naturally, like the leaves on the tree. For Colette, the leaves grew from her memory and she arranged them dis-creetly into a pattern.

Apart from the struggles and successes of the figure who now seems so dominating the 1920s saw a good deal of quiet achievement by women in France. For the first time in 1924 a woman became a doctor of letters, having worked on a historical subject, and four years later a woman became the first *agrégée* in law. During this decade several women who had been prolific writers for a long time produced some of their best work, as though the change of climate following the war had given them a new confidence. Of all the novels written by Lucie Delarue-Mardrus since about 1909 it was *L'Ex-voto* of 1922 which can be regarded as her best. The story of a girl 'pirate' takes place in a Normandy fishing community, a scene she knew well, and much later the book was filmed with the title *Le Diable au cœur*. The following year brought *Les Allongés* by Jeanne Galzy, which won the Prix Fémina, the prize inaugu-rated in 1904 and awarded by a jury of twelve women writers. Two previous books by Galzy had been 'crowned' by the Academy, but it is fair to say that this author is now remembered only for the prize-winning work which went through thirty editions on publication while in 1975 the firm of Gallimard

Amantine Aurore Lucile Dupin,
Baronne Dudevant, 'George Sand',
1804–1876, by Charpentier

Judith Gautier, 1845–1917,
photo by Nadar

Colette and her husband Willy, photo by Lalance

Colette, 1873–1954

Anna, Comtesse de Noailles,
1876–1933, drawing by Cocteau

announced a reprint. They had every reason to believe that its appeal could be as strong as it had been fifty years earlier. Les Allongés, the people lying down, are the men and women suffering from various diseases and hoping for cure or relief, at Berck, a small town in the Pas de Calais full of hospitals standing by the sea. It is well planned in three sections, each one with epigraphs taken from three very different writers: Dante, Racine, Renée Vivien. Yet there is nothing literary or artificial about it, and nothing sentimental. It succeeds, and does not date, because the author does not magnify the narrator's illness, or the collective illness of les allongés into the illness of a whole society or a whole world.

Thomas Mann was to do this in The Magic Mountain, which in fact was published the following year in 1924. Jeanne Galzy did not attempt to go beyond her range. She relates the usual, limited incidents of a hospital world but she does not write reportage. Neither does she deal in physical horrors, she indicates them with that reticence which has so often characterized women writers in France, and indeed in other countries, especially during the first part of the century. After the Second World War reticence was forgotten, too many writers of all kinds wanted to say, or rather shout, so much. But Galzy could say enough without raising her voice. She could even, in 1923, do something which now belongs only to history – she could say clearly that her woman narrator, suffering though she was, and in great pain from Potts' disease (tuberculosis of the spine), found no comfort in the idea that God existed. Efforts to 'convert' her failed. The author obviously had experience of extreme pain and hospital life, but more important was her skill in writing about the psychology of the ill and dying: 'You mustn't be ashamed of getting better', or 'For heaven's sake, let's be resurrected then, but at least not with a body!' Or even 'a day without pain is so long!' The child who died with his eyes wide open, the intelligent man who smelt so horrible: they are all here, in this novel of 240 short pages, small scale perhaps but infinitely bigger by implication. A remarkable, un-bitter book in which the author succeeds in establishing many individual relationships and several which are collective – the links between all invalids in the world and the different ones between the sick and the healthy.

Women as individuals were used to receiving attention in France and now, whenever they wrote successful books, they had to accept homage rather than balanced assessment. Reviews of books by women were tended to be more like flattering articles about actresses and a great amount of time was spent by writers of both sexes composing dedications for the signed copies of books they exchanged between each other, copies which now earn high prices in the antiquarian book market. There were more women writers in France than in many other continental countries but the highest official honours went elsewhere for the aura of frivolity still hung over France: in 1926 the Nobel prize for literature was awarded to the Italian Grazia Deledda and two years later to the much better-known Sigrid Undset of Norway for her unforgettable trilogy *Kristin Lavransdatter*, written on a historical theme of the fourteenth century in her own country.

It was still unthinkable that any woman should be admitted to the French Academy, but when the Royal Academy of Language and Literature was founded in Belgium in 1920 it was open to all men and women writing in the French language, who of course had to be elected. The very next year a French woman writer was elected: Anna Brancovan, Comtesse de Noailles, Greek and Roumanian by origin, although a native of Paris where she had been born in 1876, the year George Sand died. Proust knew and admired her in many ways, although he thought that her ecstatic search in poetry for the innocence of nature was at variance with her love for admiration in the salons. She provided him with useful material for the character of the Vicomtesse Gaspard de Réveillon in *Jean Santeuil* and the older generation in France are still ecstatic at the mention of her name, although on re-reading the poems they once admired they might not all feel such enthusiasm now. Her enthusiasm about herself was always remarkable. At the start of her autobiography, *Le Livre de ma vie*, in describing how she will tell the truth, she writes that sometimes she will not have to be modest. She quotes Boileau's remark that 'we are not equal to our thoughts' and goes on to say that 'through an aptitude that I have been forced to discover ever since my childhood I have equalled, I have outstripped my thoughts, I have flown above them'. Since she wrote that, in 1932, it has been rare and unfashionable to show such satisfaction with oneself and one's achievements; one could tolerate her attitude if one could accept her poetic outpourings, but one can't, in spite of much technical facility and prowess. But in her heyday she fascinated everyone who encountered her. Every Tuesday a group of fashionable ladies met to give poetry readings at the house of the Duchesse de Rohan and one of their most eager admirers was the young Jean Cocteau. Just before the First World War he had met Anna de Noailles through Madame Simone, the actress (and writer), and he obviously saw the Comtesse as a kind of actress too. Just as obviously, and no doubt unconsciously, she had cast herself in this heaven-sent role and so established her place in a literary-minded society. In fact, a little later Cocteau realized this himself. 'At first sight I admit she astounded me. The Comtesse was used to shining, playing a part and performing exercises that had become famous, and thanks to the credit which I enjoyed through Simone, she treated me, without the slightest preliminary, to a display which was a matter of course to her intimate friends but which was enough to make any new spectator feel like a provincial.

'I must have looked like a frock-coated Fratellini beneath a shower of hats in the midst of one of those scenes of carnage which leave the circus ring strewn with old guitars, broken furniture, soap lather, saucepans and broken china.

'Gradually I became used to it. The beauty of this little person and the graceful timbre of her voice, combined with an extraordinarily amusing power of description, triumphed over everything else, and I understood once and for all that her way of sniffing, leaning back, crossing her legs, stopping, opening her hands and flinging them away from herself as though from a sling, the gestures which strewed the floor with veils, scarves, necklaces, Arabian beads, muffs, handkerchiefs, miniature umbrellas, belts and safety pins, constituted her décor, her driving-power and in some way the props for her act.'

In fact she was a joy to the fashionable hostesses who would 'offer' her to their guests and Cocteau remembered one successful evening given by the Princesse de Polignac when he noticed the Comtesse preparing her 'act'. 'She sniffed, sneezed, burst out laughing, heaved heart-rending sighs and dropped Turkish necklaces and scarves. Then she took a deep breath, and, curling and uncurling her lips at full speed, she began. What did she say? I no longer know. I know that she talked and talked and talked and the big room filled with a crowd of people and the young ones sat on the floor and the older ones sat in armchairs. I know that the Princesse de Polignac and the Princesse de Caraman-Chimay (her friend and her sister), standing on her left and her right, seemed to be seconds in some dreamland boxing-ring. I know that the servants in their black suits and the footmen in knee-breeches and powdered wigs came closer to the half-open doors. I know that through the open windows of June, like the waltz in a film by Lubitsch or in that film where Liszt played the piano, the words of the Comtesse bewitched the trees, the plants and the stars – that her words penetrated into the neighbouring buildings, interrupted quarrels, enriched sleep, and that everything and everyone, from the star to the tree, from the tree to the chauffeurs of the waiting limousines, murmured "The Comtesse is talking . . . the Comtesse is talking . . . the Comtesse is talking. . . ." '

He wisely said nothing about her poetry and was realistic rather than cruel when he explained that 'this intuitive woman imagined she had the culture of a Goethe. The astonishing electricity that escaped from her, the lightning that played about her, the waves that emanated from her, she persisted in taking all this for intelligence.' She was convinced that if God existed she would be 'the first person to be told'. All her friends, including Cocteau and Colette, knew how much she yearned for fame – but her fame as a writer faded when she died. She lived on mainly through the memories of her friends. Charles Maurras, the critic who was unfortunately known for his reactionary views, tried to assess her poems and novels but failed to establish her as a serious artist.

She wrote because she could not stop herself from writing and she held the stage not merely because of her social position; she carried on a certain Romantic tradition associated with women writers and perhaps the unkindest thing one could say of her is to describe her as a poetess, the last perhaps, and the grandest, in France, writing of love and nature with would-be pagan freedom. Understandably she was interested in her predecessors in France, even if she was only French by education and marriage. As a child she was frightened, when visiting Coppet, by the ugliness of Madame de Staël – those paintings with the masculine face and the turban! But she was cheered to learn that Germaine had fine eyes, played the harp well and loved her parents. As she grew older she thought of Staël and Sand together and always defended them against attacks. All this she makes clear in Le Livre de ma vie, a book which compensates for the over-effusive poems, for it is a document of a kind rare today, describing a happy life lived by a privileged person aware of the happiness and the privilege and uninterested apparently in any other way of life.

Her friendship with Colette, which lasted from 1904 until the death of the Comtesse in 1935, has been quoted as comparable to that between Madame de Sévigné and Madame de La Fayette, but the distance between the twentieth-century writers was wider. It was certainly sincere on the part of the Comtesse who told Colette that she admired few people (*hélas!* she added) but she could hardly express her admiration for the very different novelist. Colette took the Comtesse's place in the Belgian Academy in 1935 and like Cocteau in his *Portraits-Souvenir* praised her highly in her *Discours de réception* and said not a word about her writing.

Yet Francis Steegmuller, Cocteau's most careful biographer to date, has maintained that Anna de Noailles exerted a sound influence over him, leading him to tone down the artificiality of his writing and become a much more serious poet. Steegmuller believed that certain phrases used by Cocteau are echoes, possibly even quotations, from poems by the Comtesse. When later Cocteau began to classify all his work as subdivisions of *poésie*, in the sense of creativity, might he not have been thinking, however remotely, of her? There is something touching about the fact that the first of his books published after his death in 1963 was *La Comtesse de Noailles, oui et non*. His appreciation of her was personal, intuitive and at the same time not unconnected with his appreciation of her social position: aristocracy, he maintained, was 'disconcerting', causing surprise, and therefore creativity.

Cocteau had met Anna de Noailles (in a taxi) through the actress known as Madame Simone, or simply Simone, born Pauline Benda, cousin of the famous critic Julien Benda. She came not of the aristocracy but of a comfortably-off Jewish family. She was born in 1877, by 1902 was successful on the Paris stage, read widely and enjoyed the company of writers. She was another example of how during the earlier part of the twentieth-century women found it relatively easy to write and find publishers if they were already literally in the limelight as actresses. To move directly from the anonymous greyness of domestic life was much more complicated; unless the woman concerned happened to have good social connections with a ready-made salon audience she had to have genius and/or irrepressible confidence and conviction in order to gain publication and lasting success. Anyone who appeared on the stage was as much in the public eye as the *grandes cocottes* who

had ridden down the avenue des Acacias in the 1890s. Sarah
Bernhardt's career was envied by many women who knew
they could not equal it, but they were determined, like her, not
to limit themselves to acting. Simone wrote plays herself,
excelled in Rostand's *Chantecler* in 1910, and in Henry Bern-
stein's *Le Secret* and from the 'thirties onwards had considerable
success as a novelist: *Le Désordre, Jours de colère* (Days of Anger),
Le Bal des ardents and many others. The second title is still in
print in 1976, and in 1960 Simone won the Grand Prix de
Littérature awarded by the French Academy.

But the novels do not go far beyond competence, although
the reader is grateful for their uncluttered presentation,
intrigued by the odd people, especially the women, that they
contain. However, as so often happened with French women
writers recently, Simone has been remembered less for her
novels, plays and memoirs than for her personal relationships.
Just before the First World War, while married to her second
husband Claude Casimir-Périer, a famous name in French
political history, she had a passionate liaison with the young
Henri-Alban Fournier, later known as Alain-Fournier, author
of the masterpiece *Le Grand Meaulnes*. He wrote to her letters full
of love and suffering, showing clearly this was no idealized
love, but straightforward sexual adoration. Fournier called her
his 'dearest love', his 'beloved wife', and did not know how he
could live without her. Simone wanted to remain free, a
professional actress and at the same time Madame Casimir-
Périer, but Alain-Fournier found no freedom in such an
existence. He was not lucky. Yvonne de Quiévrecourt, the
inspiration for 'Yvonne de Galais' in his novel, was already
Madame Yvonne Brochet. The liaison with Simone alienated
Alain-Fournier from his friend Jacques Rivière and his wife
Isabelle (Fournier's sister) and Rivière later referred to the
relationship with Simone as 'adulterous', she was not 'Yvonne'.
Both Alain-Fournier and Claude Casimir-Périer were killed in
action and Jacques Rivière died of typhoid in 1925. Simone
and Isabelle Rivière fought in the law courts from 1919

onwards because Simone wanted possession of all her previous lover's manuscripts. Judgement was given to Isabelle, but the bitterness did not stop there – it went on until 1964 at least, when Simone allowed *Le Figaro littéraire* to publish some of the letters written to her by Alain-Fournier. Their evidence was stronger than her much criticized mistakes about dates and other facts.

She lived until well into her nineties and will probably be remembered more for this relationship than for her own writing. How much did Alain-Fournier owe her, and was her own novel of 1939, *Le Paradis terrestre*, her version of the love affair? She has her role in the actress-novelist inheritance, and without her the Fournier specialist would not have been able to see him, however remotely, as a hero of fiction, he who disappeared from the real world so tragically soon.

Throughout the 'thirties Colette wrote with great sophistication in the genres which she had practised for so long, notably short, spare novels such as *La Chatte* (The Cat) of 1933 where she at last used a cat to good purpose in fiction, escaping from those self-indulgent cat descriptions which seem so time-wasting for readers who prefer people. Colette also wrote a great deal of theatrical journalism, wide-ranging and nearly always kindly constructive, for over four years. She published several volumes of evocative pieces about houses, the countryside, people in the news, animals she encountered, pieces which are now as much appreciated in Britain and the United States as in France. She wrote discursively about homosexuality, male and female, in *Ces Plaisirs* ... in 1932 (retitled *Le Pur et l'impur* in 1941), introducing people and anecdotes recognizable to most of her contemporaries. After her much-maligned first husband had died she described her years with him, or at least what she chose to remember of them, in *Mes Apprentissages* (My Apprenticeships). She also published her first collection of short stories for thirteen years – *Bella-vista* – and wrote as usual about small groups of two or three people; families, if they existed, were kept well in the background. She preferred her own family, and developed them into semi-fictional characters.

During the 1930s the literary scene was on the whole less interesting than in Britain and the United States. It was highly professional and peopled with well-established monolithic figures who had acquired fame in the 1920s or even earlier and now looked like being there for ever: Gide, Valéry, Jules Romains, Romain Rolland, Cocteau, Giraudoux, all published regularly by the *Nouvelle Revue française,* and among women writers, still Colette and very few others. Colette never contemplated the *roman-fleuve* which had become so popular ever since Rolland's *Jean-Christophe* (ten volumes of it, between 1903 and 1910), Roger Martin du Gard's *Les Thibault* (seven parts, from 1922 and going on until 1940). No writer could have been further away from that public who eagerly bought each new addition to *Les Thibault* or each one of the twenty-seven volumes of *Les Hommes de bonne volonté* (Men of Good Will) produced by Jules Romains between 1932 and 1947. But Colette wrote with amazing regularity and no year passed without a new title of some sort, for she insisted that she had to write in order to earn a worthwhile income. She had edited a series of novels for the publishers Ferenczi, but discovered no writer of great merit, despite her loyal belief in the poet Hélène Picard and later in the young Renée Hamon, *le petit corsaire,* who went out to Tahiti in search of memories of Gauguin and wrote out her adventures. By the end of the 1930s Colette had acquired a good deal of fame, and published two short novels, *Duo* and *Le Toutounier,* which were linked by one heroine, Alice. The second title was perhaps a family novel in miniature, for the heroine's three sisters are all present, two actively so, one of them, said to be modelled on Renée Hamon, far away, making films in the south seas.

One woman writer at this period achieved a long series of novels which were mainly about a group of interrelated families: this was Thyde Monnier, whose real Christian name was Mathilde. She chronicled the fortunes of the Desmichels

family, many of whom lived in what we would now call
Giono country, in the south-east of France. Unfortunately the
literary promise of her first book, *La Rue Courte*, was not fulfilled
and her *roman-fleuve* was far too melodramatic in content and
treatment. Yet in the early 1970s one of the series, *Nans le
Berger* (Nans the Shepherd), became a highly successful serial
for French television and naturally reappeared in the book-
shops with a television 'still' on the jacket. The 'regional'
novel tempted many women writers in Britain and earned
them great success, but in France such writing, although
successful too, by women and mainly for women, did not
reach a literary level of any great value.

France in the 1930s experienced a moral and political
decline which now enables the hindsighted spectator to see
some of the causes of the 1940 débâcle. Early in the decade
financial prudence had saved the country from the collapse
that occurred in Britain but the effects of world depression
eventually reached it, even though France relied on imports
less than many other countries. The right wing, especially
since they disliked the Jewish prime minister Léon Blum,
began to think Hitler was not mad after all. In 1933 came the
national scandal of the Stavisky affair, mentioned in France by
many writers long after the event. The Russian-born financier
was responsible for many shady deals and escaped trouble for
a long time because, it was assumed, he had friends in high
places to protect him. When he committed suicide the
political right wing insisted that the 'suicide' was murder – if
he had been allowed to live he might have betrayed the people
who had helped him to evade the law. The next year the mob
which marched across the Seine may not have intended to
attack the Chambre des Députés as most Parisians thought but
they succeeded all the same in bringing Daladier's government
down. One crisis followed another, the franc was eventually
devalued, civil war broke out in Spain and Hitler occupied the
Rhineland. Writers on the whole, especially the senior ones,
were still more concerned with literature than with social

change, politics and foreign affairs. However, Gide went to Moscow, Sartre studied in Germany, Camus worked in a left-wing theatre group, Simone de Beauvoir taught philosophy and in 1936 Simone Weil went briefly to Spain, as close to the fighting-lines as she could get.

These two women were not yet known as writers, although Simone Weil had a reputation as an agitator and began to publish articles on trade unionism and politics. Women still had no vote in France, although of course a few militants never stopped trying to get it. There was still no organized movement similar in intensity to that of the earlier suffragettes in Britain. The Catholic Church was a constant brake on any bid for women's independence, and the left-wing parties were not interested in repeating the campaigns of the Saint-Simon followers a hundred years earlier. Most women writers had little to say, even indirectly, about the state of the country or the world in general. They were still intensely preoccupied with the individual. There was plenty of good writing from them at various levels, but better work belonged almost entirely to the world of entertainment.

At the suggestion of André Malraux, Louise de Vilmorin began to write poetry and published her first novel in 1934, *Sainte-Unefois* (Saint Once). Her seven other novels were successful, have been translated and are still readable. Perhaps her greatest achievement was the long short story written some twenty-five years later, *Madame de . . .*, translated into English by Duff Cooper who had known and admired her when he had been British Ambassador in France. The French Academician Marcel Achard described the story as a masterpiece, possessing a 'classical strictness and a malicious grace' highly reminiscent of the eighteenth century or earlier. Its epigrammatic style is sheer delight: 'He admired her, he was not bored, she knew how to touch him, he fell in love with her and showed it.' Every page shows how much Louise de Vilmorin had inherited of French tradition, both Classical and Romantic: ' "The past

exists from the moment you feel unhappy," ' says the heroine.
' "It's possible," replied Monsieur de . . ., "but unhappiness is
self-invented." ' If the author had succeeded in keeping her
heroine alive and not let her sink into a decline and die the
book might truly be a masterpiece, but she was no doubt
consciously going back to eighteenth-century models, pre-
tending at least to point a moral and not attempting to be
realistic. Louise de Vilmorin as woman and writer gave so
much pleasure to so many people that in 1973 the French
novelist and critic Jean Chalon devotedly made her the heroine
of his entertaining *roman à clé*, *Une Jeune Femme de soixante ans* (A
Young Woman of Sixty). When he later wrote about Natalie
Clifford Barney he noticed that these two young women of
moderately advanced age did not seem to care for each other.

Madame de . . . was not in fact published until 1951, but its
author, of an old aristocratic family, had been formed by
private education and the social life of an earlier generation.
When she was beginning to write the atmosphere was changing
slowly, more girls were going on to university education,
graduate and post-graduate. But in the 'thirties French women
writers were not only still preoccupied with the individual, it
was the individual woman, in particular, who absorbed them,
not the social scene. That preoccupation was to come.

There were, however, isolated writers who deserve mention.
Few people in France or outside it spare much time for the
work of Paule Régnier, who produced several novels and one
in particular which receives glowing mentions in reference
books. It will never take wing from them and alight in a series
of classics, but it should be looked at. This is *L'Abbaye d'Evolayne*
which has been praised because it is said to show that at last
here was a woman writing about an invented experience and
not merely talking about her own personal problems and
failures. The author may have been aware of the moral and
spiritual drought current in France at the time. Unfortunately
the intensity of the book is laughable today and the style dated
and stiff. The husband Michel and his wife Adélaïde are said

to be happily married (they call each other 'vous' and have separate bedrooms) but Michel, who is a doctor, feels impelled to follow his best friend into the Benedictine order. His wife, after initial jealousy, suddenly feels that she too must join the order, it is the ideal way, the only way, for her to show her love for her husband. The situation seems worthy almost of Corneille or Racine but their heroes and heroines are real after three centuries. Paule Régnier's attempts to develop the personal and spiritual drama do not succeed. The wife realizes she has no vocation and seems to have confused her husband with God. She takes poison and as she is dying her husband wonders wildly for a moment whether he should perhaps desert God for his wife. To the modern reader the whole thing is nothing but embarrassing. It is not the novel to convince anyone that a woman can successfully write about a profound problem either beyond or within her own experience.

Personal bitterness and unrequited love seem to have been behind it, for Paule Régnier was unlucky in love, realizing after the death of a writer whom she had loved devotedly that he had loved another woman. Professor Henri Peyre has admired her and told her story. From a historical point of view it is a shock to learn that two of the best literary reviews in France, the Revue des Deux Mondes and the Revue de Paris, could not contemplate the serialization of the novel because the treatment of the religious theme would have horrified their well-educated but apparently not very open-minded readers. An erotic story would have apparently offended no one. The poet Paul Claudel treated the author as Bonaparte had treated Madame de Staël: he thought the heroine should have had babies instead of involving herself in such a tug-of-war between love of a husband and love of God on the husband's behalf. Paule Régnier eventually killed herself.

Another unhappy woman writing in France during the 1930s was Marcelle Sauvageot, whose Commentaire was a moving diary of the interior life, infinitely more satisfying than the

self-centred scribblings of Marie Bashkirtseff, fascinating
though they are. Sauvageot died at thirty-four, just before her
work was published. The young Camus was impressed by it
and this lonely young writer was in poignant contrast to all
those women who for centuries had written and were still
writing their souvenirs, often over-effusive and nearly always
composed against a comforting background which included a
husband, children, lovers. In Catholic countries the spinster
was regarded for many centuries as odd, her place in society
was not high, unless she was rich. Only too often she was
'relegated' to a life of good works against a background that
was more 'churchy' than religious. Fortunately the situation is
far different now, but during the 1930s a woman on her own
found it hard to avoid bitterness. These two writers did not
escape it.

Someone who fulfilled herself entirely through religious
writing was Marie-Noël (correctly Marie Rouget), born as far
back as 1883 and living until 1967. She wrote poems, dramas
and stories in quantity, notably *Les Chansons et les Heures*, 1920,
Les Chants de la Merci, 1930, and often set her own work to
music. She published from the 1920s onwards, during and
after the Second World War. She was not an intellectual, but
her work has been taken seriously by a vast audience in
France and much of it may well last, as long as there are
people to share her unquestioning faith in the Christian God.

The Second World War made relatively little difference to
several of these writers whose careers had begun some time
earlier. One who wrote in French but came from Roumania,
born Marthe Lahovary, better known as Princesse Marie
Bibesco, published fiction and non-fiction from the 'twenties
to the 'fifties and beyond, most of it translated in Britain,
where her personal friends included Sir Philip Sassoon,
Ramsay MacDonald, Winston Churchill and his family. She
had married Prince George Bibesco when she was seventeen
and published her first book at eighteen. This was *Les Huit
paradis* (The Eight Heavens) of 1916, about Persia, which she

had visited, and it was crowned by the Académie. The novel *Catherine-Paris*, although perhaps less obviously moving than *Le Perroquet vert* (The Green Parrot), about Russian exiles in the south of France, was the first French novel of what might be called the modern era to be selected for its readers by the Literary Guild in the United States. It merged in an astonishing way the atmosphere of western Europe, eastern Europe and Russia and in spite of its complexity reveals a lightness of touch that has always characterized a certain school of women writers. Early this century the Vienna court, Catherine-Paris found, was like an 'amateur theatrical company acting a historical play. But she thought the actors were taking incredible liberties with the text. Titus married Bérénice at the end of the first act, and Louis married Mancini. . . . The archduke in his Belvedere, with his Czechoslovakian lady, could well whistle "*L'amour est enfant de Bohème . . .*" echoing that coachman who drove Rudolf and Maria Vetchera to Mayerling. All these Hapsburg stories ended in bourgeois fashion, even the tragedies; none of the people had grown up in the school of Tacitus, with commentaries by Racine, none had learned from childhood the harsh lesson, so essential to the heart: "In spite of him, in spite of her, they left each other!" Not one of these lovers thought of their future reputation. This civilization had never had its seventeenth century.' A great deal of education and history distilled into a few lines and used to illuminate the court of the Archduke Francis Ferdinand whose assassination in 1914 was to change the world.

Princesse Bibesco continued to publish fiction and non-fiction, and never lost her popularity with a discerning audience. Her two books about Proust, *Au Bal avec Marcel Proust* and *Le Voyageur voilé* (The Veiled Wanderer), may be subjective but they succeed in conveying to the reader more about this complex personality than many scholarly works. The first was published in 1928 and recalls how, when she first met him, he frightened her; the second did not appear until 1947, after time, that creative dimension, had clarified the outlines of his personality for her. George Painter has described how, in 1908 'this astonishingly young tree-nymph from Roumania, with her violet-green eyes and talent budding into power, was received as a reigning beauty and a genius; truly, for she was both, but to her own annoyance, for her wish was not to be discovered by others, but to find herself'. Such was her insight that she 'was perhaps the first person to sense something supernatural' in Proust. After his death she realized why she did not want to dance with him, she was not yet ready to enter his strange world. 'Proust and Princesse Marthe Bibesco', wrote Painter, 'were two natives of the same land; and their touching of finger-tips at the ball was more deeply significant than the embraces of those who danced together till dawn.'

Princesse Bibesco wrote on a great variety of subjects, including several relating to Britain, and towards the end of her life published letters written by many of her friends, among them the poet Paul Claudel. Her novels are likely to appeal to women more than to men, and some readers may find her old-fashioned now, but as long as grace, elegance and tactful intelligence continue to have some virtue her work, more so in fact than that of Louise de Vilmorin, will not be forgotten. It is an example of what women could achieve before they were ostensibly 'liberated', in the days when 'liberation' usually came through the existence of a private fortune. Princesse Bibesco possessed extraordinary insight and wrote with classical, unaffected elegance, virtues which she would no doubt have possessed whatever her circumstances. But how far do material problems tend to obscure these sophisticated qualities? It is too early in the history of women's emancipation to tell. Marguerite Audoux, after all, had possessed them in her own way, and the only help she received came from a few years of Catholic education. And had she not been abandoned by her father after her mother's death she might not have received any education at all.

By the end of the 1930s the men of Huysmans' generation, had they been alive, would have been surprised to find that there were still some women with talent, it had not been a phenomenon of the early 1900s, although it should be added in fairness that the period between the two wars was dominated by the men novelists, poets and critics, and the austere editorial directors of the *Nouvelle Revue française*. At the same time many men had discreetly dropped their anti-feminist attitudes, partly because they realized they were fighting a useless rearguard action. The most discerning among them had moved forward from a partly flattering acceptance of the 'neo-romanticism' introduced by women writers such as the Comtesse de Noailles and realized now, with improvement in social status and education, women could not only show achievements comparable and parallel to those of men but at the same time comparable and different, precisely because of their feminine qualities. Divorce was of course possible by now, but this possibility did not necessarily mean happier marriage. Before 1907 Léon Blum, who was then a writer and dramatic critic, not a politician, had published his far-sighted, civilized book *Du mariage*, where he paid particular attention to the needs and rights of women. He discussed why marriage for some people was appropriate at certain times of life only and why, for instance, 'free love' did not solve all problems. By 1937 this book had gone through a hundred and twenty-eight editions.

No aspect of women's problems was forgotten. Eugène Brieux, the dramatist who had once seemed something of a male chauvinist, was nothing of the sort when he wrote *Une Femme seule* (A Woman Alone). In 1916, when the play had apparently remained unknown or unperformed in France, a translation by Mrs Bernard Shaw was published in England and Brieux wrote an illuminating preface: he was inclined to think it better if men worked and women brought up children but 'unfortunately, it happens that the wages of the working-man are insufficient for the support of a family, and the poor woman is therefore compelled to go to the factory'. This did not help children or family solidarity. Bernard Shaw is said to have overrated Brieux but it must be admitted that the French playwright anticipated an extraordinary number of the problems which are only partly solved even today. For instance, a woman may be a successful amateur writer without much trouble, but the whole picture changes once she wants to become a professional: his heroine was working on a feminist magazine. He showed the problems which the women's movement encountered from within: how to persuade them they must not work for lower wages than men, neither must they support their drunken husbands. The heroine and the other women in his play do not win: the women's trade union leads to attacks from the men, highly educated women realize they cannot necessarily find jobs without secretarial training, the heroine is forced in the end to accept life with a man, although it must be said she has persuaded him to refuse easy help and work for his living. Brieux also stated that men would have to be educated about the kind of women they would now be living with.

Writers of all kinds thought about the achievements of women and Paul Valéry, for instance, observed that the more abstract the activity, musical composition for example, the fewer women had excelled in it. But he wondered whether one day the arts might not be dominated by women, their potential was so strong. The very different Victor Margueritte, who had left the cavalry to take up professional writing, published in 1922 his novel *La Garçonne* (Tomboy), which so shocked the public that he was stripped of his Legion of Honour. His crime, in what is admittedly a second-rate book, was to show a heroine who refused to be sold in the marriage market, how she became an interior decorator, accepted lesbian friendships, tried to have a child with a handsome and brilliant dancer, failed, went through group sex, experiments with opium and cocaine – even the ageing Anatole France could not persuade the Legion of Honour that Margueritte's motives were to show how women were forced to live if they could not accept bourgeois marriage on their parents' terms. The same writer wrote three novels in a series called 'La Femme en Chemin' (*La Garçonne* was one of them), and another three called 'Vers le Bonheur' in which he discussed the ever-present, still unsolved problems: birth control and abortion. At the time, in Catholic France, these were not problems, they were social dynamite.

The attitudes in France were more violent than in England where in 1921 J. C. Squire, as he then was, edited for the Oxford University Press *A Book of Women's Verse*, suitably dedicated to Alice Meynell. By now women of thirty could vote in England, novels by women poured from the presses and the setback of *The Well of Loneliness* was some years ahead. Several of these women novelists, Rose Macaulay and Sylvia Lynd for example, wrote poetry. Mr Squire was fair and honest: 'Poetry is poetry, whoever writes it. But it is a fact, at least so far as my observation goes, that people do feel curiosity about women's contribution to the arts, and that this curiosity is common to all kinds of persons, from those who exaggerate the differences between the sexes, to those who seem to think they can eradicate them. I myself felt this curiosity when I conceived this anthology: and it would be stupid not to admit it.'

There was curiosity on the other side of the Channel, too, and women's contribution to the arts had achieved a remarkable variety and sophistication. At the same time, as Françoise Parturier observed, thinking of the mid-'thirties, 'Colette did not vote, her gardener voted as Maurice Goudeket did. Tramps voted, Coco Chanel did not, Stavisky voted, Simone Weil [who was twenty-six in 1935] did not.' In Belgium, where Marguerite Yourcenar, subject of the next chapter, was born, women did not earn the right to vote until 1948, though in 1919, through a reflection of some national guilt feeling, votes were given to mothers and widows of men killed in the war — as though to replace the men themselves.

Unfolding Eternity

Historical novels have been, still are, as popular as 'contemporary' novels in most countries and each category earns its devotees and fanatics. Once a 'contemporary' novel has ceased to date it can in a secondary way become 'historical' but a good historical novel is always, on a different level, 'contemporary', for it is inevitably about people, and if readers do not share their times they share basically their nature, however different the ordering of their life.

France in the twentieth century has produced a vast number of costume-film heroines by way of efficient commercial novels but the French language has also been used by several outstanding women writers in this genre, including Zoë Oldenbourg, who was born in Russia and in La Pierre angulaire (The Cornerstone) (1953) wrote a masterpiece. Intermittently, over a long period, Marguerite Yourcenar, born Marguerite Crayencourt in Belgium in 1903, of a French father and a Belgian mother, wrote historical novels with an imaginative dimension. Her early books, published from 1929 onwards, were hardly noticed, some were obscured by the approach of the Second World War, some not published and not translated into English at least until well after its close.

The short Alexis was the first to appear in 1929 when the author was twenty-six, although she had written it earlier. When she thought of revising it later she found very little change necessary but realized that the book, the 'portrait of a voice', was still relevant, for society had not changed as much as people imagined. How many people still had the same problem as her hero, whom she admitted to have been a real person, although she had moved the story back in time. The subtitle translates the problem: *Alexis ou le traité du vain combat*. A man who does not realize his bisexual nature, or fails to come to terms with it, goes through terrible unhappiness and makes others unhappy too. The author herself thinks of Gide's *Corydon*, at least one commentator has mentioned Cocteau's *Livre blanc*: the latter shares the sadness of *Alexis* but is crude and sentimental in comparison.

The 'portrait of a voice' is in fact a long letter (but still a slim volume) addressed by Alexis to his wife, in which he attempts to explain his nature by describing his childhood and his early life as a student away from home. The problem of bisexuality, rather than homosexuality, was to preoccupy the author all her life; hence the 'vain combat', one that is now discussed more openly than ever before but not often written about by young women nearly fifty years ago.

Marguerite Yourcenar made her start as a writer with a subject that was hardly easy, but severe as she has always been about her own writing she did not condemn her treatment of it in this early book. From that time on she rarely stopped writing, but was sometimes dissatisfied with her achievements and would forbid the reprinting of a book. The prose poems *Feux* appeared in 1936 and two years later she wrote *Le Coup de grâce* in strange circumstances: while desperate attempts were being made to forestall the Second World War she was staying at Sorrento in the hotel where Ibsen had written *Ghosts*. She was moved by the naïve frescoes (now vanished) which had been painted on the walls, showing him, complete with 'beard, spectacles and frockcoat, crowned by Muses or Spirits of Fame in a very 1900 style'. And she had always admired him deeply. Within a few weeks she wrote this short love story set during the Baltic wars of twenty years before. She might have relied on the memories of her older friends but her method was different. Old copies of illustrated magazines were not enough, she even studied the military maps of the time. Her method was automatically that of the historian for she has always refused to be led astray by personal impressions, which can only be subjective. She has even said that if she were writing about the events of May 1968 in Paris she would not rely on her personal memories – she was in Paris at the time – but study contemporary documents, hoping to find copies, among other things, of graffiti scribbled on walls.

Even before *Le Coup de grâce* was published she had written the first version of her 'contemporary' novel *Denier du rêve* (Coinage of Dreams), published in 1934 and dealing with fascism in Italy. She was not satisfied with it and admitted that such an enterprise needed technical skill that she did not possess. When she returned to the book some years later she had found that 'the novel annoyed me through its awkward transitions between lyricism and realism, through the clumsi-ness of the dialogue and its excessive stylization, through the poetic commentary which was often indiscreetly included instead of convincing, accurate detail'. She rewrote the book in 1959 to remedy the defects and because the themes still meant a great deal to her. She also wanted to show how certain myths remained close to everyday life. The earlier version had been fairly well reviewed, although it had not sold, but the author could not refrain from quoting one bad review by a Paris critic whose politics were far from hers. When discipline had been restored in France, he believed, 'this novel will represent in the museum of ideas, along with other more important remains, a nice little feminine sample of romantic, cerebral liberty'.

But Marguerite Yourcenar has been little concerned with self-vindication, she is the reverse of the journalistic writer who moves easily from one subject to another, she thinks continually round the ones she has chosen and at the same time does not believe that anything she writes belongs to her alone: 'unlike most of my contemporaries I consider a book, even the most personal, to be a partly collective achievement: everything in us goes into it, but also everything we have caught sight of or guessed at, books read and journeys undertaken, the observations of others as much as the experiences undergone by the writer himself, the marginal notes written by the proof-corrector and by readers friendly or hostile. We are too poor to live entirely on the productions of this uncultivated entity we call "I".'

In fact the author came back to her novel yet a third time in 1961 when she was invited to dramatize one of her books. No sooner was her dramatization finished than the theatre company evaporated, but she had learnt a good deal and felt even closer to her characters than before. She wanted to talk about what happened to them after the action was over (Jane Austen felt the same way about her characters) but was forced to content herself with an indication of where and when they died.

The *Memoirs of Hadrian*, her best-known book so far, certainly outside France, came in 1951, after eleven years which had seen only the translation of *What Maisie Knew* and revisions of other work. Eleven years was a short time, not only for the research, but mainly for the establishment and maintenance of the author's attitude which makes Hadrian not merely a Roman emperor of the second century B.C. but a man who tells his life-story and involves every reader in his memories and musings in some way. Everyone can identify himself and what is more interesting in a story concerned basically with male homosexuality, herself in some way or other with the central figure of this autobiography. Again, the author took up one of her early ideas for the second time. An astute research mind could have produced the fabric which is the backing to the story but only controlled imagination could have composed the actual tapestry which is gradually revealed to the reader. The author did not dare include dialogue because she maintained that nobody knows how conversations were conducted at that time.

The book is all the richer because the reader has every chance to argue about a few controversial points: could Hadrian really have seen so far forward into the middle ages and predicted events in the Near East? There is no means of telling: but pity the reader who complained that it was impossible to pile up sesterces one on top of the other because the raised shape of the Emperor's head protruded too far. The author took the point with interest but said that she had only mentioned forty sesterces – for she had experimented and piled up these very coins to see how far she could go – and when she reached forty her pile had fallen over. In the note at the end of the book she outlines her method – and a novelist in any genre can only envy such persistent practicality.

A mere amassing of historical fact could easily have been lifeless, but Marguerite Yourcenar enriched it not only with her imaginative interpretation but with a knowledge of painting, sculpture and architecture which she used as no mere décor but as living colour. Her second great novel L'Œuvre au noir (The Abyss) was not published until 1968 but its hero Zénon had already appeared as far back as 1934 in a récit which the author entitled D'après Dürer. The same collection (La Mort conduit l'attelage – Death draws the Yoke) contained other pieces based on work by El Greco and Rembrandt and it should be remembered that Marguerite Yourcenar also wrote an important preface to Piranesi's 'Prisons'. The title L'Œuvre au noir was the term used by the alchemists to describe the separation and dissolution of a substance. Reading L'Œuvre au noir, set in the sixteenth century, one is continually aware of the dominating colours in Flemish painting, but if Zénon grew out of Dürer the Flemish parts of the book are more reminiscent of the world of Rembrandt.

A projection of Hadrian's life had involved the evocation of a pre-Christian civilization; now Marguerite Yourcenar found it necessary, in the life of Zénon, to remember most of the important people living at the time – not only in art but in philosophy, theology, medical discovery; neither could she neglect mysterious figures such as Paracelsus and Nostradamus. Not only individuals but groups are included – the Anabaptists and the Adamites for example. Chronicles of the period were consulted for details ranging from outbreaks of plague to anatomical dissection and sexual orgies.

Marguerite Yourcenar lived with this book for some forty years. The three stories based on painters which had been at its origin had been part of a vast novel 'conceived and in part feverishly composed between 1921 and 1925, between my eighteenth and twenty-second year'. The achievement seems almost superhuman. With her usual honesty, her professionalism and passion for truth she wrote (in a note following L'Œuvre au noir) that her details about the book's genesis might 'displease' her readers because they came from herself and during her own lifetime, but she thought that some readers might be interested. 'What I want particularly to emphasize here, is that L'Œuvre au noir, like the Memoirs of Hadrian, was one of those books undertaken in early youth, abandoned and taken up again depending on circumstances, but with which the author has lived all her life. The only difference, which is entirely accidental, is that a sketch for what was to be L'Œuvre au noir appeared thirty-one years before the completion of the definitive text, while the first versions of the Memoirs of Hadrian did not have this good or bad fortune. Otherwise, and in the same way, the two novels were constructed over the years by successive excavation work until finally, in both cases, the work was composed and completed all at once.' She herself felt distinct advantages in these long relationships between an author and a character chosen or imagined during adolescence. But these characters do not reveal all their secrets until the author has achieved his or her own maturity. She believed this method was rare and felt she should explain it in order to avoid bibliographical confusion.

She then, as with the Memoirs of Hadrian, explained her system of documentation which is so much more than a mere bibliography.

Is the second 'big' novel a success? Never was it so hard to give an answer, for it is not easy for even a sophisticated reader to grasp the scope of the book. To enter into the mind of Hadrian, in a way that combines the real and the imaginative, might seem a more difficult, near-acrobatic feat, even though such a term could never be applied to Yourcenar. Yet Hadrian is truly the 'portrait of a voice' and the book reaches more readers more directly because there is only one voice, a unity. L'Œuvre au noir is concerned with one man, but the strands which make up his personality are so complex, and drawn together over such geographical and social distances that the reader could become more preoccupied with the strands than with the knot. At the moment interest in the mysteries of alchemy is strong but there is no clear sign that the twentieth century will succeed in its corresponding problems where the seventeenth failed. The life of Zénon is concerned with flux, change, dissolution, the story achieves a confrontation between alchemy and invention, and there could be no simple outcome. Zénon commits suicide but we are not convinced that this ending is inevitable. He has tried to find and preserve some lasting truth and since he believes it may lie within the body he is preoccupied with all aspects of physical existence. Is some spiritual dimension missing? The author comes to no presumptive conclusion.

Whatever the verdict on both Hadrian and L'Œuvre au noir – for in both cases it may change – the books are the proof that Marguerite Yourcenar is one of the most remarkable writers of this century. She is an imaginative historian, a poet and a woman who has no difficulty over the convincing portrayal of a man. She succeeds because she sees men as they really are and does not assume that their masculinity is total and exclusive. She has examined the evidence of their nature so carefully that however complex the character under examination or construction she achieves a cohesive portrait.

In the same way there is an extraordinary cohesion about all her work. When she was about seventeen she wrote a short play Le Dialogue dans le marécage (Dialogue in the Marshes) which was published in the Revue de France in 1932. No less than thirty-seven years later she included it – her very first dramatic writing – in the first volume of her theatrical works, mainly because she found echoes of her early novel *Alexis* which she wrote about the same time. She found the resemblance mainly in the hesitant search for a *prise de conscience*, a 'need for lucidity which cannot be separate from the need for moral perfection'. She was aware of influences from her early reading – the emotionalism of Maeterlinck, the *sensualité* of D'Annunzio, and the Japanese Nō plays which she had just encountered. She realized that she was young enough at the time to indulge in a kind of 'ingenuous virtuosity' and present all possible aspects of the situation, including the perpetual movement, in her heroine Pia's case, between 'so-called real life' and 'so-called dream life'. As a result, she adds, the psychological theme is treated as though it were a musical theme. Another reason which led her to republish the twenty-page drama is that it represents her first attempt to describe an old man, the first of many such portraits in her work. She modestly added that as she herself was now older she was in a stronger position to judge the merit of her achievement.

The 'dialogue' is based on an anecdote reported by Dante in the *Purgatorio* – a young wife, Pia, was exiled to an unhealthy castello in the Maremma by a jealous husband and died there. The aged husband, Sire Laurence, who says he was never young, goes to see her. She does not recognize him at first and is ready to give him money and food as she does to beggars. She is not even sure he is her husband. She is happy alone and prefers not to return to the town. But Sire Laurence is not hungry. Pia closes the dialogue by saying 'He isn't hungry? . . . Perhaps this beggar is sad. He should be given some wine, or else a rose. . . .' The rejected wife has rejected the man who rejected love and the short play is a study of how the solitary life can be satisfyingly rich.

Marguerite Yourcenar's cultural horizons are wide. She has translated Virginia Woolf's *The Waves*, which has had a deep influence on French writing since the 1930s, she has translated and prefaced the poems of Constantine Cavafy, of Hortense

Flexner too. She has written about negro spirituals, about translating Pindar, she has interpreted such different writers as Oppian of Syria and many from the Far East. It would be a mistake to think that she has taken refuge in the past, for she is deeply interested in some of the most crucial problems of the modern world – over-population, pollution and the destruction of wildlife. Although she hopes, for instance, that natural fabrics and vegetable dyes will not be lost to the world, she is in no way interested in attempting to turn back the clock: she is a realist and thinks that the human race generally should be more realistic than they are at the present, for too many people seem unable to see how busily they are destroying themselves.

Living in the United States as she has done for many years, and sometimes teaching, she has never deserted Europe. She sees it perhaps more clearly from further away, although obviously she visits her own continent regularly. It is likely that her work will become better known as this century progresses and its classical depth will prevent it from dating. Simone de Beauvoir's writing may well seem like a form of intelligent journalism in comparison. Yourcenar's understanding of bisexuality is of great value in the social climate of today, for how much unhappiness has been caused by the failure of men and women to understand the nuances of personality which had been only dimly perceived before by the modern world, by the picturesque nineteenth-century speculations about the androgyne? Hadrian thought carefully about the whole feminine character as it appeared in wives and mistresses. He believed that passionate lovers of women were more concerned with the temple and the accessories of worship rather than with the goddess herself. He found women too preoccupied with material detail while 'A man who reads or thinks, or a man who calculates, belongs to the species and not to the sex: in his best moments he even escapes from what is human. But my women lovers seemed to be proud of thinking only as women. The spirit, or the soul that I was seeking was still no more than a perfume.' Marguerite Yourcenar was well aware that this attitude was coloured by the period when Hadrian lived. But she thought it was still only too accurate in the present world of false values: 'For reasons in part natural and biological, in part certainly social,' she said in 1971, 'a woman accepts too often the artificial image which the society where she lives reflects back to her, she consents, as though with enjoyment, to shut herself up closely within interests which are often artificially feminine, instead of being in everything, and magnificently so, a human being who is a woman, *un être humain femme*.' She would with pleasure have written a book in which the central character was a woman of the ancient world, but she realized that their life was too restricted and that insufficient evidence is available to us about how they lived and thought.

Eventually Marguerite Yourcenar told her own story, in *Souvenirs pieux*, published in 1973, using the word 'pious' as Virgil used it when writing of *pius Aeneas*, he who respected and loved his family and his ancestors. Her search for the old family home in Belgium, overtaken by destructive industrialization, her reverent description of her strange literary uncle Octave Pirmez, known as 'le solitaire d'Acoz', the little town where he had retired and where he died at fifty in 1882. Until she wrote this more than understanding portrait he had been consecrated in my old *Encyclopédie Larousse* as follows: 'His books, which were few, can hardly be understood except by tender and passionate souls.' She also described how her parents met and married and the infinite number of family details are more absorbing than any novel. Such is the author's talent that one finds this family quite as fascinating as one's own, and the description of how Fernande, her mother, was brought up, gives some idea of how dangerous it was, in Brussels in the 1890s, for a girl to be caught reading French novels. The girl's family became anxious for she was in danger of being thought *originale*, slightly eccentric. 'Her very superficial culture, which she tried to improve by reading everything she came across, including the dangerous yellow-backed novels, frightened mothers: a young person who has read *Thaïs, Madame Chrysanthème* and *Cruelle Enigme* is no longer entirely marriageable. Too often she would recount historical anecdotes which delighted her, about personalities whom her dancing-partners had never heard of, such as the Duc de Brancas or Marie Walewska. She asked an old priest she knew to teach her Latin; she succeeded in construing a few lines of Virgil and since she was proud of her progress she mentioned it. She even admitted having bought a Greek grammar. Since nobody supported her, or even approved of her activities she stopped them, but Fernande had erroneously acquired the reputation of being a young person with ideas, which she was not.'

(In *Thaïs* Anatole France told the story of the courtesan who became a saint in the fourth century, Pierre Loti's heroine was a geisha. The third title is heavy with drama, and Marie Walewska was Bonaparte's Polish mistress. The Brancas family, of Italian origin, included many strange figures, notably the one who told Louis XV he had learnt to think in England. But the King did not understand what he meant.)

The sad thing is that all the knowledge of her family had to come through her father, more distant relatives and through her own research, for her mother died when she was a few days old. When her father told an old Jewish antique dealer what had happened the man reflected for a moment, then asked if the child had lived. When told yes, he replied that it was a pity.

A pity perhaps for the child to hear this remark when she grew up. But the situation may have been at the source of Marguerite Yourcenar's own personality as it comes through in her books: self-reliant, balanced, objective, dignified, able to interpret the past and link it with the present and the future. For once it is no criticism to say that she may never have been young in the casual, ordinary way. Somehow she knows all about youth just as she knows about age, and she herself escapes from age because her writing possesses an enduring, solid quality rare in the fragmentation of twentieth-century living. She has known how to smooth out the folds from eternity – *l'éternité pliée*, as Cocteau once described time.

And in case anyone should think that a woman who has spent so much of her life studying the past should have lost touch with the spirit of poetry this poem must surely prove the freshness and individuality of Marguerite Yourcenar can survive years of historical research and transmute them:

Le Visionnaire

J'ai vu sur la neige
un cerf pris au piège.
J'ai vu sur l'étang
un noyé flottant.
J'ai vu sur la plage
un sec coquillage.
J'ai vu sur les eaux
les tremblants oiseaux.
J'ai vu dans les villes
des damnés serviles.
J'ai vu dans la plaine
la fumée des haines
J'ai vu sur la mer
le soleil amer.
J'ai vu dans les cieux
d'insondables yeux.
J'ai vu dans l'espace
ce siècle, qui passe.
J'ai vu dans mon âme
la cendre, et la flamme.
J'ai vu dans mon cœur
un noir dieu vainqueur.

The future also is folded into eternity.

❋ 7 ❋

As Intelligent as They Are

It was the phrase Simone de Beauvoir used in conversation with Francis Jeanson, reporting another conversation she remembered from some years earlier: 'Colette Audry (I don't know if I've written it, but it was she who reminded me of it) wondered, when we were both teaching in Rouen, what could be done so that men would recognize us as their equals: "Well, we have to be, there's no problem!" For me that was understood, one had to be as intelligent as they are, that's all. . . .'

Is it unfair to quote it? Not really, for she never spoke or wrote idly. The phrase illustrates one of her deepest and lifelong preoccupations, how to free women from being the second, subsidiary, subservient sex, to free them from that psychological, social prison which had been constructed by men. Sometimes the prison walls were transparent and sometimes the women themselves had not even asked for the key to the door. She has stated fairly recently that The Second Sex lay close to her heart and it is surely for two things that she will be remembered: her place in the history of feminism and her personal history as a woman.

There will never be any need to tell that story for since she expended a quarter of a million words telling it herself nothing is needed for future readers except a brief set of notes listing possible cuts – which she would never have permitted – and an occasional explanation or correction from the outside. Women in particular have enjoyed the three autobiographical volumes and especially the first, which is the story of a girl growing up in France and a girl growing up anywhere. Even if the relationship with her father is not so unusual as she seems to think, it is told with honesty and obviously affected her whole life. The other intriguing relationship is that with God, a common enough story and a sad proof of Beauvoir's limitations, for she never learnt to understand her quarrel with Him, and none of her substitute religions seem to have brought her any genuine fulfilment.

Of her intelligence there was never any doubt but how strange that she sould say, even casually, that women had to be as intelligent as men. Some men are 'intelligent', some women too, but all depends on how the term is defined. If the problem of the 'feminine condition' were concerned only with 'intelligence' understood as I.Q., how easy it would be. The problem is complicated by emotive and psychological factors which may have a biological origin. Simone de Beauvoir's personal story, of which surely no detail has been left untold, is by no means a convincing proof that an intelligent woman has 'no problems'. She herself has said that one can never lose one's childhood and she has obviously never lost the taste for being a centre of attention.

How would she have managed if she had ever felt emotionally insecure? She moved directly from the warmth of her family to the warmth of her relationship with Sartre, she was never without a particular type of support which is only partially a question of money. Françoise Giroud, in her autobiography Si je mens (If I Lie), makes a pointed reference to the fact, but, when 'all is said and done', Giroud has never pretended she did not enjoy being a woman, whereas Beauvoir often resents her sex but has been prepared to use it in the way described as 'old-fashioned feminine' when necessary. She has even been observed as jealous, especially where Sartre was concerned.

Reading the autobiographical descriptions of life during the 1930s it seems pitiful that the French intellectuals could not see the political horizon more clearly and Simone de Beauvoir does not seem to have thought for herself. She waited for Sartre and others to talk about their feelings, and although she is hardly likely to have disagreed it seems strange that she never wanted to initiate action, as Simone Weil did, even if the 'action' in this case was muddle-headed. At the same time only a genuine member of the bourgeoisie could have made such efforts not to be bourgeois. When she and Sartre discussed the question of marriage they decided that there was no point in creating two sets of obligations, two sets of in-laws. One family each was enough, they thought, and no doubt they were right; no doubt she was right too in saying that her relationship with Sartre was the most successful aspect of her life, but there is an irritating smugness about her attitude.

Inevitably there has been much talk about this marriage of true minds and inevitably too people have asked whether the name of Simone de Beauvoir would have been half so well known had the serious, influential and brilliant Sartre not always been in the background. The answer is of course yes, but the long association has meant that each partner has indirectly drawn attention to the other's existence and work while the personal sexual side of the relationship has attracted attention from people who were merely intrigued, even shocked – it was easily possible in the 'thirties and 'forties – as well as those who believed that philosophers could hardly be human. Women who like to see women in the limelight, whatever the circumstances, were and still are devoted to Beauvoir.

She illustrates with uncanny rightness the genius of the French for producing, with perfect timing, a woman whose name is inextricably linked with a specific era, decade or generation. There has been no shortage of women writers in other countries and sometimes an English or American woman has been identified with a particular period: Elizabeth Barrett Browning and George Eliot, the Victorians who were all the more 'Victorian' because they flouted Victorianism, or Dorothy Parker who *was* the 'twenties. But the French have neatly produced the ideal symbolic woman to coincide with almost every period of change in social life and literature. Simone de

Beauvoir reached a wide public in and beyond France because she personified the new emancipation; a woman could be cerebral yet attractive to men. A woman could discuss philosophical and social problems and yet be perfectly capable of writing readable novels or memories of childhood.

Thinking back now over thirty years of her writing, it is strange to realize she had published nothing before *L'Invitée* in 1943, but she was busy teaching, learning, and enjoying life. Its English title *She Came to Stay* was a bad start because the whole concept of the *invitation* was lost. Perhaps the most obvious sign of inexperience is one shared by a great number of women novelists and somehow avoided by most men – the book starts, if not from a false premiss, at least from one that is never entirely justified. The heroine Françoise, involved as she is with her work and her lover and his work, would obviously not invite the infuriating Xavière to stay so close to them, or be so inhumanly patient for so long. When Pierre suggests the invitation Françoise protests for a moment, but feebly, is soon overruled and the subject is apparently forgotten. Yet there is so much to enjoy in the book that we can forgive its near-unacceptable basis and thankfully accept the rest.

First of all it is a book about women, maybe for women, for there is not a great deal for men to enjoy. Pierre may walk in the shadow of Sartre, but he is lucky that Françoise is so devoted to him. It is *her* book. If men do not have the patience to read several hundred pages about an odd *ménage à trois* they can at least enjoy, if only on a technical level, the remarkable way in which the novelist is able to write an illustration of various philosophical theories and yet still be a readable story-teller. Nothing exists, Françoise feels at the start of the book, if she is not there to see it, and at the end of the book she feels she has become a person, chosen herself, by doing something. What she did was to kill the girl whom she had accepted to live close to her and her lover. She had already thought, many pages before the end, *il faut la tuer*, and that is what she did. She had even tried to solve the triangle problem by being seriously ill herself, but she had survived.

The end of the novel, if taken literally, is unconvincing, for Françoise would not have murdered Xavière by turning on the gas. She could have liquidated, destroyed her somehow, but not this way. Nothing she thinks, says or does could persuade the reader that even for the sake of existentialism would she kill a girl who had acquired a share in her lover. In any case she loved Xavière. The relationship between the two girls is the most absorbing part of the book: never obvious, an undercurrent which sometimes ripples the surface.

There is one aspect of the book which I can never forget – among all the parties, the champagne, the wine, the coffee, the tea, the scenes backstage, the cafés, the restaurants, the hotel rooms; the dancing, which is more than mere background colour. The characters dance because they are young and however deeply they may be committed to their theatrical or literary work they are more conscious of their sexual relationships than anything else. So the characters watch theatrical dancing with much play of masks, Spanish dancing in a restaurant, most absorbing of all they dance together, at parties, at the negro dance-hall. Significantly the irritating, emotionally parasitic Xavière dances well, while Françoise is aware of her clumsiness, her lack of grace, her failure to let go. The story is in the dancing, and it is as though the author, publishing her first novel at thirty-five, put all her youth into it. Since she herself has stated that the book is about the attempt of another woman to break up the Sartre/de Beauvoir relationship then one can assume there is a good deal of herself in Françoise.

No critic would condemn the documentary novel out of hand, but most novel readers are unashamedly looking for entertainment only. In a sense the documentary novel does not become dated as the years pass, it acquires an additional life because it grows into history, while the autobiographical aspect, if any, is suddenly illuminated from within. This novel is a telling picture of France on the eve of war but it is more valuable for its individual characters who are neither mere symbols nor straight portraits of real people.

L'Invitée does not make many direct statements, and its ending is no more than a kind of curfew, but it tells the reader indirectly a great deal about its author. It was a pity perhaps that she had to discuss the book, along with nearly all her other work, in her autobiography but she could resist no temptation to talk about herself and probably believed quite sincerely that she was illuminating a situation of general interest.

After this first novel eleven years went by before *Les Mandarins*, her fourth, won the Prix Goncourt in 1954. It has been described as essential reading for anyone in the future who wants to know how the Paris intellectuals lived during the Occupation; enemies of the author and her novel say it will give a totally false impression. Everyone knows it is a *roman à clé* and again Beauvoir prolonged her book by discussing it in her autobiography. Those who really care about its historical or biographical truth can find plenty of material for research and many French people who lived through the Occupation without any detailed knowledge of politics or manoeuvring by the intellectuals have found it accurate enough. It is a landmark among the novels of the time and clearly a landmark among novels by women.

Essentially, if one accepts that vague phrase about being 'as intelligent' as men, then this book proves its author to be an extremely intelligent person, although ever since the early rivalry with Sartre at the Sorbonne no one had ever questioned the fact.

As she approaches seventy France has a Minister of the Feminine Condition and it would be unfair not to acknowledge that this post might never have been created without Simone de Beauvoir's contribution to what could be called feminism. Not everyone would agree that she has gone about it the right way. The scholars wonder at the unscientific presentation of *The Second Sex* which does not seem ever to have possessed an organized bibliography and frequently quotes that perceptive but totally unscientific book, *The Pure and the Impure* by Colette. Suzanne Lilar has written about all the errors it contains in *Le Malentendu du deuxième sexe* (The Misunderstanding of the Second Sex), but few people are likely to read it and Lilar has been condemned in France as a 'masculinisant', in other words she is not a fanatic feminist and, some would say, she is objective and fair.

Beauvoir has looked at the way women live all over the world – in China, the United States and North Africa. She has written about the Brigitte Bardot syndrome, she genuinely cares about working conditions for women and the all-important problems of contraception and abortion. Along with many other people she believes in the re-structuring of the family and above all in the sharing of parental duties. Has she clouded the issue by too much subjective writing, too much concentration for instance on her self-conscious love affair with Nelson Algren, who seemed to have been chosen as a 'suitable' writer-lover for he dealt with the social problems of Chicago? His appearance in *The Mandarins* and the auto-biography lacks the illumination of a single smile and he later wrote to an American journal saying laconically that as far as he was concerned it was an affair like any other.

What too was her motive in exposing the death of her mother to the whole world? and how strange that such an intelligent woman has been so afraid of death, like any middle-class housewife dyeing her hair in the hope of keeping her husband's interest. Did philosophy teach her nothing? How touching to think that during the Occupation she was actually forced to cook for the first time in her life and as she wrote to the sound of the low gas under the casserole she suddenly realized the pleasures experienced by a house-wife.

Yet all this is very unfair. She has written too much but it is never dull, and most of it is courageous. Her essay *Must We Burn De Sade?* was a stimulating contribution to modern writing about the divine Marquis. She seems to have little sense of humour but photographs show a well balanced face and a glorious smile. She was entirely responsible for the success of Violette Leduc, helped many writers, women and men, and in that mercifully short novel *Les Belles Images* achieved more than many numbers of *Les Temps modernes* and many tracts had done: what is the consumer society worth, and surely a mother can bring a daughter more happiness through love than by insisting on stereotyped success?

'Maman,' asks Catherine, aged eleven, 'why do we exist?' So much of life has been falsified, a sunny garden has become merely a pretty picture. Three generations of women, the two older ones struggling with husbands, lovers, careers, the girl who wants to cure the ills of the world and befriends the child who has no mother: the professional woman who thinks about office work at home and about home problems when in the office. The starving Greek peasant who had nothing to sell except rotten eggs, and the destruction of life by publicity. None of this is out of date and if this unpadded novel seems to point out too many problems too obviously, it does not matter. Through the heroine Laurence the author inevitably tells so much of her own story as it was, and, if she had had a daughter, as it might have been.

Simone de Beauvoir stated at the end of her second book of memoirs that she had been cheated, and later had to explain what she had really meant. She has never lost her dignity, even if her discussions about 'the second sex' were sometimes misguided. Time alone will tell if one is 'born a woman', or whether the 'feminine condition' is forced on women from the outside. The future may find her lacking in warmth, in literary invention and spiritual depth. In spite of her long training in philosophy she has remained constantly subjective but through this very subjectivity she has probably helped many women to learn more about themselves. When all is finally said and done, she will surely be forgiven for that remark about being 'as intelligent as they are'.

And as this goes to press the news comes that she has asked the Scandinavian-born Mai Zetterling to coordinate the production of a television documentary film, based on *The Second Sex*.

8

You've Never Been Hungry

Anyone could say 'You've never been hungry' to anyone else but the fact that Simone Weil said it to Simone de Beauvoir in the late 'twenties gives it a stimulating context. Simone Weil was a year younger than the other Simone and they were both students at the time. They seem to have met only this once, when Simone de Beauvoir was at the Sorbonne and Simone Weil, who was studying philosophy at the Lycée Henri IV, happened also to be at the Sorbonne for a course. Simone de Beauvoir was intrigued by the younger Simone, who was already noted for her intelligence, oddness and strange clothes, usually a long cape or a masculine type of tailored suit. The description of the meeting given in the *Memoirs of a Dutiful Daughter* says a great deal about both women. 'China had just been devastated by a great famine and I had been told', wrote Beauvoir, 'that on hearing this news she had wept: these tears earned my respect even more than her philosophical gifts. I envied a heart capable of beating over the whole world. One day I succeeded in approaching her. I don't remember how the conversation began; she stated firmly that only one thing mattered in the world today: the Revolution which would make it possible for everyone to eat. I replied, in a manner no less peremptory, that the problem was not how to make men happy but how to give a meaning to their existence. She looked me up and down: "It's obvious you've never been hungry," she said. Our relationship went no further. I realized that she had classified me as "a spiritualistic petty bourgeoise" and I was angry about it . . . I thought I had freed myself from my class.'

Simone Weil might have been 'a petty bourgeoise' too. She

had been born in 1909 into a comfortable Paris home where her father was a doctor. He came from Alsace, his wife had been born in Russia to a family who had originated in Vienna and the province that was formerly Galicia. Both families were Jewish but neither of Simone's parents followed any religious practices. Until she was eleven their daughter thought that the word juif (Jew) was a word used by Balzac to describe a moneylender, and all her life she found it hard to think of herself as Jewish because she had not grown up with any idea of what the term meant.

She almost did not grow up at all, for her health was bad from the beginning and became worse. But no amount of health trouble could hinder her schoolwork, her reading or listening, and at the age of ten or so she seriously announced that she was a bolshevik. She learnt quickly but envied her elder brother André who became a brilliant mathematician and was so advanced in the subject even when a boy that he only attended school for literature classes. When on holiday by the seaside he would teach himself Greek, holding a grammar book in one hand and a shrimping net in the other.

For a time Simone felt inadequate and inferior to this remarkable brother and is supposed even to have thought of suicide – but this was probably a teenage crisis. In any case her own intellectual activity occupied her entirely. Before passing her Baccalauréat in 1925 she was studying the sociologist Durkheim, writing poems in class and reading *L'Humanité*, the communist newspaper. While staying in a hotel in Switzerland that same summer she befriended the hotel staff, discussed politics with them in the evenings and told them they must form a union. She was sixteen at the time and some of the guests did not approve.

In 1924 girl students were allowed for the first time to enter the famous Lycée Henri IV in Paris and so in 1925 Simone began to attend it, especially for the course in philosophy conducted by the famous teacher Alain Chartier, who usually called himself Alain *tout court* and was well known through his

Propos, in which he used a near-aphoristic style to express what was a highly individual doctrine, although he himself did not claim to have established any neatly coherent system of thought.

Simone Weil was one of three girls attending Alain's course and one of her fellow-students, Simone Pétrement, was later to write the fullest account of her short crowded life so far published, tracing in detail how she learnt, worked and thought. From Alain she inherited and kept all her life a devotion to Plato and also to Descartes. He taught not only philosophy and its history but psychology (which according to him implied logic, moral philosophy and metaphysics) but also concentrated on a literary subject, which in Simone Weil's first year happened to be Balzac. Her work occupied her totally and Alain soon realized that she was destined to academic success. She kept many of the essays she wrote for Alain and Simone Pétrement has noted in particular one of them in which she was discussing 'Beauty and Goodness'.

A moral act, she maintained, is not an act 'which conforms to this or that rule, but a free, unpredictable act which is a creation like a work of art'. She discussed the famous story of Alexander in the desert, refusing to drink the water offered to him because his soldiers had none. Each saint, she added, had behaved in the same way, refusing 'all happiness that would separate him from the sufferings of men. . . .' At this stage it is safe to say that Simone Weil had not thought too much about Christianity and its saints – although she had obviously read all the essential texts – but this sentence, written when she was seventeen, expressed a conviction which never faltered and in fact became an obsession.

As time went on at the lycée her work was often praised, although the Latin teacher grumbled; her eccentricity was criticized, especially since she still wore the same odd masculine-type clothes, and she was suspended for one week, possibly because she protested (by putting up notices) when the *censeur* decided to separate male and female students in class. Like Simone de Beauvoir she was a dutiful daughter in the sense that she loved her parents and never had any intention of hurting them, but it is possible that at times she almost forgot she *was* their daughter – she might have preferred to be their second son. During 1926 she wrote an odd letter to her mother in which she regarded herself as grammatically masculine and signed herself 'Your respectful son'.

In all ways Simone Weil remains unclassifiable, she will always be a quandary, especially since she was one of those people whose life and writing cannot be separated, each explains the other, as far as either can be explained. Did she want to be a man, a rival to her brother? More probably she regarded herself as outside sex and on one occasion at least she announced that she was not a feminist; this was probably because she was bold enough and strong-minded enough to behave exactly as she wished in any given set of circumstances. She did not ask for rights, she took them. She even had more problems than she knew about: in spite of her brilliance she was given the minimum pass mark for her diploma at the Sorbonne (a short thesis written during the first two years of study) and the examiner was accused of not wanting to appear too favourable, for he was Jewish, as she was. At the same time he had every intellectual and personal objection to what she had written about 'Science and perception in Descartes', for she was deeply concerned with the problem of whether science can lead to equality and freedom for everyone.

She survived the examinations for the Agrégation but was not highly placed. Her known left-wing political views made her unpopular with many and earned her the title of 'the red virgin'. When she decided to apply for a teaching post she was not placed in an industrial town, as she had hoped, but in the cathedral town of Le Puy, some 260 miles from Paris south of the mountainous area of the Auvergne. The authorities threatened in fact to send her as far away as possible so that 'nothing more will be heard about her'.

A hope that was more than forlorn, for she had not been in

the quiet town for long before she was deeply involved with the teachers' trade unions. She had recently attended a three-day conference of the Confédération Générale du Travail in Paris, immediately contacted active trade unions in Saint-Étienne, the big manufacturing town forty-five miles away and very soon she was attending meetings and writing articles on trade-union topics. Her whole existence was dominated by her feelings for the underprivileged and she tried logically to put her ideas into practice. When she insisted on paying her charlady 'trade-union' rates it was not very clear who fixed these rates and nobody was more embarrassed than the cleaner herself. She helped anyone in trouble, gave away money, and a local communist who was also a work-shy drunk soon thought he had discovered how to live – but she was not taken in for very long. When she befriended the unemployed in Le Puy who could find no work beyond stone-breaking for a pittance there was serious trouble. She was regarded as an agitator, threatened with disciplinary action by the education authorities and possible removal from the girls' lycée where she was teaching.

The authorities, however, had reckoned without one thing – it had never occurred to them that Simone Weil's schoolgirls adored her. They had not taken long to see that she was not like other teachers – she did not speak very clearly and there was an odd clumsiness about her, but she had the gifts of a true teacher for making everyone want to learn and even gave an extra course on the history of mathematics. Instead of the expected demand for her removal from Le Puy the authorities were faced with a petition from the girls' parents who unanimously asked for her to stay, while teachers from the school and also from the boys' school wrote to the local press in her support. There was nothing attractive about Simone Weil in the ordinary superficial way, she never attempted to please and totally neglected her appearance: but she attracted, irresistibly, because she gave the whole of herself to her cause: that nobody in the world should lack education or food or

shelter, that nobody must be underprivileged. Her unselfish-
ness was identified with subversion and as a result a preacher
in the cathedral of Le Puy attacked her in one of his sermons
while a Parisian weekly stated that the Jewish Mademoiselle
Weil was a 'Moscow militant'.

She was touched by the support she received, unaffected by
hostility, but she left Le Puy at the end of the academic year.
Since she was determined to continue her own political education in a practical way she visited Germany during the summer
and was horrified by what she saw. At the same time she felt
that she had lost all respect for the communist party and found
it 'almost as blameworthy as social democracy'.

Her next academic post was at Auxerre, again a peaceable
town in the Yonne to the south-west of Paris. Again she had no
intention of keeping away from trade-union activity and
ordinary working people. The *proviseur* of the boys' lycée saw
her with some of the workmen who were carrying out repairs
there, and she even learnt from them how to do soldering. In
spite of the devotion to her students which nobody could
deny she received bad reports from the inspectorate who criticized her teaching methods and especially her 'tendentious'
approach to so many aspects of her subject. She could not
possibly have taught without saying what she felt about
social and political organization. But a method was found
of bringing her work in Auxerre to an end: philosophy would
no longer be taught at the girls' school and any pupils
who wanted to take this course would go to the boys' lycée
instead.

The next holiday was spent in Spain where Simone was
delighted by a fishermen's cooperative: when she found one
man reading *Faust* Part II she enthusiastically made him a
present of Rousseau's *Confessions*. Back in Paris she wrote some
articles which attracted the attention of Trotsky, among others,
and later that year she was to meet and argue with him. Her
teaching post from 1933 to 1934 was at Roanne in the Loire,
in reach of Saint-Etienne which she knew well from her year

at Le Puy. According to Simone Pétrement her relations with the school authorities were good and it was one of her pupils at Roanne, Anne Reynaud, who later published the book of *Leçons de philosophie*, based on Simone's lessons and the notes she herself had taken.

However, after three years of teaching Simone was now so immersed in political work and writing that she was aware of a change of direction within herself. Her commitment to the underprivileged was altered but she felt that as a teacher she was not close enough to the people she so much wanted to help. She was deeply concerned about the state of France and wrote to a former pupil that the country was living under a dictatorship. She criticized all political programmes, even those of the left to which she felt close, and she had had bitter interchanges with the communists. She now felt she could not understand the cause of ordinary working people unless for a time at least she could live and work as they did. *Seeing* the way they lived, and visiting a mine near Saint-Etienne, was nothing like good enough for her, for she regarded second-hand experience as useless. She did not see herself as a satis-factory analytical theorist about social conditions, as so many of her contemporaries among the intellectuals saw themselves. She insisted that she must take an ordinary job in a typical factory and by December 1934 she had found one, through a friend who knew the director of an electrical construction plant in rue Lecourbe, the long street which cuts right across the 15th arrondissement of Paris.

The director himself had been at the Ecole Polytechnique and since he was seriously interested in the improvement of industrial conditions he was well placed to understand Simone Weil's attitudes. He explained the situation to the foreman and asked him to keep an eye on her. She herself and many others have written about her year in industry and a strange story it is, depressing often when she notes the resignation of so many workers, especially the women. Yet she found the comradeship she had hoped for, no class barrier and no sex barrier; if she

stayed there only a few months this was the result of her own
bad health and an injury to her hands, for she never lost her
extraordinary clumsiness.

In mid-April 1935 she took another job in the Boulogne-
Billancourt area to the south-west of the city and found a bad
atmosphere which justified the worst of her fears. She noted
that most people were in a state of slavery and since she herself
could not reach the required production she was sacked after a
month. A new job eluded her and even she, who ate next to
nothing, realized that she was hungry and could not afford to
eat. She found it difficult to walk and stand in queues outside
factories.

No wonder perhaps that she has been described as neurotic,
masochistic. She was in some ways immature, as though there
had to be some compensation for her intellectual brilliance.
She was more than anything else determined to see her plan
through to the end and her will-power was such that nothing
could stop her, not even the murderous headaches from which
she suffered all her life.

She was even prepared to use sex-appeal in order to find a
job – she who always reacted at once against the slightest
display of sexual interest by men. She happened to hear that
at the Renault factory the man responsible for taking on staff
was susceptible to attractive young women and so anxious was
she to be accepted there that she even asked Simone Pétrement
to make the best of her with rouge and lipstick. And she
looked so handsome that her friend regretted that normally
she took so little interest in her appearance. She was taken on
at Renault – the rumour had been correct, the foreman liked
the look of her. For a few months she struggled on, and by
early August she left, aware that she had seen industrial slavery
and felt herself becoming part of its inescapable humiliation
only too easily. She had seen no way of improving conditions
for her colleagues and she was more pessimistic than ever
about the future. But at least she had put into practice the
advice she gave to a former pupil, in a sentence which explains

her whole personality: 'The reality of life is not sensation but activity — I mean activity in both thought and action.'

She returned to teaching and a post in Bourges, visited factories and tried with only moderate success to write in a works magazine. By 1936 she was totally preoccupied by the civil war in Spain and naturally there was no means of keeping her away from it. She who hated war was even photographed carrying a rifle and knowing her clumsiness her friends kept out of her way when she was carrying it. She admitted that her bad eyesight would probably prevent her from shooting anyone if she aimed at them. This same clumsiness caused her to spill a bowl of boiling water over her foot, she was sent to hospital, suffered at the hands of a Spanish doctor and had her father not intervened she might have lost a leg. The international group with whom she had been training was almost entirely liquidated soon afterwards at Perdiguera.

Back in Paris her attitude was one of strong pacifism and Simone Pétrement noticed that her taste in music and art was changing slightly, moving away from anything that implied a show of force. She began to prefer 'gentle' painters such as Giotto, Masaccio, Leonardo and Giorgione while among composers she singled out Monteverdi for special admiration. Two long trips to Italy in fact called out her love of good music (inherited from her mother), art and architecture. At the same time she would go to industrial centres and watch the workers entering or leaving their factories, but it looks as though unconsciously she was seeking a new dimension, a new approach not only to their problems but to her own. She wrote to her parents and told them about a mountain oratory she had visited, above Assisi, formerly a hermitage of St Francis. She was shown round by a young Franciscan, 'glowing with faith', and he told her a story: the 'story of a woman who in the fifteenth century had gone up there dressed as a man, had obtained admission as a Franciscan and had lived there for twenty years; it was only after her death that they discovered her sex; and the Church beatified her.' She told her parents that they had 'nearly lost her for ever' and added 'If I had known this story before going up there, who knows if I wouldn't have done the same thing?'

During 1937 and 1938 she taught at Saint-Quentin, which satisfied her need to be at the same time close to Paris and in an industrial town. She wrote several important articles, but did not publish them all, as a reaction to what was happening at the time, notably the setbacks to the insurgents in Spain and the collapse of the 'popular front' in France, due mainly to the financial policy of Léon Blum. Simone Weil was no mere political commentator, the interest of her writing at this period is in how far she could see ahead, she saw through the war that was coming, the 'victory' that followed but then there would surely be the 'revenge of the colonial peoples'.

At this period, despite her intense interest in the political scene, her horizon was no longer limited to what she considered the fatal errors of all governments, starting with those of the French. Other aspects of life began to absorb her. Her love for music may have been an important link between what appear to be two eras in her life, although there was never any clear split between them. She had heard Gregorian chant in Switzerland and was so anxious to hear more of it that in the spring of 1938 she succeeded in visiting the Benedictine abbey of Solesmes, where she followed all the Easter celebrations. It was here that she met two young Englishmen and one of them, John Vernon, talked to her about Shakespeare and more particularly about the English metaphysical poets. Many of her admirers have thought that from this moment she was converted to Christianity but inevitably with her the situation was never as simple as that and those who were fairly close to her think that the 'revelation' of Christ's existence and presence took place much later that year and was probably less dramatic than is often thought. She began however to read the metaphysical poets carefully and it was no doubt in the autumn that while reading Herbert's poem *On Love* that she felt Christ to be with her.

At this point Simone Weil becomes an influential mystic for some, while others, unaware of or suspicious of any spiritual or religious dimension in the world, feel they must part company with a woman who had until then seemed an interesting political theorist, even if she had a masochistic devotion to possibly unnecessary practical experience. The important thing is that her thought would most probably have evolved in some way even if she had not been so moved by contacts with the Catholic Church. It is possible that her experiences in factory work and the feelings that war must inevitably engulf Europe and the entire world would in some way have orientated her thinking away from politics and trade union activity into a different direction. As though aware somehow that time was not on her side she read widely in the field of comparative religion, although she never lost sight of Plato, whom she probably revered more than anyone else. She read the few surviving ancient Babylonian texts, absorbed all she could of oriental religions and later became passionately interested in the Cathars.

Much has been recounted of her meetings with churchmen, especially Father Perrin, and her complex, mingled reactions to the question of adherence to the Church: gradually she came to see that the Christian faith meant more to her than any other, she felt drawn to Catholicism and wanted to be baptized. At the same time she felt logically that she was not ready for acceptance into the Church. Her lucidity never deserted her, neither did her wish to work with her hands as so many other people did. During the autumn of 1941 she was living in a half-ruined cottage in the Gard while she worked with the local wine-harvesters. She felt that after her experience with industrial workers she should know something about conditions in agriculture.

In discussion with churchmen she was often argumentative and never accepted any aspect of doctrine at second hand. She would argue not only with the living but also with the dead, starting with St Augustine. But all the results of her arguments, with churchmen, and with herself, are in her books and note-books, none of them destined to appear until several years after her death. *The Need for Roots, Waiting on God, Gravity and Grace,* these and the two volumes entitled *Notebooks* are some of the most exciting books of the last generation, embodying as they do the reflections of a brilliant mind which for once was not closed to the spiritual dimension.

Her life was identified with her beliefs. She was thirty when war broke out. She refused to register as a Jew because she did not feel herself to be one and, more important, she regarded her refusal as a protest against any form of segregation. As a Jew, however, she was forbidden to take a teaching post under the Vichy government. She refused to queue for food and to eat anything that was not acquired with official food coupons. 'Whatever would Socrates have thought of the black market?' she would ask.

Her preoccupation with theology did not affect her involve-ment with the underprivileged. She accepted life in un-occupied France for a time and only consented to go to New York with her parents because she realized it would be easier to reach Britain that way; her ambition was to help the French cause by working for the Free French in London. After a brief stay in the United States, during which she went regu-larly to a Baptist church in Harlem, she achieved her ambition, and worked in Carlton Gardens. She even worked out two extraordinary plans which she thought would help the forces in action. She wanted to join a group of parachutists who would come down in the occupied zone, and she also wanted to organize a kind of suicide squad of nurses who would rescue the wounded from the battle area soon enough to save lives – but obviously the nurses could not all hope to survive. As ever, she remained far-sighted, she accepted the current position and policy of General de Gaulle, but the thought of a Gaullist party after the presumed military victory filled her with anxiety.

In London she became more detached from normal life than

ever and wrote with extreme speed some of her most important essays and stray thoughts. She lived in a small room in Holland Park and as usual she did not eat – she insisted that she could not eat more than what the starving French, as she imagined them to be, were eating in the occupied zone. She had been in England since the autumn of 1942 and by the following summer she was seriously ill. She died of TB and heart failure in a Kent nursing home, after the Middlesex Hospital realized they could not save her. A priest was supposed to come from London to take the burial service, but he never arrived. Maurice Schumann, whom she had known and liked in London, a Jew converted to the Church of Rome, knelt down and read some prayers from his missal.

Most of her published work is classified as 'theology', but like her own personality it cannot be classified, and in that is its value. Her thinking achieved an extraordinray synthesis of past, present and future. She did not try to be unorthodox, but she was, because she could relate logically the most diverse themes and illuminate all of them. To the logic was added that quality which can only be described as 'spiritual', although that too is hard enough to define. As materialism proceeds on an obviously self-destructive course it is not surprising that Simone Weil continues to gain in influence, especially perhaps in England, home of the metaphysical poets who had meant so much to her. She had discovered in the course of her reading that mystics of all religions spoke the same language, but it had never occurred to her that she might be considered one herself.

What is achieved by giving the whole of oneself to humanity? Can one achieve only a kind of masochistic sacrifice? Surely not, for Simone Weil chose her own destiny. She could possibly have come to terms with 'ordinary' life if she had wanted to, but she could not accept what was ordinary, it fell short of the greatness she found in Plato, the dramatists of classical Greece, Descartes, Monteverdi, to name only a few of the figures she admired. The fact that she also admired T. E.

Lawrence shows her incapacity for orthodox intellectual attitudes and she, who was not in any way given to hero-worship,
never questioned his greatness. One of her interpreters,
E. W. F. Tomlin, finds it strange that many of those preoccupied with the search for a kind of spiritual life today have
tended to prefer the 'apocalyptic visions' of Teilhard de
Chardin. They are, unfortunately, 'easier' to accept, there is
less personal and practical involvement, it is all comfortably
far away from trade-union meetings, political demonstrations
and attempts, as Simone Weil attempted, to help prostitutes by
trying to study the conditions in a brothel. Comfort, as she
knew, tends to destroy, and if she destroyed herself it was only
because she thought her work more valuable than her own
person. Her pace was too fast, she outstripped life in her
thirty-six years; ironically it is probably through her capacity
to satisfy spiritual hunger that slowly, by some complex
moral process, some of the world's material hunger will be
satisfied this century.

There are other unanswered, perhaps unanswerable questions. Was her intensely caring nature due to her womanhood,
was she truly a woman, and could such a personality have
belonged to a man? If Simone Weil had been born a man she
would probably have expended more energy and effort on
remaining alive, men seem to cling more egocentrically to
life, or else choose to die in a more violent way. A man endowed with a nature like that of Simone might probably have
done the practical manual work without such physical effort
and would probably have identified himself to a lesser degree
with the people he cared for and worked with. Back in the
seventeenth century Fénelon warned against women's tendency
to extremes, and it is part of that feminine quality which leads
to total involvement with the chosen cause. The British writer
Peter Hebblethwaite saw Simone Weil as the patron of
'winter-time' Christians, the phrase used by a German theo-
logian to describe those who believe in a Christian God but
cannot cross the threshold into the Christian Church. This

latter-day saint believed that if she did so she would lose contact with unbelievers, those unaware of their spiritual need. She knew that the effects of spiritual and material hunger are not so different as they might seem.

9

Moderato

For more than a decade after the late 1940s the world's literary critics anatomized the work written in French and known as the 'new novel'. The word 'new' no longer has the same relevance but the discussion still goes on. The pre-history of the phenomenon, the precise degree of innovation, every aspect of the authors involved, singly and collectively, together with their literary relationships between each other, the net achievements, if any, within literature and beyond, have been analysed passionately and closely discussed both in France and abroad. The 'new novel' was not the first innovation of the twentieth century and could not have happened unless there had first been the surrealist explosion, with its exploration of the unconscious, the child mind and the abnormal mind. Earlier still there had been attempts to understand and present the 'stream of consciousness', attempts which had first been made by Edouard Dujardin in France, by Dorothy Richardson in England and of course by Joyce and Virginia Woolf. Everyone has consistently forgotten Dorothy Richardson, who aimed to portray the feminine stream of consciousness, and the same fate overtook Djuna Barnes, also an innovator. So far women writers in France had been so consistently subjective that they had rarely been innovators on a grand scale. Many of them added something new or at least renewed in whatever they wrote, or their work would be totally forgotten, but their innovation was usually unconscious. Gradually they introduced new types of subject-matter but they were not much concerned with form. They wrote naturally and ignored the more technical aspects of literary fashions.

There is no doubt about the most obvious precursor of the 'new novel'; she was a woman and like most pioneers she was not recognized at first. Unlike pioneers in many other fields, however, she won appreciation fairly quickly and enjoyed success both in her own right and as the theorist and spokesman of this new kind of writing. Nathalie Sarraute is senior to both Simone de Beauvoir and Marguerite Yourcenar and she was not French by origin. Her parents were both Russian and met at the University of Geneva where they had come to escape the chills of anti-Semitic feeling in their own country. Their daughter Nathalie was born in 1902. Family circumstances and her studies took her to Germany, France and England and she was able to study the classics of four literatures in the original language. Her studies in history at Oxford were cut short at her father's request and apparently she regretted the punting as much as the study. In Paris she studied and practised as a barrister and from the age of thirty onwards, that is from 1932, she thought about writing. Seven years later she published a set of short pieces which she called *Tropismes*. It apparently received only one review in a minor Belgian newspaper, justifying its earlier rejection by two large publishers, despite admiration from the elderly Max Jacob. In 1947 came the first of her literary studies, including the brilliant essay 'From Dostoievski to Kafka' and in 1948 there followed a novel, *Portrait d'un inconnu* (Portrait of Man Unknown), which was dignified by a preface by Sartre. In spite of his support only four hundred copies were sold.

Since that time she has published (by 1975) in all six novels, several plays (which have been performed) and a great number of essays and articles about the hinterland to her own work and that of the loosely constituted group of 'new novelists' – Robbe-Grillet, Butor, Pinget and others. She has also given interviews in many countries and taken part in discussions covering all this work and many aspects of literature in general. The significance of the 'tropisms', the basis of her work, has been explained many times, and notably, of course, by herself. The biological term – an English word first used in 1899 but not officially in the French language – is concerned with stimulus and response to stimulus, and Sarraute is preoccupied with all that is happening under cover of our general external behaviour, conversation and methods of communication. The fringes of our consciousness, the way we think round things, the way we say one thing and half-know that we mean something else, the basic absurdity of how we occupy our lives: all this is her material. Buying a house, writing a book, talking trivia: these are themes rather than plots and there is no point in the reader expecting people in the books – there are people, but one can hardly call them characters – to do or say anything that seems obvious, external or active. They won't. One can be sure however that the inherent hypocrisy and false values which are indirectly criticized are not those of one or two eccentric individuals but those of the whole middle class, where all this unimportant but intrusive activity is magnified until it occupies far too much of life. Appreciation of Sarraute's work depends first of all on one's capacity for enjoying technique in itself and how far one can actively enjoy the small scale, with its large-scale implications, the study of lace-making or micro-assembly.

Sarraute did not invent the study of tropisms, even if she defined and classified the activity within literature and devoted herself to it. Not surprisingly, women writers in particular had already approached this area. Perhaps Katherine Mansfield and the later Colette (notably in *Duo* for example) had been able to catch at thoughts and words which hung in the air without being spoken, but they were still basically concerned with narrative in a way Nathalie Sarraute would regard as old-fashioned. Her 'characters', if that is the correct word, are depersonalized entities from whom the writer extracts words, thoughts and responses.

In her four intriguing and important collected essays of 1956, *L'Ere du soupçon* (Age of Suspicion), she had a good deal to say about the half-formulated thoughts that occupy the ordinary mind and the 'suspicions' that accumulate there. It might sound like half a life, half a world, and if her horizon seems limited it is consciously so. She was inclined to think Virginia Woolf old-fashioned and 'naïve' when she wrote in the 'twenties that the future of the novel could only be psychological. British literary critics in turn thought Sarraute naïve in making such a statement. Could she perhaps have underestimated someone, a woman, whose influence as an innovator in France at least is still remarkably high? Sarraute's attitude was analytical, not emotional, yet she obviously believed that the psychological novel, after so many centuries, had no future. She has maintained in the same set of essays that she and the school of new novelists have been influenced by the technique of Ivy Compton Burnett, but surely this stilted, repetitive style, which apparently impressed many people as witty, funny and revealing, is superficial and ordinary compared with the conversations in, say, *Martereau* or *Entre la Vie et la Mort* (Between Life and Death). It is intriguing for the British to observe foreign reaction to their writers, and the reverse is no less true. Sarraute's work brings the reader not action, drama or speed, but a prickly, shifting mass of colourless half-expressed images indicating a form of communication. It is perhaps not possible to come closer to formulating the actual way in which the mind talks to itself. It has often been suggested that the 'new' novelists as a group seem to have searched out techniques comparable to those of painting and Sarraute has been described as a pointilliste; yet her dots do not often achieve a luminous quality and the shapes are rarely fixed for long. She did not intend them to be. She was without doubt the innovator who initiated the new school of writing and was able to develop triumphantly within it. Her work is enjoyable in an obsessive, concentrated way, provided that she is not regarded as a novelist. A *littérateur*, more than *un écrivain* or a writer. She is an analyst even in her creative work and even more interesting perhaps when she is actively analysing, theorizing about world literature in her essays. Instead of asking 'What kind of a novel does she write?' it is more to the point to ask 'Is this a novel?' and inevitably one begins to ask 'What is a novel?' Nothing is newer than her newness and the charming, dignified Russian woman has quietly broken open the tired codifications of literary critics and writers. The French language, the language of analysis and nuance, seems remarkably appropriate for her work. Although she has expressed herself brilliantly in the several other languages she knows it seems right that she should have written in the most highly evolved of the Latin tongues.

Those who cannot easily focus on this type of writing can still appreciate all that Sarraute has to say about the 'new novel', which she anticipated almost entirely on her own, and about such key figures in the history of the novel as Joyce, Proust, and Faulkner. Analytical she is before anything else but she does not approach literary problems in the traditional desiccated academic way. She cuts through established thinking and although she presents her thought with classic impersonality the actual lines of thought are personal enough, showing her to be coolly individual, unafraid of true novelty. Intellectual conformity has never interested her and her attitudes are especially stimulating when one disagrees with her. Nearly forty years have passed now since she wrote off the 'psychological' novel as old-fashioned and yet the terms 'novel' and 'psychology' seem almost inseparable at various levels. But even if her own books will never sell in thousands (unfortunately her publishers still rate them in hundreds) it is fair to say that the novel will never be the same again, and the related discussions: what is a novel? and when is a novel not a novel? have been violently renewed.

New Sarraute still is but she has become a classic within her lifetime; extracts from her books are included, with detailed commentaries, in histories of literature intended for schools, the once-scrapped *Tropismes* was reprinted with some additional material (although without at least one piece) in 1957 and her devotees will discuss eagerly which of her books they like best. Les Fruits d'or (Golden Fruits), a satiric novel about the writing of a novel, received the Prix International de Littérature in 1964, a year after its publication, while virtually all her books and plays have been translated into several languages. She herself composed the 'blurb' for her novel Entre la Vie et la Mort in 1968 and in doing so explained much of her method. 'This book', she wrote, 'is concerned with writers and writing, but it is not, as might be supposed, an autobiography.

'Here, as in most novels, experiences which have happened, might happen or are merely possible are mingled to a point where it would be difficult even for the author to separate them.

'The reader who follows his usual method of looking everywhere for characters, who wastes his time trying to understand the movements and tropisms which make up the substance of this book will see that his efforts to fit them into suitable places have led him to construct a hero, made up of disparate parts, who can stand on his feet only with difficulty.

'Neither is this work in any way an art of poetry. It shows some phases of a desperate fight, whose conclusion is always uncertain, on one of the terrains where life and death confront each other with the greatest degree of dissimulation, that where a work of literature takes root, grows or dies.'

There is one paradox: although French seemed the right instrument for her writing the French atmosphere is in no way limiting. These are people talking, not merely French people. Although the range of the work may seem narrow, although many readers will always feel they have been cheated out of true nourishment, those who have found that their optique coincides with hers will read and re-read her books continually. Have feminism and the role of women concerned her? Hardly at all, but it is possible that only a woman could have consistently, exclusively and successfully have worked on the micro-assembly of words and tropisms for so long.

After which I feel compelled to be honest about one aspect of Sarraute's work as it affects me personally: I admire it intensely but cannot enjoy it. I feel as Raymond Radiguet felt fifty years ago when he wrote (and repeated) his complaint about the French preoccupation with cerebral literature. 'Since 1789 they've been forcing me to think. It's given me a head-ache.' And how I envy Mary McCarthy, for she seems to have enjoyed reading Sarraute as much as I enjoyed reading her now famous essay 'Hanging by a thread'. Perhaps my response to Sarraute is related to my allergic reaction against Ivy Compton-Burnett which has exiled me to the deserts of Boeotia for ever.

In the days when discussion of the *nouveau roman* was as new as the novels themselves some critics would include mentions of Marguerite Duras whereas others condescendingly thought her output beneath their notice. There was a non-gentleman's agreement that they were commercial, or, what was even worse, 'books for women'. That was a long time ago, when Duras, at the age of nearly forty, had published six novels but not yet her best work. The scenario for the film *Hiroshima mon amour* brought her well-deserved recognition as a film writer, although she maintains she should have been advised how to make more money out of it. By 1975 she had published al-together about twenty novels and collections of stories, plus one play, two volumes of short plays, three film scenarios and in more senses than one she had come a long way.

She was born in Indochina in 1914 and saw a good deal of the Far East. Her father was often away and as a child she was aware of his absence. Until she was sixteen all her friends were Vietnamese, two years later she left to study in Paris, remem-bering her childhood mostly with horror. The beaches were beautiful, the mountains too, the little pagodas were calm, so were the people; but these men and women were exploited and often ill. She remembers stories about a child with leprosy, a disease so empty of pain that a doctor could drive a knitting needle through his patient's limb and receive no reaction. She became so terrified of leprosy that she only freed herself of fear by writing about it. She saw a black panther a hundred yards away and she and her brother ate little alligators. After a childhood spent close to the jungle she was later unable to walk into a wood. Was it surprising that after spending so long on the fringe of an alien world there was so much alienation in her books?

Study at the Sorbonne, a marriage that lasted eleven years, a son, divorce, later treatment for alcoholism. All this went into the books, indirectly, and since 1943, the date of her first published novel, there has been an impressive degree of evolution in her writing, obviously following the changing pattern of her own psyche. Two years earlier Raymond Queneau had read her first manuscript and although he realized her merits as a writer the book was refused. Plon published *Les Impudents*, Gallimard accepted *La Vie tranquille* (A Tranquil Life) in 1944 and waited six years for the next book, *Un Barrage contre le Pacifique* (Sea of Troubles). Each novel gained in clarity and concentration. *Les Petits Chevaux de Tarquinia* (The Little Horses of Tarquinia) seemed a notable advance and critics quoted Hemingway and Virginia Woolf, which may be hard for the Anglo-Saxon reader to accept. But the feeling of isolation, non-effectiveness, was stronger.

When Queneau completed his report on *Le Square*, a dialogue in a public garden between a maidservant and an old man, he wrote: 'M.D. shows a concern for the renewal and deepening of her art which is rare among women writers. Perhaps she has been influenced by Compton-Burnett; one thinks also of certain tendencies in the contemporary theatre (Beckett, Ionesco and even Tardieu); but these are not so much influences as pretexts in the search for her own originality.' Compton-Burnett again: that author might have been as much surprised as most readers of Duras to find herself quoted in this context.

In 1958 *Moderato cantabile* was published by the Éditions de Minuit and is still her best-known novel, skilful enough to fascinate both traditionalists and avant-gardists alike. It uses elements of violent crime, obsessive sexual fascination and hints of alcoholism in a new type of combination. The 'new novelists', with the exception of Sarraute, had tended to use incidents of murder and sudden death partly to attract the reader and partly to express their urge to crack the skull of the traditional novel. Duras has recently said that she no longer recognizes the books she produced before this one, writing them often in a few weeks. She has described the experience behind her change of style.

It was 'a very, very, very violent erotic experience and – how can I put it? – I went through a crisis which was . . . suicidal . . . that is . . . what I recount in *Moderato cantabile*, that woman who wants to be killed, I lived it . . . and from then on the books changed . . . I even thought about it for two years, two, three years. I think that the turning towards . . . towards sincerity happened then. And, as in *Moderato cantabile*, the personality of the man I was living with didn't count. In fact, it wasn't a story . . . , a love story, but it was a . . . how can I put it? . . . a sexual story. I thought I wouldn't get over it. It was very strange. Because I've told it from the outside in *Moderato cantabile*, but I've never spoken of it otherwise.'

She broke away from her more or less conventional life, consciously aware for the first time of what she wanted. This book has been filmed, but not with her participation, and she would like to re-film it herself one day, using a restricted budget. The novel is now studied in Britain by students of seventeen to eighteen at university entrance level and surely Duras should no longer complain that she and her books are misunderstood and attract misogyny.

The prolific output of Duras has been sometimes considered along with those of the 'new novelists', sometimes ignored, and not only by men. The experience behind *Moderato cantabile* was obviously deeply traumatic, so much so that something of the pattern is repeated in later books, occasionally even more removed from reality, as in *The Ravishing of Lol V. Stein* and *L'Amour*. The special techniques of the novelist went into the film scenario for *Hiroshima mon amour* and in return certain aspects of film technique came into the later novels. Even the

Simone de Beauvoir, 1908–

Simone Weil, 1909–1943

Nathalie Sarraute, 1900–,
photo by Jerry Bauer

Marguerite Duras, 1914–,
photo by Jerry Bauer

most reactionary reader, who would not agree with her political and social theories, must surely admire the skill with which she expressed it, and a few famous sentences from this book deserve quotation: 'The remains of the salmon are offered round the table again. The women will devour it to the very end. Their bare shoulders gleam with the solidity of a society firmly built on the certainty of its rights, and they were chosen to fit this society. Their strict upbringing demands that they temper their excesses through major concern about their position.' While the women happily eat up the mayonnaise 'Men look at them and remember that these women embody their happiness.' Few women would have written like this before Duras, they would probably have fallen into the well-known trap of excess. This novel, in which every word, every sentence counts, is only sixty pages long in the edition specially prepared for use in British schools.

The work of Marguerite Duras will keep a place for itself, although it is too early to say precisely what kind of a place. It is in itself written *moderato*, giving an effect of moderate speed, and *cantabile* because it sings, fascinates. This singing quality, which has little to do with the actual use of words, will not be obvious to everyone, the music belongs to an elusive register, not calculated to reach the average ear, hence perhaps the use of a non-current musical term to describe it. Duras writes not only for the printed page. She writes also for the eye that can invent a décor behind her words and an ear that can hear overtones beyond them. Her search to present dialogues parallel in time may never be successful because the dimensions of the novel obviously cannot be stretched beyond a certain point but in a masterly way she has used the resources of the novel to the ultimate and the result is still classifiable as a novel, with a narrative appeal.

Her creation of atmosphere is masterly and rarely did anyone work with such limited material. These limits are not necessarily the physical limits imposed on French theatrical and cinema productions by lack of material and money and leading to influential achievements. Marguerite Duras's limits are self-imposed, the result of selection which appears almost obsessive. A sea coast, a distant town, a hot night in a Spanish hotel, all these décors are chosen carefully and the few details are adequate. People walking, dancing, and never accompanied by anything which is not strictly necessary. Film directors such as Antonioni have probably influenced her more than other writers. Isolation, alienation, stillness and the exploration of certain aspects of language, in particular the resources of the present tense, for once revealing the true possibilities of what is also called the narrative present, the graphic present: this is used brilliantly, although one drawback is that the results in English are not always satisfactory. Since the present tense is not easily and normally used in this way in English without a carefully established context its unvaried use in certain translated work of Duras looks 'literary' or artificial and therefore the achievements of the author are partly lost.

All the work of Duras possesses an individualistic, inherent dramatic quality and had she not been writing in the age of the cinema she might have been almost wholly a dramatist. She has in fact written a good deal for the theatre but she would surely not have been interested in the 'traditional' drama. She would have looked ahead. In France women have had much more success as actresses than as dramatists and it was not before the mid-twentieth century that they could easily acquire the necessary practical experience to become playwrights. Duras's early plays are now well received in Britain at least, but the public took its time learning her 'language'. As film writers and directors women in France have achieved a good deal and Duras's contribution is internationally famous. Not only did she bring her talent as a novelist to the screen but she has now brought her experience of the cinema into the novel. In her novels she has remained a novelist if only through her sensitive tact and taste, a feeling for form to which she has clung throughout all her experimentation. There is a choreographic quality in much of the writing of Le *Vice-consul*, for example, which possesses an inescapable sense of ordered movement.

This is an impressive novel, one of her most memorable, expressing bitterly, but again obliquely, what she feels about old-fashioned colonialism. She develops the telling contrast between Anne-Marie Stretter who could be regarded as a successful, 'respectable' prostitute and the Indian beggar woman who in spite of her misery knows a limited kind of happiness, taunts others with her happiness and survives. This is a novel of mysterious, unresolved meetings, not only between East and West, or between men and women; it illuminates, with a chiaroscuro of sadness and humour, an attempted meeting between the vice-consul and himself.

In the novels of Nathalie Sarraute the reader is hardly concerned with the sexual differences between the characters but in the work of Duras the male–female polarity often dominates. It may be a destructive force, but neither side can resist or escape it. The author said recently that she now spent more and more time with women, she had made a film showing how women spend their day, and one woman critic has discerned in the work 'the power of feminine desire; a power of calm and silence which many men find alarming for they do not know what it will lead to'. They also find the later novels uncomfortable reading because the sexual tension is hardly ever resolved. No doubt some women would react in the same way; but only a woman could have written these haunting books.

The traditionalists who claimed that the 'new novel' was never very new must surely accept now that the novel – outside popular commercial writing – may never be the same again. The two women writers associated with the group, one closely, one distantly, have made individual contributions, both working in areas of their own, both aware of what was going on about them in literature and in life, but basically they were interpreters and not mere absorbers of influence. Sarraute has been a theorist, Duras has said that she has no

theories about the novel and sometimes forgets the details of
what she had written less than a year before. Without them the
new school of writing might have seemed a secondary recru-
descence of surrealism without its poetic dimension, but
through them there entered an element that was 'feminine' in
the best sense. Men find more enjoyment than women in what
is aggressively 'new'; they relish an infinity of inconclusive
experiment and have not the slightest objection to losing
touch with the world of materialistic or psychological reality.
Would any woman have written, as Michel Butor did, 6,810,000
litres d'eau par seconde; *étude stéréophonique*? Whatever Sarraute and
Duras have felt about psychology they have always known
their own potential; they have unconsciously limited themselves to what they knew they as individuals could do well.
They wanted to remain in control of their writing, the performance must be 'moderato'. If it can have a singing tone, all
the better. The 'new novel' is a chapter in history, the writers
may never reach a vast public and the film writer (who has
now directed films on her own) has so far acquired more of
an audience than the analyst, but both will grow in stature.
They have consistently shown courage and shirked nothing;
perhaps Queneau would never dare to say again that women
do not often renew and deepen their style of writing. Sarraute
and Duras have proved what women can achieve simply by
working hard and by remaining essentially themselves. Duras
is particularly conscious of the latent strength of women which
is only just coming to the surface and has stated that she sees
nothing in the 'history of liberty . . . that has gone forward
as fast as the women's liberation movement'. She believes too
that only women write 'completely', and perhaps it is only
women who write at all, for men writers tend psychologically
to be 'women' too. Which leaves the men, writers or not,
with plenty of scope for argument.

10

Casebooks

Writers and their work have always occupied more journalistic space in France than in many other countries because the writing itself is news, not just the people who produce it. The Anglo-Saxon world – outside the literary critics – is prepared to give inquisitive, voyeur-like attention to writers, especially of course women writers, but little to what they write. How much easier it is, and how much more entertaining, to reproduce in any medium both a painting and the likeness of its painter. To reproduce even a short story takes a good deal of space and although a poem may be shorter its readership is miniscule. A novel or an imaginative non-fiction work could, until the economic crisis of the 1970s, appear in a pruned state in a magazine or newspaper, provided it was accompaned by a large enough illustration, preferably coloured. The future for this kind of publishing is now uncertain in any country and writers who are not primarily entertainers will count themselves lucky if they are allowed a little space in the one remaining imaginative medium for words, sound broadcasting. Words may need translation, colour and line do not. After the Second World War the press in France gave a great deal of space to writers. Sartre, Simone de Beauvoir, Camus, Françoise Sagan and others, while winners of literary prizes are always sure of attention, however discredited the complicated prize-system has now become. It so happened during the 'fifties and 'sixties that two writers, both women, were 'made' by the press and treated as 'cases', while their work was assessed from a psychological and social angle.

One of these writers had begun to write at the age of seven and became known two years later. The other was a teenage delinquent who died after three successful books at twenty-nine. They were both adopted children, their parents were unknown. The poems of Minou Drouet came from France to Britain and the United States at high speed and such was the controversy about them and their authorship that after thirty or so mentions in the French press there was the *affaire Minou Drouet* and a whole book called precisely that, published by her publisher a year after her first poems had appeared. Twenty years have gone by since then and young novelists – mainly girls – have continued to appear in France, although few have lasted. No other young poets have made the headlines for so long. The French educational system may be a little less rigid than it was but it still seems to produce more publishable writers in the adolescent age group than any other. Poetry competitions and creative writing classes in many other countries produce anthologies but little more. The Latin teenager apparently matures earlier than those of most other cultures and seems to acquire more experience of varying types – practical, emotional and intellectual – more quickly. This had happened to Rimbaud in the late nineteenth century and to Raymond Radiguet just after the First World War. When Aldous Huxley prefaced Kay Boyle's translation of *Le Diable au corps* in 1932 he pointed out that of all the arts writing, to be successful, depended on practical experience of life, whereas music, in which many very young people have always excelled, and still do, was of all art forms furthest from reality. It might be fair to add that poetry is on one level further from reality than fiction, and it is important to remember in this connection that Minou Drouet was a musician. That music brought 'revelation' to Minou Drouet was in fact the starting point of her story.

That story seemed far from reality and what most people would regard as normality. Mademoiselle Claude Drouet, a spinster of forty-nine living in Brittany, adopted a little girl called Marie-Noëlle who had severe eye-trouble. She had been drawn to the child because she herself had lost her sight for a time when younger.

Claude Drouet, who now called herself Madame, lived with

her elderly mother, who drew rent from the ownership of a few houses, while she herself worked as a teacher, usually giving private lessons. She also published a few articles and at least one story in the local press; she wrote a long poem but failed to publish it. One day her adopted daughter, known as Minou, now aged seven, heard the pianist Lucette Descaves playing Bach in a radio programme and realized that her life was transformed. She immediately wrote to Lucette Descaves who was intrigued, met the child and gave her lessons. All that Minou had known of music so far had been a few lessons with local teachers but now she won a prize for her playing in a local competition. She began to write short poems and lyrical letters, addressing them to Lucette Descaves. Life had indeed changed. She recovered full eyesight after a dangerously complicated operation in Marseilles and by 1955 the publisher René Julliard saw the child's letters to her pianist friend and teacher. He and his wife met her and also received letters from her, no ordinary letters. She wrote more poems, strangely mature. The literary critic and Academician Pasteur Vallery-Radot supported René Julliard in his conviction that the child had genuine literary talent, so in 1955 Julliard printed a few copies of her work for private circulation.

The story got about, the press, from the women's magazine *Elle* to *Paris-Match* and the austere *Le Monde* took note of it and examined the mysterious circumstances behind this writing. There was one sinister figure – Madame Drouet, who had some reputation as a clairvoyant and a palmist and admitted that she had chosen Minou for adoption not only because she had shared her eyesight trouble but because the lines of her hand promised a bright future. Many people insisted that *she* had written Minou's poems, handwriting experts were called in, a psychotherapist pointed out the abnormal upbringing of a girl living closely with a middle-aged adoptive mother and her mother, and not attending school very regularly owing to various health problems. She also mentioned the dependence of abnormal children on music.

On the literary value of Minou's poems some of the most interesting remarks came from André Breton, the veteran surrealist being well placed to judge poems written by a child in unusual circumstances. Their originality, he said, had been over-estimated but he praised 'the remarkably spontaneous qualities, the gift of harmonic *enchaînement*, the vivid images', he appreciated the unrestrained sensuous appreciation of the concrete world. Breton has been regarded as something of a reactionary as far as women's writing is concerned and he limited his conclusions on the literary merits of the poems by saying that no woman since Marie Noël had shown such lyrical strength. He especially appreciated the touch of humour which ran throughout the work and then went on to say that in his opinion no child could have written these poems unaided. He was convinced that 'A certain timbre of life that has been lived cannot in any case affect life that is still to be lived'. He was more interested in Madame Drouet than in her daughter. He respected her attempt to re-live her life through Minou and to make 'their two hearts into one', admitting that he found the problem of how 'the current passed between the inducer and the induced' much less interesting, while 'The question of fraud in mediums cannot . . . arise in judicial terms or even in those of conventional morality'.

Other child prodigies and their short creative lives were mentioned by journalists and critics, one elderly lady whose work as a small girl had been admired by late-nineteenth-century writers was interviewed. It was proved by various experiments that Minou could write when her mother was not in the same room and she even wrote a long poem in a London television studio in the presence of her translator only. Most of the time she behaved like a normal little girl, sometimes she was observed to behave like a somnambulist, to say or write extraordinary sentences as though she were receiving 'messages' in some occult way. There has never been any 'explanation' of the whole affair but two things matter – the best of the poems are of literary interest often because the word–idea associations are so strange. Minou Drouet was obviously repeating and relating things she had heard or read without understanding them but like a latter-day surrealist she created something precisely out of this particular type of non-cerebral association. She had been brought up in an abnormal atmosphere and by the age of nine or ten was used to being a centre of interest and making theatrical appearances. The poet Jules Supervielle himself even encouraged her to go to a congress of poets in Italy in his place.

She began to show a dangerous number of talents. She sang and played the guitar on the music-hall stage, wrote songs, stories for children and also in 1968 a children's book called *Ouf de la forêt*. As though suddenly she needed to escape from literature for a time she became a nurse and later wrote a novel, partly based on her own experiences. This was *Du Brouillard dans les yeux* (Donatella), which begins with a heart-rending description of a child gradually going blind. The child, oddly enough, is a boy. Then suddenly there is a heroine, herself as a nurse, who tries hard to save the life of a little Arab boy. The novel ends as one chapter of her own personal story began, the heroine fell in love, got married and lived happily ever after.

From time to time after her 'literary' career as such was over she occasionally wrote down experiences which showed how far she had been a 'knowledgeable' child, the child who knew when people were going to die, the child who had curious affinities with animals, and if one accepts the existence of 'second sight' she possessed it. But if she had not been adopted by a single woman – a situation illegal in most western European countries – and if the late René Julliard had not risked his reputation as a publisher no one would have known about her. No comparable 'case' or affair seems to have happened in Europe since the Second World War, or if it did nobody fed it into the publishing machine. The case of Nathalia Crane in the United States does not seem to have been quoted as a possible point of comparison. This American

girl published *The Janitor's Boy* in 1924 when she was not yet
thirteen and it received high praise. The poems were even
credited with metaphysical qualities; she later published several
more volumes and some fiction but her name now belongs
only to reference books. Obviously the French journalists were
just as interested in the young poet as in the poetry, but at
least the actual poems were quoted in newspapers and magazines. By the time Minou Drouet published a second and third
book of poems the work was often repetitive but apart from
the mystery of its true source it retained a style of its own, that
of a 'somnambulist', the critics continued to say, but a style
and a technique none the less:

River

For my friends the Salvas

You were the dancing
two times table,
you enabled my fleeting brain
to learn to count as a game.

You were the geometry
revealing to my gaiety
lines and their witchery,
the curving line which can
link the fish to the fisherman
the circle where each stone thrown
rings the singing ricochet,
the teasing parallel lines
of your banks which could
put a girdle round the earth
and never ever meet;
oblique are your ferns,
straight your poplars,
though you twist them with your laughter;
I love your old wooden bridge,

the perpendicular line
which the wind from time to time
gives a kind of tummy ache.

. . .

Water, your rhythm started
in me the unending quest
for an otherwhere, and there I know
a game, I can throw a stone and deck
with a blossoming rippled navel
the body of the stretched-out sky.

Albertine Sarrazin also wrote poems, but they were not the
most striking part of a second literary casebook in France,
some ten years after the Minou Drouet affair. In 1937 a child
was born in Algiers and handed over to the Assistance
Publique. On her birth certificate the names of her parents
were indicated by two dashes – they were unknown, but the
father was thought to be an Arab and the mother a Spanish
girl. The child was given the name of Albertine Damien and
when she was four she was adopted by a colonel in the army
medical service and his wife. The couple, who had never had
children, decided on this adoption late in life and six years
later the Colonel retired, leaving Algiers for Aix-en-Provence.
They had given their daughter the name of Anne-Marie, she
had gone to school willingly enough and seemed gifted,
playing the violin and writing a journal, but when at the age
of fifteen she was sent to the lycée at Aix she tolerated it for
three weeks, then ran away. She was then sent to a kind of
approved school, known as *maison d'éducation surveillée*, where she
took her Baccalauréat at sixteen, which was young. She had to be
escorted to another building to take the oral examination –
which she passed with good marks – and suddenly she was
tempted: she saw a back door standing open, she disappeared
through it and in two days hitch-hiked her way to Paris. The
temptation to escape had not dated from the day of the
Baccalauréat – she had made a pact with another girl from the

approved school, ironically called 'Le Bon Pasteur', that they would meet by the Obelisk in place de la Concorde, on November 1st, 1953. Her friend kept her word and for the next few weeks the two girls managed to survive by one means or another, including stealing and prostitution. Albertine had been raped at the age of ten, she was not afraid of men. In mid-December the girls tried to rob a dress shop by threatening the manageress with a loaded revolver. It was not Albertine who was carrying it, but her friend, who suddenly took fright, fired and wounded the woman. A few days later they were arrested, Albertine was sent to the well-known prison at Fresnes for two years' preventive detention. During 1954 she began to write poems, and the notes which were to grow into a journal. During this period she passed the second part of her Baccalauréat, again with mention bien.

In 1955 she was tried by the Cour d'Assises dealing with cases of minors, was sentenced to seven years' imprisonment and dispatched to a prison school at Doullens in the north-east of France. At her trial mention was made of the journal she had been keeping for some time and her adoptive parents gave up their adoption, indicating that they were 'too old' to look after her adequately. Since she was now nineteen, she began to work for the next state examination, known as the propédeutique, a preliminary to higher studies.

She did not realize that she had already provided 'copy' for writers other than crime reporters, for in 1956 her hold-up adventure was described with all its sociological implications – 'subversion, total irreverence, pointless revolt' – in an article by Jacques Senelier called *Passage des Etoilées* for the first number of a new literary review edited by André Breton, *Le Surréalisme, même*. Albertine herself was able to read a great deal and filled pages of a green exercise book with her journal which she later called *The Times*. She was already seething with an ambition to write but she had no intention of spending her life in prison. When threatened with punishment in the spring of 1957 she could no longer bear it. She managed to escape by climbing the prison wall. She jumped down the thirty-foot drop on the other side and broke the astragalus bone in her foot.

At this point her own writing tells more than any list of facts, and like Violette Leduc – but how different the terms – she now wrote everything that happened to her into three autobiographical books. Most of her letters and journals have now been published too, adding a gloss to her fiction, all of which was fact, giving even more depth to descriptions which seemed hardly credible, in what her publishers listed as 'novels'. *L'Astragale* describes all that happened after she found herself lying on the ground, outside the prison wall, but hardly able to get up and walk because of her swollen, aching foot. Everything seemed predestined, for the truck-driver who stopped and gave her a cigarette, a lift and shelter in his own home was an ex-prisoner, Julien Sarrazin. Hardly had they met and understood each other, hardly had she had some treatment for her injured foot, provisional but life-saving, than they fell in love. Julien's family were warm-hearted, fed her, lent her clothes. Through a hundred small details she knew he had been 'inside'. She had to see the world in a new way now and realized it wasn't easy to forget the prison routine, the oddly cosy prison security. She had learned to love girls and realized the women she had known in prison had turned her 'away from simplicity, from even the most superficial friend-ship'. Reality was distorted, she knew. She had seen so little of the world, reading and dreaming had replaced life, she knew she was 'bursting with images!' As a friend of Julien's drove her out of Paris she felt paralysed at the thought of 'freedom'.

Life and prison had come to mean the same thing and now she could hardly see life as anything else, even though she had discovered Julien. The police wanted both of them; Julien was caught first in March 1958, and while he was in prison at Boulogne Albertine began to write to him. He was not allowed to receive the letters and she gave them to him on his release in the summer. He must have been amazed when he eventually read them, he was in love but he had not known he was in love with a writer. All her reading and journal-keeping seemed to have some point now, one person at least was going to read what she wrote.

When Albertine began to write to him she had obviously not forgotten all she had read in the prison library. She became lyrical. 'Perhaps we'll be restored to each other, perhaps we never will be, perhaps it'll be the road, for both of us, what does it matter? There's no world for our journey.'

'Oh dear one so like me, like me with the scars of life barely healed on you. . . .' She describes how she had 'chased after money because it gives the illusion of possessing something, I've done all the bad things I could because I have to destroy furiously everything that makes you jealous.' But she admits that her attempts to be 'bad' were a failure – she stakes her last throw on love.

For four months in 1958 they lived together, having sworn never to leave each other again. They barely had time to grow used to one another. In September they were both arrested for petty thieving, sent to separate prisons, and not allowed to communicate.

Julien Sarrazin had had a grim life and seemed just as surely destined to crime and prison as Albertine. He was thirteen years older than she was, the seventh in a poverty-stricken family of eleven children; he loved his mother, hated his violent father. During the German occupation of Paris he had kept his family alive by stealing food, with his brother, from loaded goods trains on their way to Germany, and in 1943, at the age of nineteen, he was sentenced to fifteen years' hard labour, made longer by attempted escapes. Naturally, on his release in 1953 he could find no work and was reduced to stealing again.

Julien was soon released and the couple decided to marry, although Albertine had to go back to prison at Amiens to finish the sentence interrupted by her escape from Doullens. Marriage made letter-writing and visiting much easier. She was released under escort for the marriage ceremony, in

February 1959. She had wanted a religious ceremony but it was not possible, mainly because the couple could not live together. For the previous two months Julien had written to Albertine every day, she had been allowed to reply with the regulation two letters a week. After the marriage came another whole year of letter-writing – she was now at Soissons – adding up to several hundred printed pages, every one of them absorbing.

Albertine's style had become much less 'literary', although her vocabulary was wide and she obviously read more and more, for she was still studying; she refers to the French classics, Villon and Verlaine, to Tagore, Charles Morgan and Jean Giono with equal ease. Pierre Daninos she found was 'good for morale'. She listened to radio readings of The Jungle Book or poems by Lorca. Every detail of her prison life was to go into her novels later. One of the few details she changed was to imagine in her book La Cavale (On the Run) that when she was married Julien too was in prison, an 'improvement' on reality, for he was free at the time. Ever since 1955 she had regularly seen a psychiatrist, Docteur Christiane Gogois-Myquel, who had encouraged her to go on with her writing and even shown a few pages to the publisher Jean-Jacques Pauvert.

She had patiently listened to her, refusing to be put off by reports that Albertine was 'violent, crafty, perverse' and given to play-acting. She hoped she could help her, merely by listening, in her passionate struggle to transform her dreams into reality and to subdue the hypersensitivity of which the girl was apparently deeply ashamed. Since the age of eighteen Albertine had changed greatly, she had been a podgy, short-sighted teenager but now she seemed fragile, the intensity of this extraordinary inner life shone from her huge dark eyes. She had been very sure of herself in some ways for a long time and had even explained to the judge in 1955 how she saw life: as though quoting Edith Piaf, she regretted nothing. If one day she felt remorse, she said, she would make sure the judge heard of it. But she had a moral code of her own – she had never let down a friend.

In June 1959 she had to show how much she loved Julien, for even the long, detailed, loving letters from his wife could not keep him away from the old temptations which he shared with her. Out of boredom more than poverty he began to steal again, was injured in a fight and found himself in prison at Pontoise. He told her it was 'the old virus'; she forgave him, naturally – she was relieved he was still alive – and continued to write lyrically cheerful letters. Occasionally the prison censor would add a bureaucratic note that foreign words were forbidden – they were rarely more than endearments, such as (in English) 'my little rabbit' and on one occasion the censor remarked that there were enough words in the French language – there was no need to borrow from others.

In December 1959 Julien was transferred to the men's prison at Soissons and the two felt closer to each other; they could hear the same church bells and the same blackbird singing in the morning. The letters went on, and some were even secretly passed by other prisoners through visitors. Julien was released first in September 1960 and a month later he collected Albertine from prison. She was surrounded with cases, boxes and manuscripts – the accumulation of two years, most of it spent writing. For nearly an hour they sat on the pavement and looked at each other.

A few months later she was writing to Docteur Gogois-Myquel about all the notes she wanted to make into a book but in April 1961 she was again arrested, although she may well have been innocent this time. Two years more in prison for her, and a lot more reading and writing; another spell inside for him. While she waited for his return in a Provençal cottage she achieved part of her ambition: she succeeded in doing free-lance work for a local newspaper. Nothing happened in her area, she complained, which was true perhaps until the day she stole from the supermarket, intent on stocking up the larder for Julien's return. Tins of crab, a bottle of whisky – the court said she had good taste and back to prison she went, sorry only that her latest crime was so feeble and that she wouldn't be waiting on the prison steps for Julien when he was released. He came to meet her when *she* was released and offered her a rose. When they reached home she was pleased to see so much fruit on the table and he admitted, yes, that he had only allowed himself one kind of theft – on his way home from night work at a local tomato juice factory he 'did' the orchards. . . .

The books are full of these incidents, many of them barely 'edited'; again here is a woman writer who invented nothing, she merely wrote down what had happened to her. Jean-Jacques Pauvert published *L'Astragale* and *La Cavale* in 1965. At twenty-nine she knew and wrote that she had spent a quarter of her life in prison and practically everything she wrote was about being in prison or suddenly and briefly out of it. Not one day of her life could be called 'normal' for even after two books she could hardly believe in her own success or her own happiness. Perhaps the most rewarding quality in her writing is her irrepressible optimism. You catch it at once and you catch all her excess and extravagance and excitement, despite the usual dreary details of prison life. If words had not been her very life, how could she have written *La Cavale*, with its several hundred pages of prison *argot*, repetitive but always lively, full of contrasted people, fellow-prisoners and staff, and how could anyone have read it? The description of Albertine's love story and her wedding from prison takes wing from the book like a flight of birds across a dark estuary. In 1965 *La Cavale* won the Prix des Quatre Jurys in Tunis and became a talking-point in France. The public could not resist the personality of Albertine Sarrazin, they seemed unmoved by her criminal record and perhaps they envied her.

There was a chance that Albertine might have won the happiness for which she seemed to have such a capacity. Surgeons had provided her with a new astragalus and by the time her first two books were published she hardly limped at all. At the same time she wrote her third book, *La Traversière*, which ends with a description of how she found a publisher and signed her first contract. The excitement, the gaiety and the tears: anyone who has ever known what it is to have a first book accepted for publication, unexpectedly so, after a long wait, can relish this. In 1967 she was found to have a tubercular kidney. An operation failed to save her, she went back to hospital, writing cheerful letters, and died. She was barely thirty.

Since her death her poems, her letters and the journal *The Times* have been published and if some of this activity seems over-pious it is understandable. She had loved life so much that those who loved her were tempted to prolong it on her behalf. She had loved life more than fame: 'Ne *chantez pas pour la gloire*', she wrote to the singer Myriam Assimov. '*Il faut bosser pour le plaisir ou l'artiche mais jamais pour la pomme des autres*'; 'Work for your own fun or for the sake of art, never for other people.'

Albertine Sarrazin was intensely feminine, irrepressibly optimistic and rescued from her loveless childhood by her writing. In her novels she seems over-talkative, repetitive, unaware of balance and form and yet somehow achieving it because the tone of her voice soon grew natural, and unliterary, it was so full of the sweet-and-sour of life, although her life was so limited. She was hungry for living, she equated living with writing. 'You see,' she wrote, cheerfully and proudly on the manuscript of one of her poems, 'it's a sonnet!' She was a born writer and one can only conclude that if her approved school had not taught her to obey any orthodox code of ethics it had taught her to enjoy reading and writing. One is left wondering what would have happened if she had had an 'orthodox' existence: but the reality was not such. Her own 'reality' is best found in the journal, immensely serious and less excitable than her other work.

Without the years in prison she might have needed some other overwhelming experience before she could have become a writer. Jean Genet – although comparisons are dangerous here – after all wrote nothing before he was in prison. It was

the intensity of this restricted life which developed her obsessive need to write. There is no moral to this story. 'Prison is
nothing, it's probably our destiny', she wrote to her psychiatrist. If in fact she is remembered as a writer it is ironic to
think that she owed her success to a life of law-breaking. She
could only write about what she knew but she never wrote
about crime in the abstract. She never learnt what guilt was,
for she stole as a child might steal. From time to time she was
a prostitute and from time to time she drank too much. No
moral, except a reminder of the literary potential of immaturity and amorality, known about, talked about as a therapy,
but not often written out in such casebook detail as here.

11

Gazing at a Landscape

The eminent Belgian writer Suzanne Lilar, adventurous in creative writing and criticism, married to a statesman-lawyer, has an equally adventurous daughter, Françoise Lilar, whose real name remains only a starting point in the Bibliothèque Nationale card-index catalogue, which refers the reader at once to Françoise Mallet, now Françoise Mallet-Joris de l'Académie Goncourt. She was born in Antwerp in 1930, and the first thirty years of her life were busy enough. At the age of nine she wrote a novel, at fourteen and fifteen she wrote poems which were published a little later as *Poèmes du dimanche*. At fifteen she accepted her first lover and at seventeen she ran away from home with a playwright. She then married someone else and studied in Philadelphia. When she was eighteen her first son was born, the next year she divorced and studied literature at the Sorbonne, back in Paris. Then in 1951 came her first novel and the year after that her second marriage, followed rapidly by her second divorce. In 1954 a third marriage, to a painter her 'conversion' to the Church of Rome and, by 1960, three more children.

The novel of 1951 was *Le Rempart des Béguines* and so, three years before critics, publicity specialists and readers of all types had become used to the existence of Françoise Sagan, Françoise Mallet, as she was called at the time, became one of the first young women in France to write on themes which at that time English language publishers vaguely called 'contemporary'.

Apart from the youth of its author however the novel has little in common with *Bonjour Tristesse*. The heroine admittedly is young and the story is related with such intensity that the reader is tempted to say that it must be *expérience vécue*. The young Hélène, aged fifteen, is fascinated and dominated by her father's mistress Tamara. Hélène is deeply in love with her until suddenly Tamara lets her down: the woman who had seemed to Hélène the incarnation of freedom and independence from men and from society in general, suddenly accepted her lover as a husband and was delighted – she was only too pleased to find respectability and dwindle into a wife. Hélène's disillusion is total. Tamara, now at the turning-point of her life, shows her latent cruelty and destructive despair, she beats Hélène with a belt and lapses into drunkenness in a lesbian night club. The book has lasted infinitely better than *Bonjour Tristesse* because it has more depth of characterization, description and interpretation. It caused less shock in France when it was first published because the heroine was naïve and loving, not cynical like the Cécile of Sagan's first book. Perhaps Françoise Mallet as an author seemed to be too grown-up, and in any case the publicity machine was not yet well enough organized to give the book the 'full treatment'.

In addition to the women several secondary characters in the novel are all convincingly presented: Max, an artist friend of Tamara's, Hélène's father, very much the Belgian businessman. There is also a grotesquely funny lunch-party when the narrator's grandfather unexpectedly brings his 'companion', the plump, middle-aged, peroxided 'Madame Nina', whose profession is only too obvious; there is much more to the novel than a lesbian relationship. This relationship in itself has none of the hothouse atmosphere created by Violette Leduc in *Thérèse et Isabelle*, it is much more complex, for Tamara we know has been well enough interested in men and is now preoccupied with marriage. As for Hélène, who had grown up without a mother, she has entered the world of sexual emotion but her development is only starting – her feeling for Tamara was a stage on the way, she has still to discover herself.

The maturity of the book lay first of all in its balance, the contrast between the intense emotional experience and the

placid solidity of the décor. The bourgeois home of Monsieur
Noris, and particularly the odd house that gives the book its
title, is all 'real' but does not obtrude on the story, it gives
it colour, relief and a 'frame'. As in the work of Marguerite
Yourcenar, also of partly Belgian origin, the reader can never
forget the Flemish houses, furniture and painting. In those
days of the early Sagan novels, where so much seemed 'superficial' – deceptive though this impression was – Françoise
Mallet immediately seemed to offer more depth, and the impression lasted. *Le Rempart des Béguines* needed a more expressive
title in English – it was feebly called *Into the Labyrinth* – and as
more books followed it looked as though readers who were
not drawn to the 'new novel' – it had been 'new' from about
1948 – could find satisfactory entertainment, and much more
than entertainment, from the work of Françoise Mallet-Joris,
as she later became. A group of stories followed the first novel,
then came another novel set in Belgium, *La Chambre rouge* (The
Red Room), with the same heroine, on bad terms with
Tamara (who is now her stepmother) and suddenly in love
against all odds with a sophisticated Parisian who makes a
condescending visit to the town to see a play. The climax of the
story would guarantee its success with anyone who enjoys
sensationalism: her heroine is left to come to terms with
herself after a night spent with the man who now no longer
wants her. The 'red room' was a lush bordello room, complete
with a heavy theatrical décor of obvious aphrodisiac type.
The novel also contains a description, almost embarrassing in
its fidelity, of a theatrical occasion in a provincial town, a
wonderfully living 'kermesse' and a walk by Hélène and Jean
through the zoological gardens.

One reason why these two novels provide so much more
than entertainment is that they present a study of disillusion
without cynicism, and the reader feels that the author, in
addition to her heroine, is now 'grown up'. At the same time
the author made it clear that the commercial success she had
achieved so quickly was by no means her main concern. At a

commercial level she had found what appeared to be a 'formula', but having found it and used it she regarded it from now on as merely one element built into her technique and her thought. Françoise Mallet-Joris has consistently written what she wanted to write, remaining untouched by the vague complaints of hopeful publishers. She was preoccupied from early in her career with depth, not speed or sensation, and her books became more and more complex. She won fiction prizes in two successive years, the Prix des Libraires in 1957 for *Les Mensonges* (House of Lies) and the Fémina for *Café Céleste* in 1958. By now the adjective 'Balzacian' had been applied to her by a French critic and if the author found this surprising it is not difficult to see how the epithet was justified. It is comparatively easy to write descriptions of the external world and a generation ago every schoolchild was more or less made to write out a 'sunset' or an 'autumn scene' as a literary exercise. During the nineteenth and early twentieth centuries the romantic novelist, the realistic novelist, writers of all schools had written their descriptive pages as though destined for inclusion in literary anthologies. After George Sand women writers in particular have embarked regularly on novels which failed because there was too much description, too little action, and dialogue that was always inadequate and usually unconvincing. The great 'set pieces' of description in France have nearly always been written by men – Hugo, Balzac, Flaubert, Zola, Cendrars, Giono – as though sheer muscle and stamina were needed to produce a kind of literary architecture, a construction that convinces by its precision and solidity. The Belgian writers of the late nineteenth century were known to overload their work with descriptions. Colette is famous for her descriptions, especially of nature, yet when analysed they are always short, they are evocations, descriptive effects achieved by a detail here and there, for she approached landscapes and houses as she approached people, indirectly. Marguerite Yourcenar's descriptions are never long, they appear to be more objective and are the product of long and careful selection

while the colours of her palette tend to be limited – vivid and
dark; details are few and never lyrical.

Françoise Mallet-Joris is not afraid of approaching her
subject head on. Her descriptions are never static or dead
because people are usually close and there is always movement.
She has claimed that she writes slowly and with difficulty but
her descriptions at least seem to show how much she enjoys
looking at buildings, crowds, people. 'These balconies', she
wrote, while describing the extraordinary building where
Tamara lived, 'were linked between the floors by a female
colonnade, whose head supported the balcony above while the
legs went round the window in a half-circle. The effect was a
truly monstrous entanglement, a kind of marine temple worn
by the waves. . . .' The artist had even added shells here and
there in mosaic. 'In order to complete the maritime illusion a
smell of mud and fish blew into the street from time to time,
for the Rempart des Béguines was very close to the little
fishing port.' The kermesse in *The Red Room*, the chain store in
Café Céleste, these descriptions are masterly and somehow do
not betray the amount of work behind them. None of them
are too long and as the author continued to write they became
even more carefully integrated with the development of the
story so that the reader was taken along without saying, half-
aloud, 'I'm going to skip this description and see what the
people are saying or doing. . . .' It is a waste of time trying to
read this author too fast and anyone attempting this method
will have to turn back in the end and read everything he has
left out.

Her early novels were obviously written by a woman but if
the later ones had been signed with an androgynous pseudonym it might have been possible to accept them as the work
of a man. They are part of the 'liberation' of women because
they are the unfussy proof of a woman's achievement. Too
many women complain about their status and too few produce
work which would automatically improve it. Françoise Mallet-
Joris has shown more concentration and evolution in her work

than any other author who began with a popular success while still very young. Having mastered the art of description for instance she soon stopped practising it, as though the references to Balzac had embarrassed her. Most of all she insisted quietly on being herself and after the success of *Les Mensonges* in 1956 who could have expected *Les Personnages* (The Favourite), a historical novel, written in a completely different style, about a mistress of Louis XIII, who left him to enter the Church? The straightforward yet dramatic treatment earned praise for the author from leading writers in the genre such as Mary Renault.

The inescapable key-figure in all her work, especially the early books, is the young heroine, who is always fiercely individual. She has a strong sense of the ideal, and how much more complexity and depth than those silhouette figures who people the novels of Sagan. One French critic has described this heroine as 'a slim, wild adolescent, tense and proud, absolute, daring, impassioned, acid'. This is certainly true of Hélène in the two early novels, Alberte in *House of Lies*. And who could forget that short story *Cordélia*, about the girl who escaped from a fair and refused to show gratitude to the people who thought they had been kind to her? She had been a beggar, but when asked to play the part of a beggar in a kermesse, she revolted. As Françoise Mallet-Joris became more mature, and tired of the attempts by journalists to make her explain her work and her relationship to her characters – *Letter to Myself* is a salutary warning to people who ask questions about books they have not read – this heroine has appeared as a more complex figure, sometimes as a caricature even, but she has never faded away.

Another link between the novels, often in fact personified partly in this heroine, is the hatred of dishonesty. The author never attempts to provide an easy answer. Mere revolt against authority or convention for instance will not necessarily help anyone find their true identity, every individual has to make the journey in solitude, and it is no good expecting that political theories or belief in God will necessarily help. The 'programmes' put forward on all sides are seen in the end to be totally naïve, but this feminine voice never shouts out the conclusions, it keeps calm and lets them reach the listener slowly.

Each book so far has revealed Françoise Mallet-Joris as an author serious about her craft and at the same time endowed with a splendid, kind-hearted sense of humour. The only disconcerting thing about her appears to be her range. She admires Virginia Woolf because each book was a new departure. Her work could never be described as experimental in the sense that it was concerned, like that of Nathalie Sarraute, with exploring and recording an aspect of the human mind hardly examined so far. Her experimentation was at a different level and she was not merely concerned with the individual in his or her lonely state, foiled or baffled by a basic failure to communicate.

She was ready to communicate about herself, her own life, personality and family in *Letter to Myself* and *The Paper House*, but of course the family scenes read very much like fiction. The more memorable ones are all funny: we see the author trying not very effectively to deal with the complicated love-life of a Spanish maid or an *au pair* girl who played the flute very well as the piles of unwashed dishes grew higher and higher around her. Other people's houses had curtains; one day, the family thought, they might be lucky enough to have curtains too – if mother were not so busy, or so occupied with things that mattered more, such as long talks with her children about Life, Love, God, all the things one would like to talk over with one's family, if they will ever give one the chance. Françoise Mallet-Joris has in fact written very well about children. Women writers have always been expected to do so, and many have achieved it delightfully – Christine de Rivoyre for example – but just as a woman is not necessarily a good mother a woman writer is not necessarily able to handle her child-characters with understanding. Mallet-Joris learnt to do this very well in *The Paper House*, with mother at the centre, human, humorous and hard-working. The book has more to say about bringing up a family than the many well-meaning, informative, technical books on the subject. It is about the Mallet-Joris family but also about every family, while unlike most 'wholesome' books it is funny in a highly individual way and surprisingly enough just as entertaining as stories of adultery or assassination.

The author has been as productive as Françoise Sagan, but so far Sagan has made only one departure – *Scars on the Soul* – from a fairly predictable straight line. Françoise Mallet-Joris has never lost her preoccupation with honesty but her changes in technique are perhaps bewildering to everyone except her. By the early 1970s this technique shows a kind of deliberate fragmentation possibly influenced – although the author would surely deny it – by the developments in fiction-writing generally since the end of the Second World War.

In 1973 came *Le Jeu du Souterrain* (The Underground Game), a complex book reminiscent in part of an early *nouvelle*, *Le Souterrain*, and seemingly a puzzle with too many pieces and yet, at the end, too many gaps. But if one reads it slowly, the only way to read Françoise Mallet-Joris, apart from the more obviously autobiographical books, it unexpectedly reveals itself as her richest and most satisfactory book to date. The hero, Robert, the writer who is prevented from writing – or thinks he is – through trying to help solve the problems of others, is exceptionally well portrayed, proving as the earlier books had done that the author has a rare advantage over so many other women writers – she is more than capable of presenting men who cannot be labelled 'typical male character drawn by lady novelist', i.e. her men are not cardboard figures, not mere symbols who exist so that the well-drawn women characters can find someone to talk to. Their faces, voices, clothes, ideas become clear to the reader, but never in a long list, details are added imperceptibly and never surprise us for we are convinced we already know them.

As for Robert in *The Underground Game*, the author is concerned
basically with the presentation of a moral portrait; although
towards the end of the book she mentions 'his beautiful eyes,
feminine and over-gentle, their lashes too long for this virile
face', it is more amusing and relevant to note the absent-
minded gesture which we could have expected of him: he
meant to send back the dried-up smoked salmon but absent-
mindedly ordered another bottle of wine instead. Robert is
worth thinking about because it is he who keeps this complicated book together. A novelist who cannot write his novel,
and hovers between his unsatisfied wife, his mistress, and his
interest in a man in an obscure village who becomes obsessed
by his endless and no doubt pointless excavations in search of
buried treasure – are these the symbols of inadequacy, alienation, sexual failure? The author would probably be the last to
know and the reader, if puzzled, must adapt the 'symbolism'
to his own needs. There is so much else to enjoy – a complete
send-up of the literary and journalistic world achieved by
apparently idle statements such as 'A poet should never read
Le Monde', and the complex portraits, the unforgettable, sad-
dening fée Mélusine, an eccentric, penniless, ageing spinster-
researcher who sleeps in the corner of a vegetarian restaurant
kitchen, the only old lady who never feeds the sparrows.
There is the equally unforgettable Anselme, the 'convert' who
tries to convert everyone else and embarrasses the priest by his
only too relevant quotations from the Bible. The children hold
sophisticated conversations and Manuel is 'the only little boy –
or adolescent – in France whom one can still seriously ask if
Corneille portrays people as they should be, and Racine, as
they are'.

The novel gives the feeling of a kind of moral impressionism
– all these people seem to behave so oddly (except to themselves) and in an old-fashioned way the reader keeps on
looking for a pattern, a meaning. The 'meaning', to the author,
is surely her refusal to insist on meaning. She keeps elements
of suspense running through this book – will this marriage

last, will that love affair go wrong? Will Monseiur Sorel ever find the treasure? But as far as conclusive narrative goes the reader is only allowed to see that the Robert–Catherine ménage will survive. As a Catholic the author had to find some resolution, some hint of moral satisfaction for the reader, but in her quiet way Françoise Mallet-Joris is no longer interested in 'obviously satisfying' aspects of fiction, even if she is not 'obviously' an experimental novelist.

It is impossible, in reading the early Mallet-Joris novels, to escape the architecture and painting which must have formed the décor to part of her youth. In these books she achieved a representational painting of her own, she described the buildings, or scenes such as the kermesse which is a twentieth-century version of a traditional event. 'Representational' here is far from a derogatory term, for obviously good painting in this style does not merely represent – it uses the reproduction of an image, *vraisemblable* in varying degrees, for its own artistic purpose. But an artist's style evolves, and so does that of Françoise Mallet-Joris. Continental writers, more so than those of the Anglo-Saxon countries, tend to be closely aware of what is happening in painting and some of them have unconsciously used parallel techniques – as far as this is possible – in writing. The theorists of the *nouvelle vague* are consciously aware of this but Françoise Mallet-Joris probably not, however closely she had looked at painting. By the time she wrote *Le Jeu du Souterrain* it is obvious what has happened – she 'paints big', as many painters have done since the 1950s, and she no longer describes, she alludes and suggests. Bigness here means a vast number of people, a group of themes which seem unrelated, almost defying any effort to bring them together. What does it mean? asks the exhibition visitor in front of a painting that does not follow the obvious rules of verisimilitude. Why, asks the reader of *Le Jeu du Souterrain*, does she write like this? What is she saying? All that is needed is acceptance. The book is what it is. Thirty pages before the end comes the subtitle: 'The word "end" '. 'It isn't that people object to happy endings. It's rather that they don't want things to end.'

She goes on: 'And if you take a realistic standpoint, then they're not wrong. Things rarely finish. Unclouded happiness and irreparable unhappiness are rare. . . .' And a little later the author writes of painting, in a highly relevant way: 'You gaze at a landscape, you paint it, and on the canvas of the greatest master, the enigma remains in its entirety, the question is asked. Only bad painters seem to find a solution.' Françoise Mallet-Joris asks many questions and supplies few answers. Eventually she ends her book neatly enough, happily enough to satisfy the most conventionally demanding reader. Robert forgets his mistress because he has 'found' his wife again.

This is no 'solution' to all the problems posed in the book but the reader can use this ending as he wants. The security of married love? Is this a Christian, Catholic attempt at a 'solution'? Will the renewed happiness of the couple spread over the social scene like rings on the water? Perhaps, but there is a limit to the water, an edge to the pool.

There is no limit, however, to the talents of this author. She aims high, she accepts self-imposed challenge and she has a remarkable control over a highly disparate mass of material; her material now means not a young heroine but a collection of men, women and children, never people in isolation but inevitably people of all kinds in the unsolved, unsolvable entanglement of contemporary life. Mallet-Joris is a deeply responsible person and succeeds in passing on a kind of message; her early technique of the head-on description has given way to the approach that is most effective because it is indirect and full of humour. She has developed a range of techniques far wider than that possessed by most writers in the French language today, women or men, but she never displays them with bravura. Such behaviour would strike her as undignified. Her ideal is to be natural and that is why she is unconcerned with writing whatever her public might expect of her. She will not retrace her steps and there will not be another 'red room'. She finds no necessity to explain herself outside her books. She avoids sensationalism and consciously writes in a low key; if at any point she seems in danger of becoming 'earnest' she is suddenly so funny and always so truthful that all is forgiven.

Late in 1975, when the whole existence of the Prix Goncourt and the voting system were violently attacked in Paris, Françoise Mallet-Joris was selected as the possible victim of a fire-bomb attack. Fortunately she escaped. Was she chosen because she was considered to be 'square' now, a representative of the establishment, or because an attack on a woman was still thought to be more newsworthy? In any case, she cannot escape the young heroine and by early 1976 she was reported to be working on a television adaptation of that girl who was 'born' in 1900, the girl who pursued her creator to the end of her life: Claudine. She may even have been among the ancestors of Hélène, Alberte and the other Mallet-Joris heroines.

12

Opération Jeunesse

In June 1939 the roads out of Paris were crammed for there
seemed little hope now of avoiding a war. Most people were
travelling south, obviously, and one car going in the opposite
direction met little competition. The car contained a Monsieur
and Madame Quoirez. Madame had insisted on this journey
because after settling her children well to the south, in their
grandmother's house, she had to go back to collect her hats.
She did not see how she could get through a war without them.
That at least is what her daughter said more than thirty years
later and if she invented the story it is in keeping all the same.
The family came from Cajarc, in the Lot. The daughter was
four at the time and later went to a convent in Lyon. The
family did not escape the Germans entirely, the children
remembered later how they had been made to stand against the
wall because they were suspected of harbouring resistance
workers. They sheltered Jews from time to time in their apartment but since their mother hated cellars they never went
down to them during air raids. On one occasion only she
thought it might be better for the children to go – but that
was the day she had been to the hairdresser's.

Her daughter Françoise remembers the day when Germany
invaded Russia, for it happened to be her birthday. Otherwise
she recalls vitamin biscuits, little work at the convent and a
lucky escape from a German bomber after swimming in a
countryside pool. Her mother was more concerned that her
other daughter should put her clothes on before running away.
After the liberation Françoise suddenly found that war and its
aftermath were not straightforward, not all black and white;
this was when her mother accused the French of behaving like

Monique Wittig

Minou Drouet   Françoise Mallet-Joris

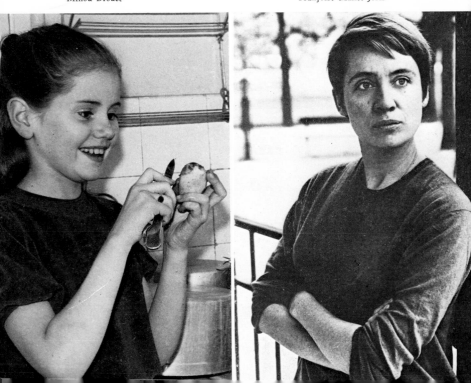

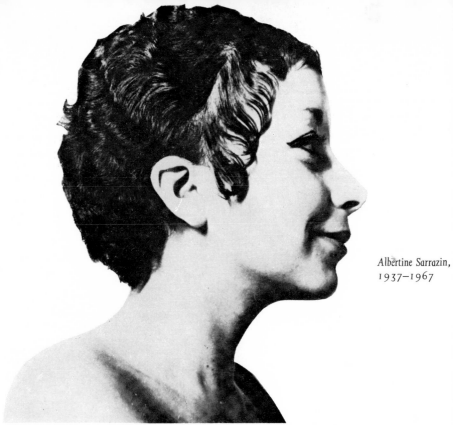

Albertine Sarrazin,
1937–1967

Albertine's drawing of
the prison at Doullance

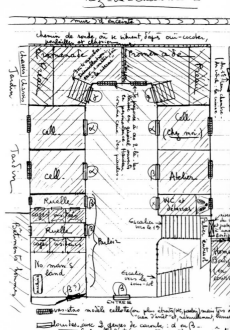

the Germans, because they had shaved the head of a woman collaborator. She reported that this was 'the first time that Goodness appeared to me much more complicated than I had thought'.

Back in Paris she went to a school across the road from her home, and so hated wearing socks that she would take them off in the hall before entering the school. She refused to go to any lessons that bored her and after 'hanging' a bust of Molière on the back of a door (the Molière lesson had been boring) she was expelled. Cleverly however she managed to secrete the vital letter before her parents saw it, so they did not know. She got up regularly at eight o'clock and for three months pretended to go to school. During the First World War Raymond Radiguet had set off to his lycée every day and spent the time reading in his father's boat on the Marne. Françoise Quoirez read on the quais, in the buses, everything, everywhere. She distinctly remembers having read Maurice Sachs's splendid memoirs Le Sabbat when she was a small girl. She read Gide, Cocteau, Prévert, Sartre and Camus, and after reading Anouilh's plays she stopped writing the historical dramas which she would read aloud to her mother, who always fell asleep. She eventually achieved her Baccalauréat, although when it came to the English oral she could not utter a word and was reduced to acting Macbeth with such terrifying effect that the examiner gave her a good mark (her story). She wasted a year or so at the overcrowded Sorbonne, spent her time talking to friends and to people she met casually anywhere. She wrote poems, realized they were no good and tore them up. Between Paris cafés and their country house in the Lot she wrote a novel, and rewrote it five or six times. A few years earlier she had begun one and forgotten all about it: but it began with a car accident.

The new one also contained a car accident, but not at the beginning. The whole book was a beginning, for it was the invention of Françoise Sagan, named after the princess who figured in Proust's great novel. She had been eighteen when

she wrote the book and sent it to two publishers simul-
taneously. The skilful René Julliard telephoned at once to say
he would publish it. The other publisher telephoned later in
the day, too late. In John Murray's office in London Mrs Osyth
Leeston picked a copy at random out of a batch of several
novels and read it until three in the morning. Knowing
nothing about the author or how she was to be received in
France she told her directors that they must publish the book.
It won the Prix des Critiques, literally went round the world
and in the English-speaking area at least it kept its French
title. It could only have come from France.

With the launching of *Bonjour Tristesse* the mechanism of the
launch became almost as important as the author and the
book. Not since Bernard Grasset had published Radiguet's *Le
Diable de corps* (Devil in the Flesh) in 1923 had publicity about
an author reached so many people. It was impossible to avoid
the book, and the era of the young author, which had indeed
lapsed since Radiguet's early death, began again now in
earnest, all the more so because the author was a young girl.
The publicity machine had had more experience in dealing
with the rags-to-riches type of story than any other and some
readers abroad in particular could not realize this story was
about moderate riches to more riches, and of a different kind.
The story that this pretty girl with the slightly masculine head
and hair-style had stayed at the Savoy without bringing even a
toothbrush with her was somehow less memorable than the
legend that she had once kept pigs on her father's farm. No
wonder Sagan was later known as the 'Bardot of literature'; the
publicity machine that was now geared for action had been
modelled on the most successful one known so far, the one
that dealt with the dream-machine, Hollywood.

Cocteau said that *Le Diable au corps* was a classic, the typist
liked it, so did he. It is true that typists and non-typists have
enjoyed *Bonjour Tristesse*, but re-reading it twenty years after its
first appearance is a strange experience, for neither story nor
characters seem even faintly credible to a middle-aged reader

who has of course by now read all the other Sagan novels. But give it to intelligent older teenagers and they respond at once: fresh, clear, fast-moving, they find, even if the car-accident suicide is contrived, something of a cliché. It could only have been written by someone whose eyes were wide open, someone who recorded what parents did without any surprise or comment, someone who seemed born adult and probably pessimistic, for there seems no hope that these imagined characters would ever be truly adult themselves.

Since the end of the war nearly ten years earlier some new writers had appeared and some members of the older generation were still writing. Women of all ages had been in the news. Colette had written *Gigi* in 1944 when she was in her seventies but it was not published in Paris until the following year, after the Russian-born Elsa Triolet had been the first woman to win the Prix Goncourt (a generation after Judith Gautier had been elected to the Académie Goncourt) with her stories *Le Premier Accroc coûte deux cent francs* (The first scratch costs 200 francs), an absorbing record of the resistance atmosphere, nearer to journalism than literature, perhaps. During and just after the war many young men had obviously been too occupied to become writers. The leading intellectuals – Sartre, Camus, Simone de Beauvoir – had reached early middle age and Saint-Germain des Prés was the centre of the cult they attracted. Cocteau went on writing and made films, Boris Vian was fashionable, so were Anouilh, Beckett, Ionesco, and soon Genet. Giraudoux had died during the Occupation. Several writers were in exile, several in disgrace. A new generation had grown up and as happened in the 1920s one cross-section of them at least were not going to take life too seriously – or so they thought. Existentialism and the new novel were too abstract for them, poverty and privation were boringly out of date and they were intent on enjoying themselves. Françoise Sagan explained years later how she reacted, and apart from her reaction as a writer she wasn't speaking for herself alone.

'But you have to realize that it was difficult for me in 1954 (my hour of fame) to choose between the two roles offered to me: the scandalous writer or the middle-class girl. For actually I was neither one nor the other. It would have been easier for me to be a scandalous young girl or a middle-class writer.' She was not ready to choose between two alternatives which were equally false. 'My only solution, and I congratulate myself heartily on it, was to do what I wanted to do: have a good time, *faire la fête.*' Her good time was particularly good, interrupted only by novels and plays. 'And that is the end of my story; after all, what can I do about it?' She had always been fascinated by the possibility of living fast and hard, drinking, and feeling dazed. She found that this absurd gratuitous way of life provided her with the means to escape 'our petty, sordid and cruel age'. François Mauriac had denounced her first book as 'cruel'; but she only described what she saw.

Since the fairy-story success of the first book there have been some eight more novels and various plays. There has also been non-stop controversy. Sagan had created a recurring heroine whose readers assumed to be herself and/or by extension, themselves: the spoilt, idle, bored middle-class girl who seemed always to find men, sex and money but never love or happiness. At least one London editor has complained, spitting with rage, that Sagan has been included in the *Oxford Book of French Prose* (even in a non-representative passage). There has been a theory that Sagan's novels are only read by women, all types of women from the colonel's lady to Judy O'Grady, but this is not true of France; men apparently read her for the vicarious thrill of moving among people who all have large cars, no worries about work and all the time in the world to make love and talk about love and life. The characters of Racine were not very different in their way after all, and it was Racine who provided the title for *Dans un mois, dans un an* (Those without Shadows), just as Paul Eluard wrote the phrase 'Bonjour tristesse' in his poem *La Vie immédiate.*

The disconcerting thing is that Sagan is a much more serious writer than anyone believed at the beginning, more serious than she knew herself. If her effects were casual, her methods were not. She has always known how to present her characters in a clear-cut situation within a few lines, hardly anyone or anything is described in more than one sentence and no word is wasted. Everyone has their favourites among her work – which she finds disconcerting – and it might have been wiser not to have written or published *The Heart Keeper* at all. Josée de Saint-Léger – the name she had used for her heroine in the forgotten first attempt at a novel, and unconsciously used again in two or three later ones, was *sympathique* until she became involved with the American Alain who is unfortunately never so real as his horrible mother. And one wonders how anyone could have tolerated him for as much as a week.

How right was the title of the first book since the *tristesse* has intensified and is unlikely ever to go away. Sometimes it is confused with *ennui*, as though boredom were more chic than sadness, especially when accompanied by alcohol. Sagan's books have the tempo of the times, and although the world oil crisis has now made them a little out of date car-wise they can still be read on the journey from London to Paris. They demand rapid reading but no skipping. Speed is one of the few things which helps Sagan characters to forget their *ennui*, for brief periods, and they particularly enjoy driving on their own.

Speed almost killed Sagan herself in 1957 as everyone knows, for no newspaper could resist the picture of that Aston Martin lying the wrong way up. Her parents had enjoyed their Bugattis in the 1930s but were soon outdone by their daughter who at one point owned five cars, while her heroine Josée seems to have preferred her car to her men. Sagan herself was so successful that for a time she drove into unreality: the bank no longer gave her a cheque book, paid all her bills and her staff directly. Her paperback sales are massive, but the tax demands are even more so, while after two marriages her family now consists mainly of herself and her son.

Nobody ever produced a fiercer condemnation of the consumer society nor one that was more indirect, although she may not have realized at first what she was doing. Her young people possessed so much and needed so little that they soon became bored by minor diversions such as rapid love-making in the bathroom during a party; they were reduced to working, albeit they worked in decorative but useless concerns not unlike the advertising agency in Beaucoir's *Les Belles Images*; the perpetual ballet between lover/mistress, husband/wife, older or younger couples became dangerously repetitive. *La fête* was a bore. The results of Sagan's unconscious attack were more telling than the fiercely destructive frontal attack usually more popular among men writers.

Although her novels seem as casual as the characters within them they were usually written with extreme care and absence of self or self-consciousness. Yet no one was more interviewed, criticized and written about than the author, nobody perhaps more misunderstood. She was deliberately kept behind a whisky-sodden smokescreen and for a long time hardly complained. Young writers have always been news but before the Second World War there had not been many of them. Rimbaud and Radiguet are the obvious examples in France – and they did not include many women. The public preferred their authors serious and struggling; an author who seemed neither, as Cocteau had been, was suspect, and even in the early 1970s French critics were referring to Sagan in a superior way as the most unread author of the year. It wasn't true, but she was no longer a young author, and of that she was perfectly aware. She wrote that funny and heart-breaking play *Un Piano dans l'herbe* (A Piano on the Grass) on the theme that youth's a stuff will not endure, and the admired young poet had become a successful tycoon. One is young or not, and as Henri says in the play, the *opération jeunesse* is a failure.

Of *Des Bleus à l'Ame* (Scars on the Soul) it was fashionable to say in France in 1972 that the best-seller writer had become an author. Sagan maintained she wrote a 'different' book because a riding accident prevented her from typing. Whatever the reason she spoke as herself, even relished her advanced age of thirty-seven, looked forward to the year 2010 when along with Marguerite Duras and Françoise Mallet-Joris she would award a literary prize and fly home by private helicopter. She runs through all her faults and admits that in the end she will write 'solid, interminable novels' and even descend to baroque and literary descriptions, but it seems unlikely. This gloriously funny, ironic book reveals a Sagan that few casual readers could have suspected. It can only be appreciated if one has read all her earlier novels and remembers that cheerfully amoral brother and sister Sébastien and Eléonore from *Château en Suède* (Castle in Sweden). She parodies herself with enthusiasm and in between these ridiculous 'Saganesque' incidents sums up the French social scene as nobody else has done, discusses solitude, alienation, wrongheaded notions about helping the poor, and mentions the women's movement or the President of France *en passant*, with tentative, ironic, contradictory allusions as though thinking aloud and perpetually teasing the reader. The pill is a good thing, so is equal pay for equal work, but sleeping *à deux* can give you a stiff leg.

The novels had always been sprinkled with occasional terse quotable remarks which seem inherited from the traditions of La Rochefoucauld and now there is no moralist more severe than Sagan: the French are 'well fed and badly behaved', 'conformism and snobbery slumber deep down in the beds with the same arrogant tranquillity. Nobody, ever, behaves "well" in bed, unless they are loving and loved – two conditions rarely attained.'

It could easily be proved that there is a masculine streak in Sagan, in her independence, her reticence, her cool control, but surely only a woman would have written *Scars on the Soul*, for the author only pretends to be confident, and consistently flirts with the reader throughout the book, talks about wearing 'a moral veil' and gives no more than half of herself away. It is the perfect antidote to the melodramatic masochism of

Violette Leduc and one is even forced to regret that the cheerful irresponsibility is surely not so total as the author might like to think. But whatever she writes in the future – and *Un Profil perdu* (Lost Profile) is a sad, not very good book – she will remain the writer who had the courage to enjoy herself and the courage to admit that *la fête* cannot last for ever. Like many people with a fine sense of humour she may well be deeply pessimistic. But her appointment as the leader of *opération jeunesse* was a good one, although, by its very nature, this cannot last either.

❧ 13 ❧

The Search for Love

The English writer known as W. N. P. Barbellion wrote one remembered book and its title hardly promises entertaining reading: *The Journal of a Disappointed Man*. Yet it is a moving, compulsive book, disappointment is no longer destructive when written out. Once she had published *La Bâtarde* in 1964 at the age of fifty-seven Violette Leduc was no longer disappointed, but no one had ever felt sorry for herself with such obsessive energy and she had had no time to lose the habit. This is unkind, no doubt unfair, for her life was hard for a long time and her capacity for suffering was great. She was the illegitimate daughter of a young woman who lived in a northern French village and fortunately had a mother who helped her to bring up the child. Violette's mother went to work in Paris and fairly soon made a satisfactory marriage. There was enough money to send Violette to boarding school (and even to buy her a Pleyel piano) but nothing was ever to destroy her desperate feelings of insecurity and the awareness that she could not grow up, could not be happy: her mother dominated her, the two women had a particularly intense relationship, so intense in love and possibly hate that Simone de Beauvoir said that any one of her books could be called *L'Asphyxie*, the title of her first book to be kept in print, the story of a love-starved schoolgirl.

As it was Leduc found another kind of 'mother', in Simone de Beauvoir, who seemed to need a 'daughter'. Sartre had no son but he had Jean Genet and other writers whom he encouraged, supported, defended, explained. The two intellectual leaders helped many people but without Simone de Beauvoir the illegitimate peasant girl would surely never have become the writer of at least one international best-seller and several other novels. First, however, came *Les Boutons dorés* (The Golden Buttons) which Beauvoir read in manuscript and immediately recommended for publication. Jean Cocteau and others of like reputation agreed that here was a new writer, someone to be taken seriously. So far she had hardly dared to take herself seriously, except as an object of self-pity, but despite the coolness of the critics about the book the fact of publication and the support of Beauvoir made her aware that a new life had begun in middle age. She wrote eight novels in all and three volumes of autobiography. Both aspects of her work use the same material and sometimes very little in the way of fiction has been added to fact – or fact as she remembered it. On the other hand she describes her own life in three volumes as though it were fiction, and since it was in fact stranger it is only the presence of real people, such as Beauvoir herself, or Camus, or Genet or Maurice Sachs in the autobiographies that convinces us we are reading about incidents that really happened.

It is only fair to add that *La Bâtarde*, the first, best and most successful of the three volumes, was published in France under that convenient classification *récit*, which is interpreted as fiction and used for that type of work which could not honestly be called a 'novel'. As a result the book was eligible for the major literary prizes, and this adroit editorial move was almost successful: it *almost* won the Prix Goncourt for 1964. In Britain the book was published with its French title – there is no obvious feminine version of the noun 'bastard' in its original sense – but fared much better because the publisher's salesmen could not have faced the uphill work of selling it as translated 'fiction'.

The 'fiction' really happened too, and at least one book has been a centre of controversy for a time because it was unofficially censored. The Anglo-Saxon world believed for years that anything could be published in France and that only in their protestant, puritan, hypocritical society could any literary masterpiece be banned because it was 'indecent', obscene, pornographic, liable to corrupt. There is still no clear definition in law about what these terms actually mean. The fate of Leduc's *Thérèse et Isabelle* indicates how much change there has been in social attitudes to literature.

Violette Leduc wrote an early novel which she called *Ravages*, and took the manuscript to Simone de Beauvoir. The book as it appeared in France and other countries was different from the book she originally wrote, and shorter. In the French paperback edition however it still has 371 pages. The heroine Thérèse picks up a man in a cinema, sees him from time to time, even introduces him to the girl friend with whom she has had an intense love affair, intermittent now. She marries the man, Marc, becomes insanely jealous, they part, she tries to kill herself, she finds she is pregnant, she nearly dies at the hands of two abortionists but eventually survives in hospital. She is back with her mother who had always warned her against men.

Men in fact would tend to find the book as exhausting as its heroine. Perhaps they feel a collective discomfort that a woman could be so unhappy, because she had no father, because she was ugly, felt unloved and unconsciously came to relish the fact because there seemed no escape. The indecision of Thérèse can only fascinate women and infuriate men: did she want the man Marc or not, why did she pick him up? 'I chose him, I wanted him. I feel revulsion but I can't let go. I'm not a coquette. I'm timid and I've committed myself too far. I'm not honest and I'm not dishonest. I hate sex and I don't hate it. I'm an indecisive enemy.' There is not a shred of humour anywhere and the book is only saved by its style and its vivid, unexpected comparisons. Who could forget the description of the wedding night spent in a hotel room which smelt of 'wet dog', or fail to react to those touches of poetry, the unexpected images with a lyrical quality reminiscent of paintings by Chagall: 'I love Marc in a flowering chestnut tree, I hope in a ship with roots'.

Ever since the end of the Second World War women novelists in many countries have written abortion scenes and in France they will no doubt go on doing so until the present law is changed. In 1975 it is still easy only for the rich to buy legal abortion and the result has been far too many novels about the subject and about the unmarried mother and her problems. If they have become tedious from the literary point of view their social importance is not tedious in any way and they will go on, must go on until they are no longer necessary. The scenes described by Leduc are particularly harrowing and they express the immaturity that causes so much unhappiness and prevents people, not only women, from seeing the causes of their misery. 'I want to go back to what I was before', Thérèse tells the second abortionist. And when eventually she leaves the clinic with her mother the last lines of the book show that one, not two umbilical cords have been cut:

' "Your little waist. You've got your little waist back", said [my mother].
'For the first time her words found no echo within me. I was alone. Alone at last.'

This immaturity is the key to Leduc's personality and her work. Obviously she herself grew out of it by writing, but it never left her books and the reader must pay the price, he (or more usually she) has to wade through the tears, wondering if the river is even wider than the sea. One interesting aspect of *Ravages* is the occasional appearance of a row of dots which might seem to indicate the passing of time, but in fact these dots indicate an invisible presence, a menace not only to literature in France but life in general: censorship. In her introduction to *La Bâtarde* Simone de Beauvoir reports that the publishers of *Ravages*, Gallimard, were *effarouchés*, frightened by the descriptions of the heroine's love affair with Isabelle. So they were cut, although in part they were restored in *La Bâtarde*. Beauvoir was shocked that in spite of the author's unsentimental language Gallimard could not stomach the details of this lesbian love affair. Originally a long description of it was to have appeared at the beginning of the novel and in the third volume of her autobiography, *La Chasse à l'amour* (The Search for Love), Leduc gives a histrionic display of what this excision meant to her. Simone de Beauvoir had even offered the book to other publishers, but she failed to influence them.

'They have rejected the beginning of *Ravages*', wrote Leduc. 'It's murder. They didn't want the sincerity of Thérèse and Isabelle. They're afraid of the censor. Where does the censor hang out? What are its quirks? I can't place it. The censor? it's the insensitivity of Paris. . . . The censor has knocked down my house with the tip of its finger. If I could throw myself at its feet, I would. I'd explain myself. I'd tell it that the beginning of *Ravages* was not dirty. It is true. It will only soil the person who wants to be soiled. It's love, it's discovery. Thérèse and Isabelle are quite new. They love each other in a school for three days and three nights. They don't see evil. Could the censor see it where it doesn't exist? Thérèse and Isabelle are too authentic to be vicious. There are no vices. There are ill people who need to be cured. Sex is their blinding sun. They caress each other. It's their religion. Their hell is time. Their time is limited. They are not damned. They are privileged. They exchange what they have found. They find the world between their legs. I was describing the fire, the *élans*, the grandiose rashness of Isabelle; the exalting obedience of Thérèse. . . . My ink: plasma; my pen: an umbilical cord. My typescript: a new-born child. The censor has smashed it all up. . . . The publisher is frightened of the censor. . . .' And there is much more and the publisher deserved every word of it even if the dance of the naked psyche had become a recurrent event in France and the audience was wilting.

Eventually part of the missing text was included in *La Bâtarde* and later still *Thérèse et Isabelle* was published in France, first in a limited edition and finally it was placed on open sale. Nobody could have fought harder against censorship all her life than Simone de Beauvoir and although *La Chasse à l'amour* was not published until after Violette Leduc's sudden death in 1971 her attack on the censor did not come too late, as long as literary censorship exists her words will be valid. Did *Thérèse et Isabelle* frighten the publishers because it was *about* women or because it was *by* a woman? It seems absurd that a well-written account of lesbian love should cause alarm while commercial pornographers can write and publish more or less what they wish. Again in the preface to *La Bâtarde* Beauvoir wrote that 'the restrained audacity of Violette Leduc is one of her most striking qualities, but no doubt it has gone against her: she scandalizes the puritans and the sensation-hunters are not satisfied'. In the past women do not seem to have been successful writers of pornography mainly because they are not usually consumers: in an old-fashioned way they seem to prefer love to aphrodisiacs. Only a woman could have written *Thérèse et Isabelle* and not simply because only a woman could have lived through this experience. It would have been difficult for a man to keep the balance in the description between the physical and the emotional. It is this concealed balance, plus the author's own particular type of poetry, that makes *Thérèse et Isabelle* a work of literary value. It has been said that the author was more aware of its commercial value than she would admit, and also that the publishers were not afraid only of censorship. Did they question the literary value of the piece, did they think the emotional intensity was repetitive and overwhelming? It is possible that love between two women has never been so intensely expressed and if love does not consist entirely of love-play this is something the two women had no time to discover. There are many limitations to Violette Leduc: she was hardly ever able to portray the still depths of emotion because she automatically destroyed them, she inevitably turned any smooth surface into a maelstrom of hysteria. Her heroines never have time to settle down and one wonders if they would ever want to. It is all a long way from the Ladies of Llangollen.

In any case it was a better idea to keep Thérèse and Isabelle away from the two other couples in *Ravages*, Thérèse and Cécile, Thérèse and Marc, for the reader would have been too exhausted to absorb the rest of the book. As it is much of the material appears again in *La Bâtarde* and it is easy to see why Beauvoir understood Leduc: they both had this habit of repeating in their memoirs the incidents they had already written up as fiction. There is nothing wrong with doing this but it is a method which appeals more to the student of literature than to the average reader. Of all Leduc's books *La Bâtarde* will always be the most moving because it describes in detail her childhood and adolescence, the roots of her personality, the desperate need for security through love and money. Her descriptions of real people are astonishingly memorable – Camus, for instance, in *La Folie en tête* (In Mad Pursuit), and Maurice Sachs in *La Bâtarde*. Who else but Leduc has described the situation of a bisexual woman in love with a homosexual? And did she remember what he had written in *Le Sabbat* about his admiration for American women? No matter, *La Bâtarde* is a book that no reader can forget even if the urge to tear it up and throw the bits out of the window is as intense as the scenes described. If *Thérèse et Isabelle* had been rejected earlier no publisher or censor wanted to excise the scene in *La Bâtarde* where Violette and Hermine make love in front of a voyeur.

The fate of the *The Well of Loneliness* in 1928 is well known. Even Victoria Sackville-West's reticent description of her love-affair with Violet Trefusis was not published in Britain until the early 1970s after all the people concerned were dead. It had been generally held that such behaviour was not uncommon among the aristocracy or among artists and writers (unthinkable in the middle or working class) and the rest of society usually accepted it, especially since it was not against the law. (It will never be known whether its 'legal' status was due to prudery, ignorance or unexpected understanding on the part of Queen Victoria.) It did no obvious harm, it had a kind of shocking, but not too shocking glamour. Now of course the situation is very different and some militant sections of the women's movement advocate a mass adoption of lesbianism as part of the anti-male campaign. The results are not too difficult to foresee: many women would be much happier, there might be fewer unhappy marriages and men are hardly likely to complain or even notice, for there would be no shortage of heterosexual partners.

Until the end of her life Violette Leduc needed love and support from women, she would even identify classical paintings with individual women she had adored in the past. Yet it would be a mistake to think she had no other theme. Two of her books, both short, have a different tone, as though this over-hysterical woman had been given a course of tranquillizers. However, these are still stories of obsession and lack of love. One is *La vielle fille et la mort* (The Old Maid and Death), which she wrote early, and the other *La femme au petit renard* (The Lady and the Little Fox Fur), which belongs to 1965. The old maid loves a man who is dead and does not want his body taken away from her. The *renard* is not a fox but a fox fur and the woman who owns it measures out her life not with coffee-spoons but with coffee beans and the remnants of food she can find by scavenging or begging. These are sad little books but they are not repellent: studies of degradation have been only too frequent since the Second World War and they have been valuable in drawing attention to the interrelated problems of hunger and loneliness, especially in cities. They go further, when well written, into the whole problem of human alienation. It is only when the degradation seems to be studied for its own sake, almost always by men, that it becomes tedious. Leduc wrote these two books out of compassion and in them she looked some way beyond herself, although, of course, her own experience lies behind them. If she had been able to start writing earlier her work might have acquired a wider scope, but it is too easy to forget that without a great deal of luck and help she might never have been able to publish at all.

It is easy to forget one extraordinary aspect of Violette Leduc's achievement: her mother, the original Mademoiselle Leduc – she could not even remember how her name was spelt – did not know what a publisher was. When she first worked for one, Violette had to explain to her mother that a book had to go through the process of publication, it was not merely printed. Nothing had destined her to be a writer, not even the fact that her peasant-born mother had eventually read Stendhal and Balzac. The emotional damage done by this dominating mother is a case-book story but without it Violette Leduc might never have written a line or come so far. Fortunately she found that other mother in Simone de Beauvoir ('she was almost maternal', she wrote in *La Chasse à l'amour*). The 'bastard' who had been obsessed by her own ugliness was an instinctive writer and the lack of control that had ruined her personal life made her into a writer without inhibitions just at the time when this kind of document, especially when well written, was eagerly wanted by the reading public. In the First World War she had been frightened by German bombs, in the Second World War she became rich working as a black marketeer in company with a Jewish writer who was later killed by the Nazis. The reader can only be glad he (again more possibly she) has not had these experiences, but glad too that someone had the courage to record them. Yet it would be a mistake to think that there was no artistry or selection in the writing.

Fame brought her money, which she had always avidly and unashamedly wanted. Whether it brought her happiness is another matter. When she became an international success she had outward poise, good clothes provided by French couturiers and a handsomely impressive blonde wig. Unfortunately she remained so much of a masochist that she sometimes allowed herself to be seen without it: and she was an old bald woman, even at the age of sixty. As a true Frenchwoman of the older generation she was shocked by the coarse personal questioning of British journalists, for instance. She died too soon to write a fourth book of souvenirs in which she intended to write about a fascinating subject: her reactions to success. She did not have the chance; life had cheated her of so much and now it cheated her of her farewell performance, which had been in her mind for several years, if not from the very beginning of her writing life.

✥ 14 ✥

The Two-Breasted Amazon

When the Alsatian-born Monique Wittig won the Prix
Médicis with *L'Opoponax* in 1964 she was twenty-eight and at
that stage she was still ready to talk about herself, a readiness
she soon lost. She had been brought up in Rodez in the
Aveyron and in Montmorency to the north-west of Paris. To
those who enjoy her writing it will hardly be a surprise to
learn that she contemplated a career in music and when she
had to choose between buying food and buying a record she
usually chose the record. Her musical taste was wide-ranging,
including at first the romantic composers, then Bach, Vivaldi,
Monteverdi, Frescobaldi, Pergolesi, then back to Couperin
and Rameau. In 1964 she thought Schönberg a 'complete
genius', enjoyed Prokoviev, Stravinsky, Bartók and Boulez. She
knew nothing about folklore but imagined that it would not
move her. Ballet meant little – 'all those tutus irritate me', she
confessed. Music did not become her career, she took a
degree in literature, studied oriental languages, worked at the
Bibliothèque Nationale and then in publishing. Her first
attempt at a novel failed to interest anyone, but the Éditions de
Minuit in Paris employed her as a proof-reader at a lower than
minimum wage and she was offered a bed in Robbe-Grillet's
office. She did not accept it. The firm was delighted to publish
L'Opoponax. Jérôme Lindon, whose list has included some of the
most stimulating writers since the end of the Second World War,
had given her six months' leave from the firm to write it. Most
prize-winning novels earn publicity, obviously, even if their
authors do not grow rich as a result, and this book was more
newsworthy than most because it was not a traditional novel nor
another example of the 'new novel', it was simply, rarely, new.

It is a story of children at school told in the third person through a single little girl and as one critic said at the time 'we are present at the invention of a way of speaking', *on assiste à l'invention d'un langage*. The author herself went as far as to say that her search for 'concrete material' allowed her to develop a style which lay 'between spoken and written language'. External narrative did not interest her greatly in this book and as time went on it hardly existed for her. Language absorbed her, language which never lost its function as communication but it was communication in a new way; it was the fusion, Wittig hoped, of two languages, that of childhood and that of the adult world. Many writers have used language in new ways but the result has often been a failure in communication, for disembodied words, however provocative their flight, turn into puzzles, latter-day *dada*, or a kind of typographical ornamentation, if the basic function of communication has gone. Monique Wittig maintained this communication because she is a poet and also because she has studied non-European languages, which enabled her to see further than the average writer. Her poetic quality makes her contribution genuinely exciting, even if limited, meriting comparison with the work of the new novelists who, with the exception, notably, of their two women representatives, have been unable to produce a dram of poetry between them. Wittig herself has acknowledged her debt to Robbe-Grillet, Robert Pinget and to the films of Jean-Luc Godard. If one responds to poetry one surely responds to Monique Wittig's writing, even if that response is not total, uncritical acceptance. The build-up of nouns and adjectives in her prose and the restricted use of punctuation could antagonize many readers and oddness in itself does not constitute poetic quality, especially perhaps in prose. It has been understandably alleged from the beginning that Wittig's writing is precious, self-conscious, limited in scope and surely self-destructive.

There seemed to be logic behind all these reactions and when five years later *Les Guérillères* appeared these critical arguments might have seemed justified, for the author had chosen a theme obviously destined to earn the enthusiasm of some but the ribald antagonism of many: the female guerillas are attacking an enemy who could have been friendly – on their own terms – but were not allowed to be, for the enemy consisted of men. Wittig had already invented a style of her own and now she was going to use it in the way she wanted. To join in a controversial social and sexual battle by way of a literary innovation might seem not merely courageous but unbalanced and suicidally eccentric. The 'handwriting', so to speak, had not changed, its obviously idiosyncratic features had become more striking still, there was now a baroque quality to this short book and there was a new dimension; the exclusive importance of each individual woman and of women as a group was now emphasized by the printing of a vast O on a blank page (the O of the vaginal orifice) and by frequent pages carrying women's first names from every country in the world. It was a battle-cry; all women, the book said, in its siren voice, must unite in the defence of the female principle and gradually build a collective female state.

The world of The Opoponax had been relatively accessible, for every adult reader had once been a child, even if he or she remembered a different childhood in a different way. But identification with what Mary McCarthy called 'the pearl-tressed, two-breasted Amazons' was obviously limited. Not every woman wants to be an Amazon, even with two breasts, but this book was tempting propaganda. In Britain nobody took it more seriously than Professor Frank Kermode who stressed its social and philosophical implications.

Wittig had earned her international admirers but it looks as though their intensity will have to compensate for their lack of numbers. By 1974, when she published Le Corps lesbien (The Lesbian Body), she herself had more or less fled the real world and gone into hiding. Her third novel was no story but a declaration, the proclamation of a world of women, occupied entirely with themselves and with each other. Les Guérillères had been full of aggression: how else could men be removed? – physically or metaphysically – from the existence of the women, who although sometimes condescending to mate in captivity, at this pointed hated them? In *Le Corps lesbien* the men have gone, so now there is time and space for women to live and love as they want. But the reader need not think that he – or more probably she – is to be given a kind of Utopian vision, a new, ideal Lesbos. There are lyrical, sometimes comical glimpses of this, but the main preoccupation of the book is simply and symbolically with the female body and by extension again with the female principle.

Some critics in France could not refrain from mentioning Jean Genet and his exclusively masculine world but added that his writing had immense scope, whereas Wittig's was apparently now more limited than ever. Some commentators found it almost decadent, 'trop joli', reminiscent of Pierre Louÿs or Renée Vivien. The novelist Claudine Chonez thought that the book was cruel, that male homosexuals were 'affectionate and weak' compared with these omnivorous women who enjoyed nothing so much as the dissection of the loved one's body. But it would be a mistake to take the book literally, for the author, in her intense search for ever more intensity – the infinite depth of feeling between women – uses anatomical analysis as one way of achieving it. The Marquis de Sade, having no other vocabulary at his disposal, had used physiology in his early approach to psychology. Aimiable male critics and literary historians have held that women did many things quite nicely but could not invent. Wittig, however limited her field, has invented a way of writing; it is also a way of thinking, and if it is not everyone's way that does not diminish it. The reader will love or hate it. Those who find it boring are usually those who cannot face the responsibility of commitment. It is especially convenient for men to find it boring – they do not enjoy being made redundant. Perhaps *Le Corps lesbien* is science fiction and as in the case of much science fiction there is always the danger that it might come true.

There is a new generation of women writers in France as in other countries who believe they are working for the liberation of their kind by using the battle-axe method, attacking men in general, and also those women who behave in the way described as old-fashioned feminine, accepting servile 'féminitude', as the French now call it. Their reward, understandably, is hostility all round, and they will only encourage men to go on thinking of women as unsuccessful imitators. Wittig is particularly interesting because she remains essentially feminine; her intellectual and artistic achievements are equal to those of a man and her psychology is of a different order. In *Les Guérillères* she went through what some might call a 'masculine' or aggressive phase but it is only 'masculine' in a superficial way. The pearl-tressed Amazons carry out their destruction in a symbolic manner but their attention to detail is something found more often in women than in men. Her characters are dancers. Wittig may have disliked classical ballet but like Marguerite Duras in a different sphere she is very much a choreographer in this book, ordering individuals and groups about the stage with mathematical precision. She believes women are the creative sex in all ways and that men will soon imitate them.

In *Le Corps lesbien* this aggressive period is over, love remains, love with all its emotional overtones and, thank goodness, its moments of laughter. The true aggression, however, happened somewhere between the two books, when nobody was looking: the men were removed. Jonathan Swift wrote about a world of giants, a world of dwarfs. It is possible that he could have written about a world of women, but by chance he did not. Monique Wittig did, and by chance she was a woman, an interested party. Whatever one feels about the validity of her thesis, she devised it, wrote it and surely proved beyond any doubt that a woman has inventive capacity. If she expects universal agreement with her attitude she will not get it, all of which makes for more stimulating argument.

The author's note to this third novel is well worth quoting

for it sets out how Wittig identified her thought and her language. She believes that lesbians have been silent: only Sappho, Radclyffe Hall, Sylvia Plath, Anaïs Nin and Violette Leduc (in *La Bâtarde*) have spoken for them. 'Only the women's movement has proved capable of producing lesbian texts in a context of total rupture with masculine culture, texts written by women exclusively for women, careless of male approval. *Le Corps lesbien* falls into this category.

'The descriptions of the islands allude to the Amazons, to the islands of women, the domains of women, which formerly existed with their own culture. They also allude to the Amazons of the present and the future. We already have our islets, our islands, we are already in process of living in a culture that befits us. The Amazons are women who live among themselves, by themselves and for themselves at all the generally accepted levels: fictional, symbolic, actual. Because we are illusionary for traditional male culture we make no distinction between the three levels. Our reality is the fictional as it is socially accepted, our symbols deny the traditional symbols and are fictional for traditional male culture, and we possess an entire fiction into which we project ourselves and which is already a possible reality. It is our fiction that validates us.

'The body of the text subsumes all the words of the female body. *Le Corps lesbien* attempts to achieve the affirmation of its reality. The lists of names contribute to this activity. To recite one's own body, to recite the body of the other, is to recite the words of which the book is made up. The fascination for writing the never previously written and the fascination for the unattained body proceed from the same desire. The desire to bring the real body violently to life in the words of the book (everything that is written exists), the desire to do violence by writing to the language which I (j/e) can enter only by force. . . .' She maintained that a woman could not use the word for 'I' because men used it too; if a woman wanted to express what only a woman can experience, then she must use another symbol: not *je*, but *j/e*, perhaps. 'J/e is the symbol of the lived, rending experience which is m/y writing, of this cutting in two which throughout literature is the exercise of a language which does not constitute m/e as subject. J/e poses the ideological and historic question of feminine subjects. (Certain groups of women have proposed writing *jee* or *jeue*.) If I (J/e) examine m/y specific situation as subject in the language, I (J/e) am physically incapable of writing "I" (Je), I (J/e) have no desire to do so.'

Everything she says is absorbing and controversial. Has she justified her attempt to destroy the alleged masculine orientation of language? And how far does it exist, in how many languages? There is plenty to fight about and that guerilla warfare is by no means over. In the meantime, *as a writer*, Wittig counts more than the leaders of the Le Mouvement de Libération des Femmes as a proof of achievement by a woman and in the vanguard.

In the mid-'sixties she was a modest girl with unforgettable large grey eyes who enjoyed exploring the London docks. Ten years later she tried to carry her lesbian logic throughout the production of her third book – she wanted a lesbian translator, a lesbian jacket-designer. She did not get them, but her message came through clearly enough.

A little later still many French critics began to regard her as belonging to the past, and of course they must always be on the lookout for something new, something that will bring about controversy at least, if not sales or money. 'Nobody talks about her now': it sounds like an epitaph. She may cause more surprise, she may fall silent, but her books published to date are more than mere essays in style and experimental language. They represent a serious attempt to explore the relationship between the feminine psyche and the spirit of language. Dorothy Richardson in Britain had explored the feminine unconscious, but not the technical means of expressing it. Monique Wittig has gone further, and her exploration means more than her success or failure.

✤ 15 ✤

Feminism or Death?

This was the title (less the question mark) given to one of her books in 1974 by Françoise d'Eaubonne, whose list of publications includes novels and poems. The message of the book is clear from the title and she was not the only woman writer to sound so militant, desperate and determined. Marguerite Duras had been right, at least about France, when she pointed out how fast the women's movement had gone forward. It had a good deal of ground to cover. In all other ways France had always imagined itself the centre of the avant-garde, but Finland had been the first European country to give votes to women as far back as 1906: while Frenchwomen had to wait another forty years or so.

Women are not only writing hard in France, they are publishing too; at the time of writing, 1975, they are so deeply aware of women's achievements in writing that there is at least one publishing firm and bookshop in Paris which gives as much publicity to those achievements as possible; it is run by women for women and for men if they will stop a moment to listen. The firm publishes a portrait of Christine de Pisan on several of their documents and gives away tote-bags with a picture of women on the march during the Revolution. Since these publishers are not purely chauvinistic – unlike a great many of their male colleagues – they have searched out documents about women's achievements in many countries and also about women in under-developed countries who are still living more or less like slaves, almost unaware that in time other forms of existence could be possible for them. In time, for if women's liberation is a process of social evolution, unfortunately it cannot be hurried. Françoise Giroud has been the first Frenchwoman to look after women's status (*la con-dition féminine*), a post she only accepted when the President had agreed to give her full cabinet status. Madame Simone Veil, that astonishingly effective lady, has had to cope with the problems involving birth control and abortion, problems which would hardly have been mentioned a generation ago because those who were rich enough could buy whatever they wanted and why should anyone worry about those who were not? If Françoise Giroud's ambitions on behalf of her own sex seem somewhat romantic, Madame Simone Veil, Minister of Health, is nothing if not realistic.

Realism in fact is the keynote for women's writing now, and perhaps it always has been, on different levels, outside the supply of obvious 'romance' which some people need even among the hard-headed supremely unromantic French. Christiane Rochefort's work is a good example of how a skilled writer can handle realism precisely on these 'different levels'. Her novel *Le Repos du guérrier* (Warrior's Rest), first published in 1958, was over-praised and not so outstanding as first thought. So far the British have not been able to stomach it, for up to the time of writing the American translation has not appeared here. Although it had a shaky start and an uncon-vincing ending it is probably still the best novel about an alcoholic written by a woman. Admittedly the heroine, Geneviève, is an irritating doormat woman – what sort of love could make her cling to the appalling Renaud for so long? – but it is the display of technique that makes the book worth while. Perpetual drunkenness and craving for drink soon become tedious enough when described realistically, for the subject is hardly new, but Christiane Rochefort soon leaves obvious realism behind, her forte is the way in which she intensifies unreality. Why does Renaud try to kill himself and why does he drink? Because he was twenty in 1945 and he thought that life was just about to begin: but like thousands of other people of the same age at the same date he suddenly realized that what he had thought of as life was no more than

history. 'Don't ask on whom the bomb falls, it falls on you.'
Geneviève is ten years younger and has never learned about
that old-fashioned hope. Perhaps that is why the book ends
with what appears to be her old-fashioned disappearance into
pregnancy. 'One day,' said Renaud, 'I'll write a treatise. I'll call
it *On Love*. I'll be against it.'

Christiane Rochefort allowed her publishers to tell her
readers something about herself: she was born in a working-
class part of Paris and had spent 'nearly all her time amusing
herself, that is to say painting, drawing, sculpting, making
music, carrying out disorganized studies, medicine, psychiatry,
the Sorbonne, writing for her own delight, and in the time
left over, trying to earn her living in order to survive'. She was
once press attaché for the Cannes Film Festival and was dismissed in 1968 for her 'freedom of thought', on which one
can only congratulate her. Disorganized it all may have been,
but this existence has produced several books which destroy
with an individual and essentially feminine irony all that
public hope about social organization and how to 'help the
poor'. The novel of 1961, *Les petits enfants du siècle* (The Little
Children of the Century), should be required reading for all
those who think that social security is a fine thing, and those
who think it is too fine a thing, for why should one work any
more, and how does a family with several small children live
in a high-rise apartment in the suburbs of Paris? A moving,
unsentimental, deeply ironic book told in the authentic and
inevitably unattractive voice of a girl whose mother had so
many children because she didn't know what to do. Even if
Christiane Rochefort's more melodramatic participation in
Choisir (the society that campaigned for women's right to
choose motherhood if they wanted it), and the French
women's movement is forgotten – when, that is, the movement
helps to achieve 'feminism or death' – she will still be well
worth reading for she does not write tracts, she writes novels,
she cares about people and she cares too about the way she
writes, whatever she may say about her 'disorganized studies'.

Perhaps this disorganization has preserved her from the cerebral coldness that makes well-intentioned intellectual women so tediously ineffective and unreadable.

Women writers in France can hardly escape the urge to campaign but some do it more convincingly than others. The two sisters Flora and Benoîte Groult achieved a certain fame in the 1960s with the books they wrote together, but they later began to write separately and Benoîte joined the campaigners with a book that had at least an arresting title: *Ainsi soit-elle*, arresting because in French the usual formula for the biblical 'So be it' is *Ainsi soit-il*. Each book of this kind augments the orchestra but hardly produces an authentic new note.

Perhaps the most stimulating voice of all came from Gisèle Halimi, whose own story equips her supremely well for a major contribution to the women's cause. *La Cause des Femmes*, 'cause' in the legal sense, appeared in 1973 and should be read by everyone, women and men, likely to be affected by the question of social justice for women, and that is literally everyone. Gisèle Halimi did not come from a middle-class family in France but from a less favoured one in Tunis where her father, who was entirely self-taught, had struggled to bring up a son and – *quel malheur!* – two daughters. Nobody noticed that she was top of the class at school, all attention was focused on her brother, who achieved nothing. Her refusal to do housework was as violent as her urge to become a barrister in Paris, and she succeeded. She got married and was able to conduct her cases while pregnant because luckily her robes concealed her state. She noticed that her opponents always hinted that inevitably she must lose the case, for she was a woman. Her career became more important than that of other women barristers because through the famous Bobigny case in 1972 she won a political battle for legalized abortion. The girl in question, aged sixteen, had a backstreet abortion which led to a haemorrhage. A clinic would only treat her if her mother would pay three months' salary; she was forced to give a cheque, *sans provision*, in advance. The eighteen-year-old father of the aborted child, when in trouble for stealing, told the police what had happened and they charged the girl's mother, the abortionist and two accomplices. Maître Halimi defended them, won the case and the relevant law, which dated from 1920, collapsed. The membership of *Choisir* increased at once. Many women writers had signed that famous letter of 1971 stating that they had had abortions. It looked as though the climate was changing, but it still has not changed enough. Gisèle Halimi's book is worth quoting for its fairness and basically moderate attitude. She cites Engels's analysis of the family situation and points out that the liberation of women cannot happen in isolation. Men will in fact benefit in the long run. 'Objectively, I consider that the liberation of woman is the liberation of man.' The social implications were wide: 'the liberation of women implies a change in economic structures and relationships. But also a change in the "male" form of power.' 'Man must learn to live in a different way and neither men nor women need "pretend" any more. There will be a new relationship between men and women. Everything will have changed in fact: sexuality, the sharing of work, the manner of speech. A new way of understanding life. A fair and responsible division between two equal liberties.'

Gisèle Halimi ended her book by saying that she did not believe in a revolution by women. But she saw women as 'the marching wing' of a new revolution. This was written in 1974, twenty-five years after *The Second Sex*, from which its epigraph was taken: 'One is not born a woman, one becomes one.' Gisèle Halimi brought a lawyer's fairness to a campaign in which most of the militants rarely separate the cause of women from the left-wing movement in general. A big subject, of which we have so far seen only the beginning. Women obviously have had to undertake this kind of writing on their own. Even Gisèle Halimi thought that men, with few exceptions, could not really help.

It is all a far cry from Elisabeth Barbier's *Gens de Mogador* (People of Mogador), that non-literary but readable *roman* fleuve about the emotional problems of a property-owning family in the south of France, perfect for serialization in any medium, equally far too from a whole group of books by women which reach a high literary standard, win prizes, occasionally appear in English, interest a critic now and then but lead to no excitement: the tales of Monique Lange, especially *Les Platanes* (The Plane Trees), which seems to have been created for the cinema and is deeper than it might appear, 'smoother' than any story by Sagan; the charm of Christine de Rivoyre, the reticent tales of the Belgian Maud Frère, the painful experiences narrated with finesse and intensity by Irène Monesi and Suzanne Prou, the intriguing work of Dominique Rolin, always intelligent, sometimes obscure, preoccupied with psychological duality, as borne out by *Deux* of 1975. Poets include the German-born Claire Goll and the Canadian Anne Hébert (a novelist too). Anne Huré, who was once a nun, is perhaps the first woman writer in French to use her experience within organized religion as a theme for fiction, especially impressive in *Les Deux moniales* (The Two Nuns).

It was 1967 when Claire Etcherelli published her first novel in Paris, *Elise ou la vraie vie* (Elise or the Real Life) and it well deserved its Prix Fémina. The author had used part of her own unhappy experience in writing it and it contributed another aspect of realism to fiction written by women. She had been born in Bordeaux into a poor family, her father had been killed by the Germans. The government helped her with a scholarship for a time but eventually she came to Paris and worked in a factory.

It was thirty years since Simone Weil had worked for Renault in almost exactly the same conditions, but she was not concerned with writing fiction, which she distrusted. Certainly no woman had yet written so convincingly about work at the conveyor-belt as Claire Etcherelli did, translating the boredom without being boring. Skilfully the book also tells the story of the heroine's love for an Algerian who is taken away by the police during a demonstration at the height of the crisis over the country's independence, when France was torn in two over the issue of colonial policy. Where was *la vraie vie*, real life? The author does not attempt to say, she reports the reality of life that she herself saw at first hand, the reality in which terms may change, but the basic problem, of personal and national independence, never.

In a second book, four years later, *A propos de Clémence*, Claire Etcherelli again tried to find that elusive 'reality' in writing about a woman whose book is being filmed. The heroine herself is no longer sure what is real and unreal. The background to the book is the civil war in Spain and the story is especially fascinating to any woman who has been drawn into politics through sheer romanticism – the identification between her half-formed ideals and the personality of a mysterious lover who is a key-figure in desperately serious political intrigue and adventure.

Catherine Claude particularly deserves a mention for a first novel about the French resistance movement, *Ciel blanc* (White Sky), which uses a flashback technique with particular effectiveness. It was unfortunately neglected outside France. Other names among women writers hardly well enough known so far to the non-French reader include Geneviève Serreau, novelist, film-writer and critic, Viviane Forestier, another critic, the efficient Edmonde Charles-Roux, Simone Jacquemard, Michèle Perrein, Noëlle Loriot.

At the same time Clara Malraux has published in four volumes (up to 1975) the memories of a long and unusual life, much of it spent in company of André Malraux: she was his first wife. The books, collectively called *Les Bruits de nos pas* (The Sound of our Steps), reveal a personal struggle which any woman will find absorbing: how does a wife remain a person, especially when her husband is a well-known figure constantly in the public eye? The struggle was difficult enough in the 'twenties and 'thirties, for Frenchwomen had relatively little freedom. Now women have much more, but this is a problem which cannot be solved by knowing a set of rules. It is an individual problem which women have known about ever since the days of Mary Wollstonecraft; since hardly anyone can advise anyone else, the more it is written about, the better.

The English-reading world will soon know more of Hélène Cixous, a Professor of English in France, whose massive, over-massive but masterly study *The Exile of James Joyce* has now been translated, leaving the average critic in a state of exhaustion. As for her novels, the list of which grows longer at speed, they provide the critics with impassioned delight and reduce the reader to baffled silence. Brilliant technical display, inevit-able if well-assimilated memories of Joyce, but somehow a failure to transfix that tedious but indispensable common reader, riveting him or her to the page. Women writers as a rule tend to lose too much of their essence if they consciously move too far away from the worlds of humanity and humour. Men make the move with less effort, for they are less closely identified with their writing and abstraction is less foreign to them. Hélène Cixous however is clearly at home in her enclave of word-management; the critics in France have joined her there and the reader can now look forward to the thrill of catching up. Women are so often accused of their lack of invention, but this may be because for too long all their energy has been directed into catching up with the inventions, earning themselves the opportunity to invent while at the same time finding themselves forced, in the non-literary world, to carry out the practical details made necessary by men's inventions. The contribution by women to the arts, and especially to writing, during the last half-century, has revealed their latent potential. Who can say now how far they will go in other fields? This is why it is impossible to underrate the experimental writing by women, for it is not only literary, it is experimentation in the psychological and social field, a pointer to the future.

It is impossible to list all the ways in which women have contributed to 'new' ways of writing this century, which is by no means limited to the once-new novel. Lise Deharme, for example, is an experienced novelist but deserves to be mentioned for something very different, the extraordinary little book *Le Pot de mousse* written during the Second World War which can only be described as surrealist fairy-tales. Each untranslatable sentence, where people turn into legendary animals and back again, where the word-play shows a brilliantly delicate appreciation of language, proves that if the greatest tellers of fairy-tales and fables in France may have been Perrault and La Fontaine, with Madame d'Aulnoy some way behind, at least one woman caught them up in the twentieth century. I doubt if any man could have written these stories, they have no obvious links with any aspect of the male psyche. However, Lise Deharme had been influenced by André Breton, reputed to be so hostile to women. That is a question too complex to study here, but it should be added that Lise Deharme, often in touch apparently with occult forces, was 'visited' by Breton several months after his death, and he told her that after a short horrible moment death was 'marvellous'. Lise Deharme in fact analysed briefly this strange domain, about which so few people have written convincingly. She found it necessary to rectify 'the confusion which forms between the "fantastic" and the "marvellous" (about which people say so little).

'The "marvellous" can be fantastic.

The converse is not true.

The "marvellous" enriches existence: it is a spectacular play.

The "fantastic" is a tragedy.

The "marvellous" is life.

The "fantastic" is death.

When these two are united, a door opens on to the "invisible".'

Another writer who made a serious attempt in experimental writing, this time in dual-media expression, was Elsa Triolet. This was *Ecoutez-voir*, a book which she described as '*imagé*' but not '*illustré*'. Although the pictures it contains draw the eye away from the text and the experiment is not an entire success, at least it was made, and I for one prefer it to most of her other more conventional work.

Another woman writer, working on a different level, developed a genre which may never be repeated, for it is too personal, a fusion of her own experiences as an antique dealer with fiction. This was Yvonne de Brémond des Ars, and her long list of titles, each one separately readable, was called *Journal d'une antiquaire*.

It would be hard to list the work of Anne Philippe as 'experimental'; it lies in that magical hinterland somewhere beyond poetry, but it is not prose. After the extraordinarily moving book she wrote about her husband Gérard Philippe, the actor, who died of cancer, she became a writer herself, publishing *Spirale*, *Ici là-bas ailleurs* (Here, There, Elsewhere), books as difficult to classify as they are fascinating to read.

Women have also been extremely reliable observers, and the kind who write *Les Cahiers de la petite dame* (Notebooks of a Little Lady), as Gide's friend Maria van Rysselberghe did, will be read in the future as the memoir-writers of the eighteenth and nineteenth century are still read now. One could wish too that Adrienne Monnier, who made such a contribution to the French literary scene through her famous bookshop, had written more of the *Gazettes* that are so valuable a record, especially for that uncharted period of the German occupation when most writers wrote about literature with careful avoidance of any reference to political events.

The mention of the French Canadian poet Anne Hébert makes it essential to refer to two others who are in fact better known and one especially, Gabrielle Roy, born in Manitoba, who wrote a classic first novel in 1945, *Bonheur d'occasion* (The Tin Flute) which deservedly won the 1947 Prix Fémina. Who could forget that pathetic young heroine who of all her *famille nombreuse* in Montreal is the only one, working as a waitress, to bring home any regular money? The men do little, they merely talk or hope, or eventually go off into the Second World War. The women are perpetually pregnant. The heroine is soon pregnant too, and accepts the second-hand happiness of a husband who is not the father of her child. Life is much easier in French Canada now, and surely this book by Gabrielle Roy counted for something in social improvement, especially because her method, always the most effective, was indirect.

Women began to write in French Canada over two hundred years ago, the first of them being Sœur Marie Morin who lived from 1649 to 1730. Her *Histoire simple et véritable* was not published until 1921, and then only in part, with the title *Annales de l'Hôtel-Dieu de Montréal*. Elizabeth Bégon wrote a set of letters to her son-in-law, in Louisiana, between 1748 and 1753, which were published as late as 1953 and give a good impression of what was then colonial life, but the fashionable side of it. The apparently brilliant *journal intime* of Josephine Marchand-Dandurand has not yet been published although she is known for one book of memoirs, *Nos travers*.

In 1891, Madame M. S. Van de Velde, writing on the then contemporary French novels, remarked that they were not for young girls. How surprised she would have been, sixty years or so later, to find they were written by young girls. This applied in Canada as well as in France and Marie-Claire Blais was barely twenty when her first novel was published in Quebec in 1959. To read this or any other of her novels is a shock and many readers have been alarmed by the hysterical note which shrills out from them. But the sagacious Edmund Wilson was not put off and was impressed enough to write an admiring preface to *A Season in the Life of Emmanuel*, one of the saddest novels written since the end of the Second World War. The little boy, again of a *famille nombreuse*, destined to the seminary and soon to the hospital, is, along with Gabrielle Roy's heroine, the symbol of a society that for too long could only be called anachronistic, and if it still has its problems, they are now of a different order. Significantly the women writers of French Canada seem to be better known in Europe at least than their male counterparts: the reason is that they approach social problems through family life and do not attempt to deal with larger political issues through any abstract analysis.

A study of publishers' lists during the last few years shows how many French women are writing and what efforts are being made to let women express themselves, even if they only talk into a tape-recorder about how they pass the time doing a dull job; the women writers obviously have to combine their writing with some other job or even depend on their husbands, a situation which has become highly unfashionable for many. In 1963 Rayner Heppenstall was able to write in *The Intellectual Part* that 'Women novelists, in general kept by their husbands, also function as housewives, hostesses and perhaps even mothers'. But he would hardly have dared write that ten or fifteen years later. Since so many women in France as elsewhere do not expect, do not want to be 'kept' by a partner of any kind all those who can earn money in the sidelines of writing – everything from the chaotic worlds of broadcasting to film festivals – do so. One writer of historical novels for instance keeps goats and sells their cheese to exclusive *fromageries* or restaurants in Paris. As the state of the economy forces newspapers and magazines to atrophy and dwindle journalism is not so easily available as a money-earner to everyone. So some women writers have become more than ever determined to write books that might not be literature but at least they would *sell*.

I can only hope that the stories of how they broke into what had been an all-male world are true, or at least partly true. Who was 'Pauline Réage', mystery author of the famous *Histoire d'O* (The Story of O) published first in 1954? It was an open secret for years – *tout le monde le sait*, one was told – that the author was the well-known Dominique Aury, intelligent writer and critic who for a time was assistant to the enterprising publisher Jean-Jacques Pauvert. But it has also been suggested that 'Pauline Réage' was a team of experienced writers and journalists who were determined to be successful in their pornographic pastiche, and so they were.

The Story of O in book form is not likely to fascinate everyone.

It depends if you enjoy descriptions of refined amorous torture, and whether the utterances of O's lover René strike you as entertaining. The book probably provides more amusement for the specialist in literary pornography than for someone who merely wants sexual stimulus. Whoever wrote it knew the Marquis of Sade's writings pretty well and though the result is infinitely less boring and much more graceful it is hardly an obvious aphrodisiac. The introduction to a book is best read afterwards, as everyone knows, but rarely was any introduction as fascinating as that by the intelligent Jean Paulhan which prefaces O. First of all he refers to a revolt by Barbados slaves in the eighteenth century which may never lose its relevance: they were offered freedom – but they did not want to be free. Then he goes into details that make some women feel uncomfortable while others spit with rage. A woman admits at last, he maintains, as men have always reproached them, 'that everything in them is sex, even their minds'. That old story about reaching for the whip was not wrong. Most men dream of possessing a Justine, Sade's totally masochistic heroine, but which *woman* would want to incarnate her? Psychologically the book is intriguing from beginning to end and Paulhan finds it 'mercilessly decent'.

The author added her – naïvely we shall continue to say her, until the whole story has been published – own personality. O (for orifice perhaps, or O for zero, someone with no name) is described with the usual amount of detail, but women readers will be fascinated at least by the clothes, described with much detail and obviously intended to go in and out of fashion for as long as clothes are worn. A suit with a pleated skirt, black gloves, no hat, make-up, a waspie; and O notices, even during torture, that her lover's slippers are worn, he needs new ones.

In 1954 I enjoyed cutting the pages of my numbered copy, reading finally that preface, 'The Story of O', wrote Paulhan, 'is obviously one of those books which make their mark on the reader – which do not leave him [here it seems fair to add or her] quite or entirely as they found him [or her]: which do not leave him altogether, or not at all, as they found him [again we should add or her]: strangely mingled with the influence which they exert, and changing with it. A few years later they are no longer the same books.' How true, for in 1954 it may not have occurred to many people that this story with all its physical and psychological baroque could appear in the English language, bedevilled as that language is with a paucity of vocabulary and law-making habits that defy codification. Yet this English-language version did appear and was duly picked at by literary critics. And George Steiner, on indicating in 1965 that he did not relish pornography, drew the ironic disapproval of two experts, Maurice Girodias and the publisher of O himself. Jean-Jacques Pauvert wrote to *Encounter* in London (who had published Steiner's original article) and pointed out that Steiner had not mentioned 'L'Histoire d'O, which for me, is the one and only erotic book. The reason is that literary eroticism is unimaginable for an Anglo-Saxon. The English language may be very rich in technical terms but it is very deficient for the expression of ideas, sensations and shades of meaning. Perhaps something which is an image in Pauline Réage's writing for instance, can only be translated into English by the use of blunt, coarse terms. Like the Chinese, the Anglo-Saxons have no erotic literary language. . . .' It is all contestable, there is more, but not so relevant to our theme.

If books change as they grow older, few changed so much as this one for in 1975 it was made into a successful film and packed many cinemas in Paris. It also caused Madame Giroud to resign from the board of the weekly newspaper *L'Express* because it was publishing the text in serial form. No one responsible for the condition of women could see her name linked with the heroine who adored punishment. Many French critics continue to take the book seriously and *L'Express* took the 'author' seriously by interviewing 'her': she said she was a feminist but did not think much of the women's movement. And how many of her readers will agree with what she said about men: women knew that a husband was 'one more child. Men are irresponsible like children, show off like children. Women are more "*raisonnables*".' And the author took her heroine seriously: 'She is the symbol of a love which remains pure through debauchery which is absolute': Pauline Réage also believed that O enjoyed being 'mistress of herself – quite a different thing from self-control'.

All this happened during International Women's Year, 1975. During that year the enterprising left-wing municipality of Gennevilliers, far out in the suburbs of Paris, produced a very useful bibliography *La Femme à travers les livres*, with lists, often highly specialized, of books by women and about women. Interspersed with the lists were poems by Aragon, Eluard, Nazim Hikmet and Pablo Neruda. There was also in Paris an exhibition of paintings by women artists. The French designed a well meant but unpleasing postage stamp. Contributions to the celebration of this year were more practical in other countries: in Iceland for example the women of the country refused to work for one day and life was practically paralysed. In the United States, where lesbian clubs, depressed and depressing, have become a feature of social life in some areas, women were afraid to leave their jobs for even a day because they realized they would probably lose them. In Britain books by women writers throughout the Commonwealth were exhibited at New Zealand House, and a great number of women wrote articles in *The Times*; the novelist Margaret Drabble said that boys should be taught how to cook. But in 1976 the film of *The Story of O* was still leading people – who? – to buy whips and chains.

Twenty years, in the mid-twentieth century, is a long stretch for a mysterious, once-censored author. Before the century is over we may have the story of The Story, but in the meantime there is time to work out whether O herself is synthetic, symbolic or a mere fantasy.

Whoever 'Pauline Réage' may be her women readers will enjoy the superficial aspects of her possible, probable femininity and some of them might even feel at home with the masochism. The best writers of sensational or pornographic books in Britain have not been women, as far as we know, but in the United States women have done better, for who could resist the readable and very funny Maude Hutchens, for example, whose *Diary of Love*, printed in Holland, was turned back by prudish Customs officers in Harwich in the early 1950s and appeared only in Britain after the blue pencil had removed not obscenities but brief remarks whose realism – especially from a woman – was too embarrassing to the average magistrate.

But writers in the French language were just as adventurous and produced surprises of a different kind. Emmanuelle Arsan, of Eurasian origin, the wife of a diplomat, wrote *Emmanuelle* for a bet and won it, for her book immediately appeared everywhere in cheap editions and occupied many large cinema screens for many months. It was gloriously funny (O had not been funny), its crudity was never nauseating and its descriptions of a walk through Bangkok on the way to an opium-den could stand comparison with good writing from the surrealist school at its most serious – except that the French word *sérieux* does not mean quite the same thing as its apparent English counterpart. This author did not hide behind a man's name, wrote several other books with the same heroine (or her daughter) very rapidly and a magazine (extant at least in 1975) took the name of this remarkable girl. The remarkable author was more energetic than Françoise Sagan in her choice of literary epigraphs: each chapter was given several, ranging from Dante to Nietzsche and later authors of similar status, and if the reader unaccountably becomes bored with the amorous antics of the heroine and her partners of all sexes, then a study of the relevance of these quotations is almost as entertaining.

Of the millions of people who have seen a non-shocking *Emmanuelle* on the screen probably a few thousands only, outside France, have read the book – reading is harder work than looking. But lazy readers can still half-read, half-look at magazines, and in France even a not-too-expensive women's magazine can still survive. By the 1960s nothing seemed to be lacking in the organization of the publicity machine – women were always news, writers were news, therefore women writers could be news, they were photographed, interviewed, discussed. An interesting woman was not necessarily a film star, but there was a danger that a woman writer in the news was more interesting for her looks (and her lovers) than for her books. She could have been just another kind of *femme-objet*. But just a few magazines were always on the look-out for women who might provide them with a new kind of copy. It is impossible not to mention the magazine *Elle* because it has achieved a fusion of two elements in a way that cannot easily happen in any other country: its readers were expected, encouraged, to be interested in the sex-object attributes, such as clothes, cosmetics or the absence of them. But they were assumed to have an interest in what can only be called culture, without being told at the same time that they 'ought' to be interested, it was not a separate part of life. An interest in painting, writing, any art form, was taken for granted by editors who have on the whole been more gracefully subtle than those of other countries. The editorial and educational aspects of the magazine were in fact fused, not joined together with wall nails or panel pins. I mention this technique now with enthusiasm, in the hope that it will not fade away too fast.

Yet in his fascinating study *La Femme et ses images* the novelist and sociologist Pascal Lainé was by no means pleased with the magazine for the way in which it seemed to write about feminism as a new fashion, a new means of seduction. Indirectly it crept into the advertising, and perhaps, he thought, it was not being taken seriously enough. Yet even this attitude is preferable, especially in a magazine with a young readership, to the usual one adopted by the French magazines of a more conventional kind: their message to the young is always 'attract a man, take a lover, find a husband'. When aimed at the slightly older reader the message changes: keep your children and your husband happy – that seems to be the priority – beautify your home. The concept of a woman as a personality in her own right, the idea that has preoccupied such different people as Natalie Clifford Barney and Simone de Beauvoir, is hardly represented at all, and as Pascal Lainé has pointed out, it is not clear whether women magazine readers assume the image they see in front of them or whether the magazines reflect what the editors and photographers find round about them. At the moment the scene is essentially fluid, so are the images and so is their interplay. The magazines are valuable for the way they 'fix' an image temporarily. By the time a novel is written and read, the image would have changed. Novels, plays, other writing last longer, but the magazines complement them all the same.

How much do women writers owe to publicity techniques, personal and commercial? Ever since the time of George Sand and the late nineteenth century women writers in France have been treated like actresses, inevitably with good and bad results. Sand's appearance coincided with the Romantic movement, her personality seemed ready-made to express the spirit of the age. She inherited a tradition but almost ignored it and added a new element – the involvement of work and life that led her far beyond the reticence and anonymity that had been an essential aspect of Madame de La Fayette. Madame de Staël had received publicity, it is true, but it was not altogether due to her writing and it did not always help her; and fond though she was of amateur theatricals she never acquired the glow that hovered round Sand all her life and has not faded even now.

Very different is the reputation of women writers in Britain and the United States. The medieval Margery Kempe and the seventeenth-century Aphra Behn are intriguing writers but only to scholars. Nobody has worked them into the national tradition in any obvious way. As for that handful of brilliant women – Jane Austen, Emily Dickinson, the Brontës, George Eliot, they did not really care for publicity, although they hoped for readers and success. Publicity was not, is not, necessarily appreciation, and even writers of the twentieth century do not always understand that a book is in some ways a commercial product. Time passed before Scott praised and envied Jane Austen, before the Brontës became the perpetual heroines of psycho-biography. Without publicity appreciation takes longer, but it lasts better. With publicity it comes more quickly, is sometimes misdirected, does not always last but often changes key and makes for controversy. All of which can only mean a longer if posthumous reputation for the writer because readers and critics will argue with varying degrees of ferocity over points which will become relevant singly or in interrelated groups as the social scene changes.

As things stand today, readers and critics show few signs of exhausted curiosity about the lives of writers, and particularly about their sex-lives. The sex-lives of women excited more curiosity than those of men, for according to the Christian heritage women were intended to be mothers and wifehood was merely a stage on the way. Sex outside marriage was a career and love was an undefined, upsetting thing, outside reason, which was alarming, but it was regarded as short-lived and conveniently ended by marriage. In France there has tended to be less hypocrisy than in Britain about career women such as royal mistresses or the *grandes cocottes*, the 'grand horizontals' of the late nineteenth century. Yet the French had a different type of hypocrisy: the men genuinely thought they were passionate admirers of women, thus justifying the barbarous way they treated them both in private life and in law. So the French women writers had to be cautious and proceed indirectly for a long time, few of them had Sand's irrepressible confidence and energy. Some took men's names, as the 'Bells' and 'George Eliot' had done, some took frivolous names, like 'Gyp', and some hid behind their husbands. Even in the mid-twentieth century some women in France sign their books with Christian names, 'Nicole' for example, although it is known that the 'author' of *Les Lions sont lâchés* (The Lions are Loose), that amusing satire on contemporary sex relationships, is partly Françoise Parturier, better known for her books on the 'war between men and women'.

But the photographers' flashes shine with particular brightness on the faces of women. The faces do not have to be beautiful or attractive in the conventional sense – they are assumed to be individual and deserving of attention. They cannot be dull, dullness is non-existence. The publicity machine in France works differently from the would-be corresponding system in other countries. Publicity probes may be deep, but not cheap, not crude: that is apparently, too often, the Anglo-Saxon way, which brought complaints from Violette Leduc when she visited England. Behind the endless questions of the French interviewer lies what has been called the Strasbourg goose principle of French education: the questions are not devoted for long to hobbies or gossip, they will aim at relating the person closely to the work. Those who operate the publicity machine do not forget that the person temporarily in their possession is the author of a book, and they direct the recipients of their publicity to read it and think about it. There is another point here: in order to read the book most people will actually have to buy it, for they cannot often depend on libraries. A book in France is still something to be bought with real money, just as food and wine and clothes are bought. In Britain too many people still believe a book is something to read reviews of, talk about, look at, borrow: but buying it, reading it, still have a low priority. And if anyone reacts violently to this I would say that their violence is due to their guilt.

All this is relevant to the status and success of the woman writer. The photographs of Simone de Beauvoir at the time of her early successes showed her to be human, handsome, feminine. Those of Françoise Sagan and Violette Leduc intrigued the French public who without any doubt allow writers of both sexes to have their due status as creative artists. In too many other countries this status belongs as of right to a painter or a musician because their visual or sensory appeal is so much swifter and stronger. For a writer to be in the public eye and not merely on the shrinking book-pages he or she has to be a wild success, commit a crime, have a known sexual involvement, announce a religious conversion or die. It may be a disappointing fact to many writers in Britain but photographs of attractive women writers even on book jackets are known to bring them sales. Outside the field of romantic fiction, which exists in all countries, women are still regarded too often as the sex-objects of literature. The French women writers have attained their professional status by methods which have sometimes been so indirect that they could have been called dishonest, but they never wanted the more usual method employed in Britain, where too many women writers tried to behave like men.

Concentration on the sexual life of a woman writer can have some amusing results. The life-story should draw people to the work but how often does it obscure the work altogether? Have recent revelations about Edith Wharton's love affair with Morton Fullerton increased the sales of her books, and in fact how many are in print? Detailed writing about the sexual problems of Virginia Woolf has fascinated reviewers but how many people were led to re-read *The Waves* or *Between the Acts*? Some, but not enough. When Nigel Nicholson published the account of the love story between his mother Victoria Sackville-West and Violet Trefusis how many of those who relished it turned back to, say, *All Passion Spent*, or did anyone read *Echo*, one of the novels written in French by Violette Trefusis and published by a firm which advertised on the jacket books by Julien Green and Graham Greene? It is bad, heartless and funny in its tragic story, set in a Scottish baronial castle surrounded with grouse moors, which, of course, are not at their best when described in French. But surely the reading produces more entertainment than the gossip about the writers, which is only relevant because of the books.

The theatrical-style propaganda about women writers in France, inherited from the gossip columns of 1900, from *Le*

Cri de Paris, Gil Blas and La Vie Parisienne, is now more scientific, but the operators have inherited a method, and most of all new generations of writers and readers. The indirect approach, and the precedence given to the actual writing, brings more subtlety and entertainment value to the scene, and through the entertainment the 'messages' come through to the reader.

When George Sand began to write she wanted to earn money. She wrote about herself and her experiences just as most of her predecessors among women writers had done, her research was shallow, her sense of vocation surprisingly faint, but there was in her a unique combination of forces which few people anywhere have possessed. Lucie Delarue-Mardrus's phrase about the *océanique féminin* perhaps sums up her nature. Many of the women who have followed her have continued to write in the same way, but they have gone further. If their approach to fiction, because of their heritage, is constantly psychological, they have moved into nearly every possible territory and retained all that had been won by previous generations. Historical novels in depth, theology, politics, sociology, new techniques in fiction and new ways of handling words – in developing all this they have moved constantly closer to the realism of the individual and the social group. There are some curious gaps, for so many women have written brilliantly about the countryside but they have not included the 'regional' novelists represented in France by someone like Jean Giono and by so many brilliant women writers in England and Ireland. In the same way they have not produced any study in depth of the adolescent, as Romain-Rolland did. But no doubt they will do so, and some of them are writing poetry which will surely last. The French language is so hostile to poetry, by its very sentence-structure, that it has taken time, since Apollinaire and the surrealists cracked it open, for anyone to handle it vividly. Women writers have written about love and sex (how could they not have done?), work and boredom, but they have achieved more personal and social freedom for women by hardly trying at all than by trying too hard. Some of them have been aware all the time that they were women, some have been, are, what Marguerite Yourcenar has called the 'feminine human being', *l'être humain femme*.

Women writers in France have had more to cope with than remarks like Hawthorne's about the 'damned scribbling women' or John Squire's amiable curiosity. Molière warned his audiences about bluestockings three hundred years ago and the women writers of today have not forgotten that unkind little rhyme *'Si tu veux être heureux, n'épousez pas un bas-bleu'*. Fortunately writers like Marguerite Yourcenar or Simone de Beauvoir have directed their learning into books that are alive, for they have been intent on living themselves. A scholar like Hélène Cixous writes novels in experimental vein, Marguerite Duras makes films, stage-directs at least one of her plays to be produced with film methods. As far as attitudes to male-dominated society are concerned the writers will go on being *guérillères* for some time to come.

There is a saying in France that one hardly hears now but reads occasionally in old books. *'Ce que femme veut. . . .'* What a woman wants. . . . And the second part, usually taken for granted, is *'Dieu le veut'*, God wants it; in other words, the woman always wins. There is a ring of resignation about it. One would like to think it is true, and nobody has tried harder than the French women writers to make it come true.

In 1961 Françoise Giroud wrote about her feminine compatriots as 'women of iron and velvet', who were on the way to change, how much change she did not know and nobody will ever know. These women may not have had a minister before but they have had a long line of subtle propagandists who never put forward any obvious programme, they were merely themselves. Three centuries ago Madame de Sévigné wrote it all into one sentence: 'When I listen only to myself,' she said, 'I can do wonders.' This is the message from France, extended by that iron hand in its almost invisible but indestructible velvet glove. Made of nylon now, not cotton, and tougher than ever.

Select Bibliography

General

PIERRE A. G. ASTIER: La Crise du roman français et le nouveau réalisme, Paris, 1969

ROBERT BALDICK: Dinner at Magny's, London, 1973

ANDRÉ BILLY: L'Epoque 1900, Paris, 1951

LÉON BLUM: Du Mariage, Paris, 1907; Marriage, New York, 1937

IRENE CLAREMONT DE CASTILLEJO: Knowing Woman, a Feminine Psychology, rev. ed., London, 1973

FRANÇOISE GIROUD: Si je mens, Paris, 1972; I Give you my Word, New York, 1974

GISÈLE HALIMI: La Cause des femmes, Paris, 1973

EMILE HENRIOT: Portraits de femmes, Paris, 1951

PASCAL LAINÉ: La Femme et ses images, Paris, 1974

JEAN LARNAC: Histoire de la littérature féminine en France, Paris, 1929

MARGARET LAWRENCE: We Write as Women, London, 1937

SUZANNE LILAR: Le Couple, Paris, 1963

LAURENT MAILHOT: La Littérature québecoise, Paris, 1974

CHARLES MAURRAS: L'Avenir de l'intelligence, Paris, 1927

ANAÏS NIN: The Novel of the Future, London, 1969; New York, 1970

GEORGE D. PAINTER: Marcel Proust, A Biography, Vols. I and II. London, 1959 and 1965; Boston, 1965

FRANÇOISE PARTURIER: Lettre ouverte aux femmes, Paris, 1974

MARIO PRAZ: The Romantic Agony, London, 1933; New York, 1970

JOHN STURROCK: The French New Novel, Oxford, 1969; New York 1969

G. RATTRAY TAYLOR: Sex in History, London, 1953; New York, 1973

MADAME M. S. VAN DE VELDE: French Fiction of Today, London, 1891
JOHN WEIGHTMAN: Literature of the Avant-Garde, London, 1973;
Concept of the Avant-Garde, La Salle, 1973
ANTHONY WEST: Mortal Wounds, London, 1975; New York, 1973
VIRGINIA WOOLF: A Room of One's Own. London, 1929; New York
WAYLAND YOUNG: Eros Denied, London, 1965
Yale French Studies, No. 27, 1961

Individual Authors

MARGUERITE AUDOUX: Marie-Claire, Paris, 1910
George Reyer: Un cœur pur: Marguerite Audoux, Paris, 1942
NATALIE CLIFFORD BARNEY: Aventures de l'esprit, Paris, 1929;
New York, 1970
Souvenirs indiscrets, Paris, 1960
The One who is Legion, London, 1930
Adam, ed. Miron Grindea, No. 269, 1963
Jean Chalon: Portrait d'une séductrice, Paris, 1976
MARIE BASHKIRTSEFF: Doris Langley Moore: Marie and the Duke
of H, London, 1966
SIMONE DE BEAUVOIR: L'Invitée, Paris, 1943; She Came to Stay,
London, 1949
Le deuxième sexe, Paris, 1949; The Second Sex, London, 1960;
New York, 1953
Les Mandarins, Paris, 1954; The Mandarins, London, 1957
Mémoires d'une jeune fille rangée, Paris, 1958; Memoirs of a
Dutiful Daughter, London, 1969; New York, 1974
La force de l'âge, Paris, 1960; The Prime of Life, London, 1962
La force des choses, Paris, 1963; Force of Circumstance, London,
1965
Les belles images, Paris, 1967; London, 1968
Une mort très douce, Paris, 1964; A Very Easy Death, London,
1966; New York, 1973

Select Bibliography

Francis Jeanson: *Simone de Beauvoir ou l'entreprise de vivre*, Paris, 1966
Francis Bondy: 'Notes on a Lady Mandarin', *Encounter*, 25 Oct. 1965
C. B. Radford: 'Simone de Beauvoir, Feminism's Friend or Foe?', *Nottingham French Studies*, 6 Oct. 1967; 7 May 1968
PRINCESS MARTHE BIBESCO: *Catherine-Paris*, Paris, 1927; London, 1928
Le perroquet vert, Paris, 1924; *The Green Parrot*, London, 1929
Le voyageur voilé, Geneva, 1947; *The Veiled Wanderer*, London, 1950
MARIE-CLAIRE BLAIS: *La belle bête*, Quebec, 1959; *Mad Shadows*, London, 1960
Une Saison dans la vie d'Emmanuel, 1965; *A Season in the Life of Emmanuel*, London, 1967; New York, 1969
L'Insoumise, Montreal, 1966
David Sterne, Montreal, 1967
Les Manuscrits de Pauline Archange, Paris, 1968; New York, 1970
Tête-Blanche, London, 1962
The Wolf, Toronto, 1975
St Lawrence Blues, London, 1975; New York, 1974
COLETTE: *Œuvres complètes*, 15 volumes, Paris, 1950
Some translations:
Chéri, and The Last of Chéri, London, 1953; Baltimore, 1974
Mitsou, London, 1957; New York, 1958
My Mother's House and Sido, London, 1953
The Other One, London, 1960
The Cat, London 1953; New York, 1974
My Apprenticeships, London, 1957
Ripening Seed, London, 1955
The Other Woman, London, 1971; New York, 1974
Duo and Le Toutounier, London, 1976; Duo, Indianapolis, 1975
Anna A. Ketchum: *Colette ou la naissance du jour*, Paris, 1968
Margaret Crosland: *Colette or the Difficulty of Loving*, London, 1973; Indianapolis, 1973
LOUISE DEHARME; Le Pot de Mousse, Paris, 1946
LUCIE DELARUE-MARDRUS: Mes Mémoires, Paris, 1938

243

MINOU DROUET: *Arbre, mon ami*, Paris, 1956; *First Poems*, London, 1956

Robert Parinaud: *L'Affaire Minou Drouet*, Paris, 1956

MARGUERITE DURAS: *Les Impudents*, Paris, 1943

La Vie tranquille, Paris, 1944

Un Barrage contre le Pacifique, Paris, 1950; *Sea of Troubles*, London, 1953

Le Marin de Gibraltar, Paris, 1952; *The Sailor from Gibraltar*, London, 1970

Les petits Chevaux de Tarquinia, Paris, 1953; *The Little Horses of Tarquinia*, London, 1960

Des Journées entières dans les arbres, Le Boa, Madame Dotin, Les Chantiers, Paris, 1954

Le Square, Paris, 1955; *The Square*, London, 1959; New York, 1965

Moderato Cantabile, Paris, 1958; London, 1966

Hiroshima, mon amour, Les Viaducs de la Seine-et-Marne, Dix Heures et demie du soir en été, Paris, 1960; *10.30 on a Summer's Night*, London, 1962; *Hiroshima mon Amour*, New York, 1961

Une aussi longue absence, Paris, 1961; with *Hiroshima mon Amour*, London, 1966

L'Après-midi de Monsieur Andesmas, Paris, 1962; *The Afternoon of Monsieur Andesmas*, with *The Rivers and Forests*, London, 1965

Le Ravissement de Lol V. Stein, Paris, 1964; New York, 1966; *The Rapture of Lol V. Stein*, London, 1967

Le Vice-Consul, Paris, 1966; London, 1968

L'Amante anglaise, Paris, 1967; London, 1968

Détruire dit-elle, Paris, 1969

Abahn Sabana David, Paris, 1970; with *The Vice-Consul*, New York.

L'Amour, Paris, 1971

With Xavière Gautier: *Les Parleuses*, Paris, 1974

Cahiers Renaud-Barrault, 52. 1965

CLAIRE ETCHERELLI: *Élise ou la vraie vie*, Paris, 1967; *Elise or the Real Life*, London, 1970

A propos de Clémence, Paris, 1971

JEANNE GALZY: *Les Allongés*, Paris, 1923

JUDITH GAUTIER:

Richard and Cosima Wagner: *Lettres à Judith Gautier*, ed. Léon Guichard, Paris, 1964

M. D. Camacho: *Judith Gautier, sa vie et son œuvre*, Switzerland, 1939

'GYP': *Souvenirs d'une petite fille*, Paris, 1927

MADAME DE LA FAYETTE: *Isabelle ou Le Journal amoureux d'Espagne*, ed. Marc Chadonne, Paris, 1961

Émile Magne: *Madame de La Fayette en ménage*, Paris, 1926

VIOLETTE LEDUC: *L'Asphyxie*, Paris, 1946: *In the Prison of her Skin*, London, 1973

L'Affamée, Paris, 1948

Ravages, Paris, 1955

La Vieille Fille et la Mort, and *Les Boutons dorés*, Paris 1958; *The Golden Buttons*, London, 1961

Thérèse et Isabelle, Paris, 1966

La Bâtarde, Paris, 1965; London, 1965

La Folie en tête, Paris, 1970; *Mad in Pursuit*, London, 1972; New York, 1971

La Chasse à l'amour, Paris, 1973

La Femme au petit renard, Paris, 1965; *The Lady and the Little Fox Fur*, London, 1967

Le Taxi, Paris, 1971; London, 1973; New York, 1972

FRANÇOISE MALLET-JORIS: *Le Rempart des Béguines*, Paris, 1951; *Into the Labyrinth*, London, 1953

Les Mensonges, Paris, 1956; *House of Lies*, London, 1958

Les Personnages, Paris, 1961; *The Favourite*, London, 1962

Cordélia, Paris; London, 1965

Lettre à moi-même, Paris, 1963; *Letter to Myself*, London, 1964; New York, 1964

La Chambre rouge, Paris, 1953; *The Red Room*, London, 1956

La Maison de Papier, Paris, 1970; *The Paper House* New York, 1971; London, 1971

Le Jeu du Souterrain, Paris, 1973; *The Underground Game*, London, 1974

Michel Géoris: *Françoise Mallet-Joris*, Paris, 1964

QUEEN MARGARET OF NAVARRE: *The Mirror of the Sinful Soul*. A prose translation from the French . . . made by the Princess (afterwards Queen) Elizabeth. Rep. in facsimile and ed. by Percy W. Ames, London, 1897

COMTESSE ANNA DE NOAILLES: *Le Livre de ma vie*, Paris, 1932

Jean Cocteau: *Portraits-Souvenir*, Paris, 1935

Francis Steegmuller: *Cocteau*, London, 1970; Boston, 1970

'RACHILDE': *Monsieur Vénus*, Paris, 1889

André David: *Rachilde, homme de lettres*, Paris, 1924

André Breton: *Entretiens*, Paris, 1952, rev. 1969

CHRISTIANE DE ROCHEFORT: *Le Repos du guerrier*, Paris, 1958;

'PAULINE REAGE': *Histoire d'O*, préf. Jean Paulhan, Paris, 1954; New York, 1966

GABRIELLE ROY: *Bonheur d'occasion*, Paris, 1945; *The Tin Flute*, London, 1948

FRANÇOISE SAGAN: *Bonjour Tristesse*, Paris, 1954; London, 1957; New York, 1974

Un certain sourire, Paris, 1956; *A Certain Smile*, London, 1956

Aimez-vous Brahms?, Paris, 1959; London, 1960; New York, 1974

Dans un mois, dans un an, Paris, 1957; *Those without Shadows*, Paris, London, 1957

Les merveilleux nuages, Paris, 1961; *Wonderful Clouds*, London, 1961; New York, 1974

La Chamade Paris, 1965; London, 1966; Englewood Cliffs, 1970

Le Garde du cœur, Paris, 1968; *The Heart Keeper*, London, 1968; New York, 1974

Un peu de soleil sur l'eau froide, Paris, 1969; *Sunlight on Cold Water*, London, 1973

Des Bleus à l'âme, Paris, 1972; *Scars on the Soul*, London, 1974; New York, 1974

Un Profil perdu, Paris, 1975; *Lost Profile*, London, 1976

NATHALIE SARRAUTE: *Tropismes*, Paris, 1939; *L'Ère du soupçon*, Paris, 1956; *Tropisms and the Age of Suspicion*, London, 1964; New York 1968

Les Fruits d'or, Paris, 1963; *The Golden Fruits*, London, 1967
Martereau, Paris, 1953; London, 1967
Le Planétarium, Paris, 1959; London, 1961
Portrait d'un inconnu, Paris, 1948; *Portrait of a Man Unknown*, London, 1959; New York, 1968
Entre la vie et la mort, Paris, 1968; *Between Life and Death*, London, 1970
Mary McCarthy: *The Writing on the Wall*, London, 1970; New York, 1970
René Micha: *Nathalie Sarraute*, Paris, 1966
Ruth Z. Temple: *Nathalie Sarraute*, London and New York, 1968
'SIMONE': *Le Désordre*, Paris, 1930
Jours de colère, Paris, 1935
Le Paradis terrestre, Paris, 1939
Robert Gibson: *The Land without a Name: Alain-Fournier and his World*, London, 1975; New York, 1975
ALBERTINE SARRAZIN: *Romans, lettres et poèmes*, pref. by Hervé Bazin, Paris, 1967
L'Astragale, Paris, 1965; London, 1968; New York, 1968
Josane Duranteau: *Albertine Sarrazin*, Paris, 1971
ELSA TRIOLET: *Le premier accroc coûte deux cent francs*, Paris, 1945
Écoutez-voir, Paris, 1968
LOUISE DE VILMORIN: *Madame de . . .* , Paris, 1951; London, 1956
RENEE VIVIEN: *Poèmes de Renée Vivien*, Paris, 1923–4; New York, 1975 (in French)
Y. G. Le Dantec: *Renée Vivien, femme damnée, femme sauvée*, Aix-en-Provence, 1930
SIMONE WEIL: *The Notebooks of Simone Weil*, 2 vols., London, 1956
Selected Essays, 1934–1943, London, 1962
J. P. Little: *Simone Weil: a bibliography*, London, 1973
Simone Pétrement: *La Vie de Simone Weil*, Vols I and II, Paris, 1973
E. W. F. Tomlin: *Simone Weil*, Cambridge, 1964; Atlantic Highlands, 1954
MONIQUE WITTIG: *L'Opoponax*, Paris, 1964: London, 1966; New York, 1966
Les Guérillères, Paris, 1969; London, 1971; New York, 1973

Le Corps lesbien, Paris, 1973; *The Lesbian Body*, London, 1975; New York, 1975

MARGUERITE YOURCENAR: *Mémoires d'Hadrien*, Paris, 1951; London, 1955; New York, 1963

Le Coup de grâce, Paris, 1939, rev. 1953; London, 1967; New York, 1957

L'Œuvre au noir, Paris, 1968; *The Abyss*, New York, 1976

Souvenirs pieux, Paris, 1974

Jean Blot: *Marguerite Yourcenar*, Paris, 1971

Patrick de Rosbo: *Entretiens radiophoniques avec Marguerite Yourcenar*, Paris, 1972

Index

Index

Index

Index

Index

Index

Index